PENGU

THE PENG
AUSTRAL

The Penguin Book of

AUSTRALIAN VERSE

INTRODUCED AND EDITED BY

HARRY HESELTINE

PENGUIN BOOKS

Penguin Books Australia Ltd,
487 Maroondah Highway, P.O. Box 257
Ringwood, Victoria, 3134, Australia
Penguin Books Ltd,
Harmondsworth, Middlesex, England
Penguin Books,
625 Madison Avenue, New York, N.Y. 10022, U.S.A.
Penguin Books Canada Ltd,
2801 John Street, Markham, Ontario, Canada
Penguin Books (N.Z.) Ltd,
182-190 Wairau Road, Auckland 10, New Zealand

First published by Penguin Books Australia, 1972
Reprinted 1974, 1976, 1979, 1982

Copyright © Harry Heseltine, 1972

Made and printed in Australia by
The Dominion Press, North Blackburn, Victoria

The Penguin book of Australian verse

Index
ISBN 0 14 042162 9

1. Australian poetry. I. Heseltine, Harry P., ed.

A821'.008

CONTENTS

CHARLES HARPUR (1813-68). The son of convicts,
Harpur was the first native born Australian poet of
consequence. At various times schoolteacher, sheep
farmer and Government gold commissioner, Harpur
wrote his verse under conditions of considerable pioneer-
ing hardship.

ADAM LINDSAY GORDON (1833-70). Born in the
West Indies and commemorated in London (in West-
minster Abbey), Gordon lived in Australia from 1853
until his suicide in Melbourne at the age of thirty-six.
Famous during his lifetime as a horseman, Gordon
gained wide posthumous fame in Australia for the kind
of verse collected in *Bush Ballads and Galloping Rhymes*.

HENRY KENDALL (1839-82). Born at Kirmington,
on the south coast of New South Wales, as a young man
Kendall was an ardent admirer of his predecessor,
Harpur. Unsuccessful in business matters, intermittently
unhappy in his marriage, Kendall wrote prolifically and
with varying merit. His 'Bell Birds' is one of the best-
known nineteenth century Australian poems.

VICTOR DALEY (1858-1905). Irish born Daley was
one of the first Australian poets to attempt to support
himself solely by writing. In consequence, much of his
life was passed in poverty. His work is often associated
with a kind of 'Celtic' Romanticism, though, when
writing under the *nom de plume* of Creeve Roe, he was
capable of hard-hitting, radical social comment.

CONTENTS

HENRY LAWSON (1867-1922). Lawson is the great representative Australian writer of the 1890s, one of the crucial decades in the development of Australian culture. His finest achievement is in his short stories, but in the mass of his verse are found several ballads which have achieved the anonymous status of folklore and some few pieces of more individual force.

CHRISTOPHER BRENNAN (1870-1932). The son of an Irish Catholic brewer, Brennan was the first Australian poet deliberately to connect his verse to the current of European intellectual life. From 1892 to 1894, Brennan was in Berlin on a travelling scholarship from Sydney University, and he brought back from Europe a passionate attachment to Mallarmé and the French *symbolistes*. *Poems 1913*, his major work, is a *livre composé* which amalgamates all the strands of his complex intellectual interests.

JOHN LE GAY BRERETON (1871-1933). Although his career was overshadowed by that of his close friend, Chris Brennan, Brereton had real gifts both as a poet and literary scholar. He was the first Challis Professor of English Literature in Sydney University, while his verse makes a distinctive contribution to the poetry of his generation.

JOHN SHAW NEILSON (1872-1942). Neilson is one of the 'sports' of Australian literature. Almost completely lacking in formal education, passing his life as a manual labourer, Neilson produced lyric verse of a delicacy and force to make it a landmark in the development of Australian literature.

HUGH McCRAE (1876-1958). Hugh McCrae is
perhaps one of the gayest figures in Australian poetry,
his verse always possessing its own special *élan*, even
when touching only superficial feelings or when, as in
'Enigma', it is tinged with melancholy.

FURNLEY MAURICE (FRANK WILMOT)
(1881-1942). Frank Wilmot kept poetry alive in Mel-
bourne at a period when it was fairly difficult to keep
poetry alive anywhere in Australia. His unspectacular
career as a bookseller and later with the Melbourne
University Press gave him time to produce verse which
is among the earliest to sound the note of 'modernism'
in Australia.

BRIAN VREPONT (BENJAMIN ARTHUR
TRUEBRIDGE) (1882-1955). Born in Melbourne,
Vrépont included in his varied career occupations as
varied as violin teacher and masseur. His only book,
Beyond the Claw, published when he was sixty-one,
contains some quite idiosyncratic writing for an Aus-
tralian of his generation.

WILLIAM BAYLEBRIDGE (WILLIAM
BLOCKSIDGE) (1883-1942). Baylebridge, born in
Brisbane, spent a large part of his early life in England.
During the First World War he seems to have made a
mysterious contribution to Allied Intelligence activities
in France. In Australia in his later years he lived
largely as a recluse.

CONTENTS

VANCE PALMER (1885-1959). One of the central figures of Australian literary culture for nearly half a century, Palmer was born in Bundaberg, Queensland, and died in Melbourne. He turned his hand to many branches of creative literature and *belles lettres*, but his major achievement was in the novel and short story.

PETER HOPEGOOD (1891-1967). Born in England, Hopegood came to Australia after serving with the Essex Regiment in the First World War. Thereafter he pursued a lively and independent way in both verse and fiction.

LEON GELLERT (b. 1892). In 1914, when he was twenty-two, Leon Gellert volunteered for the First A.I.F. His experiences on the Western Front gave him the material for his book of verse, *Songs of a Campaign*, from which 'These Men' is taken.

TOM INGLIS MOORE (1901-1978). Moore was born into a pastoral family at Camden, New South Wales. His own career was largely academic, with an interval for service with Army Education during the Second World War.

KENNETH SLESSOR (1901-71). Modern Australian poetry arguably begins with Slessor, whose first volume, *Thief of the Moon*, was published in 1924. His creative career was comparatively short – only one or two poems appeared after 1940. Yet the hundred or so poems of his *oeuvre* include some of the most important pieces written by an Australian in this century.

9

R. D. FITZGERALD (b. 1902). FitzGerald started to write at the same time as Slessor, and his contribution to Australian poetry is just as important. Quite different from Slessor's, his verse just as significantly helped to define the possibilities of modern Australian poetry. Where Slessor for many years remained silent, Fitz-Gerald has produced some of his best writing during the last two decades.

J. A. R. MACKELLAR (1904-32). Mackellar was born and educated in Sydney. He was establishing a reputation as both a poet and an athlete when a sudden illness led to his untimely death at the age of twenty-eight.

JAMES PICOT (1906-44). Born in England, Picot was a theological student before he enlisted in the Second A.I.F. Captured in Singapore by the Japanese, he died while a prisoner of war in Burma. His posthumous volume, *With a Hawk's Quill*, indicates a genuine 'impressionist' talent.

A. D. HOPE (b. 1907). Hope is one of the leading modern Australian poets. A graduate of Sydney and Oxford, he was until his retirement in 1967 Professor of English at the Australian National University. His verse remained largely uncollected until the 1950s; the publication in 1955 of *The Wandering Islands* was an important event in revealing powers wider and deeper than his already known capacity for witty satire.

JOHN THOMPSON (1907-68). One of the editors of the earlier *Penguin Book of Modern Australian Verse*, Thompson made a career with the Australian Broadcasting Commission in radio broadcasting. His own writing, limited in quantity, was marked at its best by poise and intelligence.

HARRY HOOTON (1908-61). Born and educated in London, Hooton came to Australia in 1924, living first in Newcastle and later in Sydney. His work has for long been little recognized outside a small personal following.

RONALD McCUAIG (b. 1908). Born in Newcastle, New South Wales, McCuaig, like many Australian writers of his generation, has made journalism his career.

ELIZABETH RIDDELL (b. 1909). Elizabeth Riddell was born in New Zealand, was married to the late E. N. Greatorex, and works as a journalist in Sydney.

CONTENTS

ROLAND ROBINSON (b. 1912). Coming to Australia from his native Ireland at the age of fourteen, Robinson was an early member of the Jindyworobak movement. He remains true to its idealism and probably no white Australian poet has more sympathetically or thoroughly immersed himself in the life of the aboriginals.

JOHN BLIGHT (b. 1913). Born at Unley in South Australia, Blight now lives by the sea in Queensland. The sea is the chief inspiration of a great deal of his best poetry.

FLEXMORE HUDSON (b. 1913). Hudson was born in Charters Towers, Queensland, but has lived most of his life in South Australia. Though never a member of the Jindyworobak Club, he was closely associated with some of the leading members of the movement, notably Rex Ingamells. His verse sometimes expresses a more direct socio-political concern than that of the Jindyworobaks.

REX INGAMELLS (1913-55). In the middle 1930s Rex Ingamells started to develop those views about the relation of culture and environment which led him to found the Jindyworobak Club in 1936. Following through his theories, Ingamells came finally to publish an Australian epic, *The Great South Land* (1951). He was killed in a car accident in 1955.

CONTENTS

KENNETH MACKENZIE (1913-55). A West Australian by birth, as a young man Mackenzie moved to Sydney, where he embarked on a career in journalism. He was one of many Australian writers to come under the influence of Norman Lindsay, although in both his fiction and his poetry he developed the personal note of his own sensibility.

DOUGLAS STEWART (b. 1913). Although he was born in New Zealand, Stewart has been thoroughly absorbed into Australian culture. In many practical ways, notably as the long-time literary editor of the Sydney *Bulletin*, he has enriched the literature of this country. His own contributions include poetry, verse-drama, criticism, short stories, and autobiography.

HAROLD STEWART (b. 1916). Harold Stewart is probably best known in Australia as one half of the mythical poet 'Ern Malley', the central figure of a celebrated literary hoax in 1944. Since that time he has published in Japan and U.S.A., and now lives in Japan.

JOHN COUPER (b. 1914). John Couper came to Australia after service in the British Army in the Second World War. In this country he has filled a variety of teaching posts, and was on the staff of Macquarie University, Sydney until his retirement in 1978.

14

DOROTHY AUCHTERLONIE (b. 1915). Dorothy Auchterlonie, the widow of the poet and literary historian H. M. Green, lives in Canberra, and until recently taught English at the Australian National University.

DAVID CAMPBELL (b. 1915). Born into a pastoral family, David Campbell has lived much of his life on the land, apart from a period at Cambridge and Air Force service during the Second World War. Much of his poetry derives from his rural experience, though recently the range of his themes has been perceptibly broadening.

J. S. MANIFOLD (b. 1915). Manifold comes from a well-established family in the Western Districts of Victoria, and before the Second World War took a degree at Cambridge. For most of his adult life, however, he has been a political radical. He now lives with his wife and family in Brisbane. He is an authority on Australian folk music.

DAVID MARTIN (b. 1915). Born in Hungary, Martin fought on the Republican side in the Spanish Civil War, and has lived in many parts of Europe as well as in Israel and India. The author of a number of novels and children's books, he came to Australia in 1949, and now lives in Melbourne.

JUDITH WRIGHT (b. 1915). Judith Wright is one of the few writers to enjoy unchallenged pre-eminence in contemporary Australian poetry. Since the appearance of her first book, *The Moving Image*, in 1946, she has been recognized, both at home and abroad, as a poet .of great accomplishments. Born in the New England area of New South Wales, for many years she lived with her family at Mt Tamborine, Queensland. She now lives in Canberra.

NANCY CATO (b. 1917). Nancy Cato was born and educated in Adelaide, where she now lives. She has travelled widely both in Australia and Europe.

JAMES McAULEY (1917-1976). James McAuley, with the help of Harold Stewart, invented the poet 'Ern Malley', whose 'posthumous' poems were printed in the magazine, *Angry Penguins*, in 1944. The hoax demonstrated McAuley's own belief in the importance of formal control in poetry. His conversion to Roman Catholicism, in addition to his 'classicism', played a significant role in shaping his poetry. The founder of the magazine, *Quadrant*, McAuley held the Chair of English Literature in the University of Tasmania until his death in 1976.

CONTENTS

Harris was one of the central figures in the literary controversies of the 1940s. He remains a lively controversialist, and produces, from time to time, some very carefully worked out poems.

T. H. JONES (1921-65). Hari Jones came to Australia from Wales. Teaching at Newcastle University College, he was establishing a reputation in the Australian literary scene when he was drowned in 1965.

NAN McDONALD (1921-1973). Nan McDonald was born and educated in Sydney. A volume of her *Selected Poems* was published in 1969.

GEOFFREY DUTTON (b. 1922). Dutton is a many-sided man of letters. As writer, publisher, and publicist, he has played a prominent role in Australian culture during the past fifteen years. A number of his ventures have been with Max Harris – notably the journal, *Australian Book Review*, and the magazine, *Australian Letters*. His own writing includes, as well as verse, fiction, criticism and biography.

ALEXANDER CRAIG (b. 1923). Born in Melbourne, Craig served in New Guinea with the A.I.F. After living and teaching for a number of years in the U.S.A., he now teaches English at Macquarie University, Sydney.

DOROTHY HEWETT (b. 1923). Dorothy Hewett lives in Sydney after many years spent in Perth, the city of her birth. She writes novels and plays as well as verse, and in all her work adapts the radical traditions

of Australian writing to the conventions of modern
literature.

NANCY KEESING (b. 1923). Nancy Keesing lives in
Sydney, and is well-known as a critic as well as a poet.
With Douglas Stewart, she collected the important
anthologies, *Australian Bush Ballads* (1955) and *Old
Bush Songs and Rhymes of Colonial Times* (1957).

ERIC ROLLS (b. 1923). One of the idiosyncratic
figures of contemporary Australian poetry, Eric Rolls
lives on the land, owning his own property near Narra-
bri, New South Wales. Recently, he has been branching
into other forms of literature than poetry.

DAVID ROWBOTHAM (b. 1924). Although not one
of the spectacular figures of Australian poetry, this
Queenslander has, for something like a quarter of a
century, been building a considerable *oeuvre* of prose
and fiction.

VINCENT BUCKLEY (b. 1925). Buckley was born
in Romsey, Victoria, and most of his intellectual life has
been centred in Melbourne University, where he now
holds a personal Chair in English. Catholic and aca-
demic, Buckley has played an important role in instilling
the quality of critical intelligence into modern Aus-
tralian poetry.

CONTENTS

CONTENTS

life as Bruce Dawe. Dawe served for nine years with the R.A.A.F. He now lives in Queensland, where he teaches at the Darling Downs Institute of Technology.

CHARLES HIGHAM (b. 1931). A migrant from England, Higham has injected a distinct note of cosmopolitan awareness and intelligence into recent Australian poetry.

EVAN JONES (b. 1931). Jones belongs to that group of poets centred on Melbourne University, and including Vincent Buckley and Chris Wallace-Crabbe, who began to make their mark on Australian poetry in the 1950s.

JOHN CROYSTON (b. 1933). Croyston is not a prolific poet, but his work is known to readers of most Australian literary journals. He is a Drama Producer/Writer with the Australian Broadcasting Commission in Sydney.

VIVIAN SMITH (b. 1933). After teaching French in the University of Tasmania (his home state), Smith has now transferred to English studies at the University of Sydney. He has published several books of verse including *The Other Meaning* (1956) and *An Island South* (1967).

RANDOLPH STOW (b. 1935). Stow's reputation
rests chiefly on his novels, but his verse output, collected
in *A Counterfeit Silence* (1969), contains at least a few
poems which seem likely to have a permanent place in
Australian writing.

Dust   424
Ruins of the City of Hay   425
Sleep   426
Ishmael   427

JUDITH RODRIGUEZ (b. 1936). Judith Green
was born in Perth, Western Australia. She has travelled
in Europe and the Middle East, and is married to Fabio
Rodriguez, a lecturer in Latin American literature.

NORMAN TALBOT (b. 1936). Norman Talbot was
born in England, and now lectures at the University of
Newcastle, New South Wales. He is married, with three
children, and has published one volume of verse, *Poems
for a Female Universe* (1968).

DON MAYNARD (b. 1937). Don Maynard has
worked in publishing and as a teacher, and has
travelled in Europe, the Middle East, and Asia.

B. A. BREEN (b. 1938). Born and educated in Victoria,
Breen is now a high school teacher in the Victorian
Education Department.

LES MURRAY (b. 1938). Murray's bush background
influences a good deal of his poetry, which is amongst
the most accomplished of the younger Australian poets.
In 1970 he won the New South Wales Captain Cook Bi-
centenary Poetry Prize with the sequence, 'Seven Points
for an Imperilled Star'.

PETER STEELE (b. 1939). Peter Steele is a Jesuit priest, and tutors in English at Melbourne University.

GEOFFREY LEHMANN (b. 1940). Lehmann published his first book, *The Ilex Tree* (1965) in collaboration with Les Murray. Since then his books include *A Voyage of Lions* (1968) and *Comic Australian Verse* (1972). Lehmann is a graduate in law from Sydney University.

CRAIG POWELL (b. 1940). A graduate in Medicine from Sydney University, Craig Powell's special interest is psychiatry.

ANDREW TAYLOR (b. 1940). A Victorian by birth, Taylor has spent several years in Italy and America. He is now on the staff of the University of Adelaide.

ROGER McDONALD (b. 1941). After a childhood spent largely in country towns, McDonald worked for some years with Queensland University Press. His first volume of verse is *Citizens of Mist* (1968).

JOHN TRANTER (b. 1943). A Sydney-based poet, Tranter's verse has been collected in the volume, *Parallax* (1970).

ROBERT ADAMSON (b. 1944). After an unsettled youth, Adamson is now living in Sydney. He is one of a

number of younger Australian poets who find inspira-
tion in the work of Francis Webb.

PETER SKRZYNECKI (b. 1945). Skrzynecki's Polish
Ukranian parents brought him to Australia when he was
four years old. He is now a teacher in the New South
Wales Education Department.

MICHAEL DRANSFIELD (1949-73). Dransfield
had his first book of verse, *Streets of the Long Voyage*,
published in 1970. A career of great promise was cut
short by his early death.

CHARLES BUCKMASTER (1951-72). Charles
Buckmaster was born at Lilydale, Victoria, and spent his
first seventeen years on an orchard in the rural district
of Gruyere. He moved to Melbourne in 1968 and, for a
time, became actively involved in the La Mama writers'
workshop. The years until his death were spent mainly
in Melbourne.

INTRODUCTION

ROBERT FROST, it is reported, once gave a lecture on 'The Anthology as the Highest Form of Criticism'. While the lecture itself has not survived, its title has the ring of truth to anybody who has ever tried to assemble a collection of other men's work. The sheer volume of material to be screened: the complex and delicate considerations competing for priority in every decision for acceptance or rejection; the problems of ordering and arrangement: these matters, responsibly approached, make the anthologist's task one of the severest tests of principle and practice in the whole ambit of literary criticism.

It is as well, therefore, to set down at the outset some of the basic principles I have tried to follow in making this selection of Australian verse. In the first place, I have not sought to make every previous collection obsolete. Such wholesale erasure of the past seems to me neither profitable nor indeed possible. My wish is, rather, to supplement and complement that sense of what is central to our poetry which earlier collections have helped to form.

I have therefore included – and without apology – a number of 'standard' anthology pieces, by poets both major and minor. Their omission would merely have obtained novelty at the expense of sanity. Generally, I have been guided not only by what personally pleases me but also by what I believe to be essential to an understanding of the development of our poetry. I have not, however, construed it as part of my responsibility to pinpoint every newly discovered feature on the map of the absolutely up-to-the-minute. The work of the very young, the exactly contemporary and most boldly experimental, will always elicit interest from readers of poetry, an interest which can merge all too readily into the culturally modish, the intellectually chic. What seems bright and shiny today may, by tomorrow, be abraded entirely away.

27

Yet no anthology can act merely as a supplement and complement to the past. By its very existence, it offers a challenge to previous interpretations of the tradition on which it builds. The challenge of this anthology may, indeed, be thought to contain an element of the contentious, and the bone of contention is buried, not very deep, in the treatment accorded the nineteenth century. When, some years ago, Douglas Stewart and Tom Inglis Moore published a two-volume history of Australian poetry, Inglis Moore devoted the whole of the first volume (278 pages) to verse from the earliest colonial period up to that of Mary Gilmore; in this book, the same corpus of work is represented by some dozen poets and accorded a scant 50 pages. Furthermore, the bush songs and ballads, so often admired for their native power, are completely absent from this anthology.

Their absence does not bespeak any snobbish derogation of their interest and achievement. It is due, in part at least, to the further application of the principle of supplement and increment. The bush songs and ballads are by now so readily available that to reprint the major items yet again would be gratuitous. Douglas Stewart and Nancy Keesing, J. S. Manifold, and Russel Ward have made the further reproduction of these products of our nineteenth century popular culture, for the time being, unnecessary.

What in effect this anthology embodies is the history of articulate, personal poetry in this country; poetry in which the individual imagination encounters a language, a physical environment, and a culture, and seeks to amalgamate the elements of that encounter within the forms of a conscious art. Where the ballad tradition has intersected the impulse towards a self-conscious art, I hope its importance has been adequately recognized – notably in the poems of Barcroft Boake, Henry Lawson, and 'Banjo' Paterson; or, in the twentieth century, in the work of Douglas Stewart and David Campbell, Dorothy Hewett and Ronald McCuaig.

'Tradition', Kathleen Raine once wrote, 'is the record

of imaginative experiences.' What, above all, I hope the
reader of this book might discover is the tradition of those
Australians who have tried to make poetry – true poetry –
out of the ingredients their circumstances offered them.
It follows, therefore, that writers like C. J. Dennis and
John O'Brien have found no place in this book: again,
not because I disregard the interest and importance of
what they did, or the delight their lines can offer, but
merely because they do not seem to me to have had that
commitment to the imagination which would have made
them, in the fullest sense, poets.

With these acts of exclusion behind me, I brought to
my selection no prejudiced views about the pattern of
development I might want or expect to find in two hun-
dred years of Australian poetry in English. My aim was,
first of all, to present what I judged to be a selection of
the best poems written in this country since 1788. Yet, as
I winnowed down my choice of what I believed to be
excellent, it became increasingly plain that certain patterns
of growth did emerge. The crudest, the most unavoidable
fact of all was that the best of the poetry written in Aus-
tralia tends to fall after a date somewhere around 1930.
The weighting of the anthology towards the last forty years
was not an arbitrary decision nor one dictated by a pre-
judice in favour of modernity; it was dictated by the
quality of the poems themselves. Concomitantly, it be-
came clear that of all the nineteenth century Australian
verse which aspired to the condition of poetry, only a tiny
amount could sustain cool-headed criticism, even when
sympathy was amply mixed with professional rigour. The
century offers a number of pieces of a minor, if faded,
charm; even more of the greatest interest to the student
of Australian society and culture. But of genuinely good
or important poems, not many more than are printed here.

The nineteenth century polarization between mass pro-
duction and minimal achievement, however, comprehends
a more engaging paradox. In spite of the domestic medio-
crity of so much of the verse of the period, it contains the

seeds for nearly all the subsequent, mature growth of Australian verse. An inspection of the dozen or so major exhibits from Harpur to Brennan will reveal with extraordinary fullness and clarity the shape of things to come. Such an inspection will constitute a large part of what I shall feel able to say by way of historical introduction to these poems – and not only because our twentieth century verse derives so intimately from the preoccupations of the nineteenth, but also for the simple reason that, as one approaches one's own present, historical analysis becomes increasingly problematic, and critical interpretation (in an anthology) correspondingly impertinent.

*

That the tradition of deliberate poetry starts in Australia with Charles Harpur there can be no doubt. The most useful perspective on Harpur's verse and the imaginative history he initiated, however, is much more open to question. The conventional way of judging our nineteenth century poets – treating them as cameras pointed at a landscape – clearly has its uses. Yet those uses are chiefly concerned with the outer trappings of poetry, its conjunction with socio-cultural desiderata. Investigation of Harpur and his successors in terms of their accurate reportage of antipodean phenomena will tell us very little about the inner continuity of Australian poetry, the workings of the imagination in this country, the way it has absorbed the physical environment rather than registered it.

Of Harpur's 'The Creek of the Four Graves', for instance, I believe more important things need to be argued than the reliability of its physical description. There is, indeed, little or no evidence that literal realism in any way commanded Harpur's primary allegiance. What, on the contrary, are the two crucially informing qualities of the poem are that it is narrative, and that it is heroic. In committing himself to verse narrative as the enabling mode of his imagination, Harpur established a tradition in our poetry at least as important as any photographic concern with flora and fauna. From 'The Creek of the Four Graves' through to R. D. FitzGerald's 'The Wind at Your Door' and James McAuley's 'Captain Quiros', one of the remarkably constant features of our verse has been the urge towards story-telling. This predilection for the narrative mode is, I believe, a principal manifestation of the attachment of our culture to some of the basic tenets of Romanticism.

The heroic aspirations of Harpur's language in 'The Creek of the Four Graves' may seem to have less radical connections with Australian culture than its formal structure; may, indeed, be explained away in terms of inert and poorly executed Miltonic and eighteenth century borrowings. Again, I believe this to be far too simple a view. Whatever the success of his style in practice, Harpur's Miltonism was the result of deeply considered choice among the large range of styles wherein he hoped to find, somewhere, a suitable home for an Australian muse. The high and stilted rhetoric was Harpur's attempt to humanize the land he lived in. Knowing full well that he was born into an Australia 'unstoried, artless, unenhanced', he hoped (perhaps naively) through his very choice of language to turn a place where people lived into a civilized society.

The narrative and the language of 'The Creek of the Four Graves' combine to realize a myth of Eden. The tale is not merely one of pioneering hardship but an image of the human condition as early nineteenth century Australia revealed it to Harpur's imagination. The Eden theme, to be sure, is universally recurring in all literatures. What give the Australian version of it its peculiar features are its ambivalent secularity and its concentration on the impediments in the way of attaining Paradise rather than on the seat of bliss itself. To conceive of a secular Eden may well be a paradox; if so, it is a paradox whose intricacies and consequences it has been the business of an extraordinarily large part of our poetry to unravel. The central preoccupation with Eden has risen to the surface of the work of at least two of our landmark poets – Brennan and Hope – and has provided images and a controlling frame of reference for scores of others.

The source of a modern Australian phenomenon – the production of a poetry largely given over to a kind of Romantic idealism in the midst of a pragmatic, even sardonic society – may well be found in 'The Creek of the Four Graves.' 'A Midsummer Noon in the Australian Forest', the other piece of Harpur's verse printed in this collection, arguably makes an equally definitive contribution to the direction and pattern of our poetic history. Too often thought of as a mildly successful programme piece, 'A Midsummer Noon' reveals its true inwardness only in its concluding lines:

> O 'tis easeful here to lie
> Hidden from noon's scorching eye,
> In this grassy cool recess
> Musing thus of quietness.

Here, the whole centre of the poem's gravity is shifted away from the Nature which is observed to the consciousness which is doing the observing. Where 'The Creek of the Four Graves' initiated the effort to absorb the Australian landscape into a usable human culture by making it the field of archetypal narrative, 'A Midsummer Noon in the Australian Forest' established the processes of the perceiving consciousness as the twin pivot of Australian poetry. Again, the processes of consciousness are among the universal and unavoidable concerns of all poetry; it is, I believe, the 'musing' quality of the Australian imagination which gives it its special flavour. In Australia, the reflexive fascination of the poet with his own perceiving powers less often reveals a stream of consciousness than something like a static, contemplative mode of knowing the world. Its characteristic metaphors are of tides and oceans rather than rivers; its implications for an understanding of personality have resulted in some of the still unsolved problems of perception and technique of our contemporary verse.

One of these problems finds a *locus classicus* as early as Adam Lindsay Gordon's 'The Sick Stockrider', one of the most celebrated and admired of nineteenth century Australian poems. The piece is a decisive failure, in dramatization. It is as if, once he had set down the opening lines, Gordon clean forgot, if he ever clearly realized, that his poem was being spoken by a dying man. A dramatized personality simply does not exist in the poem; and one of the great difficulties of our poetry has remained, even up to the present time, that of adequately imagining and dramatizing a self outside the poet's own. To be sure, it is not often, in the twentieth century, that the failures in projecting another personality into verse are as naively thorough as Gordon's, but the failures and evasions, when they occur, tend to be of the same kind as those of 'The Sick Stockrider': sentimental variations on the *ubi-sunt* motif, images of Eden enfeebled into Arcadia, done in a language which mingles self-pity and self-indulgence in equal measure.

Whatever its shortcomings, 'The Sick Stockrider' must find its way into a representative anthology of Australian verse, as much for its one-time prestige as for its prototypical failures. That prestige produced a considerable crop of imitations and was one of the forces leading to the intersection in later nineteenth century poetry of folk balladry with the creative drive of the individual imagination. A further generative poem behind the work of the 1880s and 90s was that sturdy old companion piece to 'Midsummer Noon', Henry Kendall's 'Bell-Birds'.

It is by now scarcely necessary to defend the accuracy of Kendall's observation of the Australian landscape that he knew. Far more pertinent, in the present context, is to note that the poem, within the limits of its writer's somewhat coarse sensibility, aims at synthesizing what I have described as the two pivotal concerns that Charles

Harpur transmitted to his successors in the making of an Australian poetic tradition. The minimal 'narrative' of the poem is, characteristically, a quest for the invisible and unattainable bell birds; the texture of the opening stanzas announces the enchantment which that quest initially induces. 'Initially' is important here; the feeling at which the poem arrives is all of loss and nostalgia. The movement of the poem embodies in little and at low pressure one of the great potential dangers confronting the poet in Australia. The pursuit of a Romantic idealism within the boundaries of secular behaviour, the awareness of a mysterious and inaccessible centre to human life, may well lead to doubt, disillusion, at worst, despair. The hope of a hidden paradise, together with a knowledge of the experientially extreme, rendered Australian poetry from the outset peculiarly susceptible to those agonies of consciousness which normally characterize the latter stages of a Romantic movement. In Australian poetry, these qualities have, paradoxically enough, been less a terminal symptom than a continuing and permanent condition.

Much of Kendall's output bears witness to the way such despair can become mere unhappiness in poets not especially gifted with intelligence or verbal finesse. In the other two poems printed in this anthology, however, Kendall did make genuine and significant contributions to our verse. 'The Last of His Tribe', much more immediately in contact with the aborigines than 'The Creek of the Four Graves', reaps its measure of success through the form in which its humanist compassion is cast: the brooding meditation of a lyrically sympathetic consciousness. The utter contrast, in language, conventions and subject of 'The Song of Ninian Melville', indicates one of the basic difficulties of the nineteenth century Australian poet: the problem of choosing among the proliferation of styles made technically available to him by the northern cultures. For an antipodean poet of that time, Susan Sontag's stern insight, 'Style is the principle of decision in a work of art', must have been even more difficult in application than in modern America, where, God knows, it must be difficult enough.

More positively, 'The Song of Ninian Melville' suggests a close, vigorous, and colloquial engagement with social actuality. It is perhaps unfortunate that so few of our nineteenth century poets saw that one of their best chances of writing good poems was to be deliberately anti-poetical. Both Harpur (in 'The Temple of Infamy') and Kendall (in 'The Bronze Trumpet') experimented with the possibilities of formal, Augustan satire; a piece like 'Ninian Melville' was a much rarer forecast of things to come. 'The Temple of Infamy' and 'The Bronze Trumpet' have their twentieth century descendants in, say, A. D. Hope's 'Dunciad Minor' and James McAuley's 'Letter to John Dryden'. The lineage of 'Ninian Melville' comes down to the verse of Ronald McCuaig and, more recently, Bruce Dawe.

Outside his poems, Henry Kendall's was a sad and disordered life, ending at the unhappily early age of forty-two. Yet the great example of the melancholia which was almost endemic among our nineteenth century poets was Barcroft Boake. The circumstances of his death sum up all too notoriously the conditions and likely fate of the Australian poet of his time: suicide by hanging himself with his own stockwhip on the shores of Sydney's Middle Harbour at the age of twenty-six. Boake's most famous piece, 'Where the Dead Men Lie', conventionally regarded as a vivid portrayal of the harsh face that Australia could turn towards its pioneers, also warrants attention for the note of social protest which is sounded in its closing stanzas. Yet, as one reads the poem, one needs above all to remember that Boake was a city bred Australian who turned his back on Sydney and gave himself to the bush in a barely understood attempt to clarify his subjective vision of things. The bush was for Boake as much metaphor as phenomenal reality. The insistent extremity of Boake's vision in 'Where the Dead Men Lie' seems in excess of the data that the poem offers. Boake is setting out, as best he may, the experiential horror of antipodean Romanticism, shock at an Eden which assumes the face of Hell.

Such a reading of a poem which is usually held to place Boake among the bush balladists is, I believe, supported by the less familiar 'An Allegory', also printed in this anthology. The sardonic understatement of its bitter irony finds its parallel, if anywhere, in some of the short poems of Stephen Crane. Yet 'An Allegory' is not a freak, a sport, in the pattern of Australian poetry. Its disillusion and despair are as integral a part of Boake's achievement as that achievement is of the formative history of verse in this country.

In a curious and tragic sense, Boake was a victim of his own amateurism. Only towards the end of his life was he learning something of the technical sophistication which might have protected his imagination against that all too candid encounter with his emotions out of which the best of his poems are made. The case of Victor Daley is almost completely the reverse. Supporting himself and his family entirely by his writing, Daley learnt early the deviousness which would allow the continued exercise of craft skills with the least possible drain on the true resources of his imagination. 'Dreams' is typical of his achievement, and of a great deal of the verse written in Australia in the latter half of the nineteenth century. It arrives at its ready charm with too little cost, using its formal smoothness as a protection against rather than as a means of attaining involvement.

Lightly worn Romantic sentimentality had its vogue, at this time, outside Australia as well as within. Nevertheless, the cultural forces which surfaced in the phenomenon were significantly, if slightly, different in this country from those elsewhere. Part of Daley's contribution to the growth of Australian poetry lies simply in his full-time practice of the trade of letters; his was a necessary demonstration that, if you cared enough, writing could become a career. The quality of Daley's lyrics is certainly a function of his limited talent, allied with his practical stance in the world of letters; it is most certainly not the product of a Romantic culture so generally enfeebled that it could not produce anything other or better.

Even Daley had enough of the poet in him to sometimes break through the shell of his bland technique to the creative stir beneath. When he was not exploiting his well-known 'Celtic' lyricism, he was capable of writing, under the *non de plume* of Creeve Roe, passionately felt and pointedly direct poems of social protest. When Creeve Roe's force of feeling combined with Victor Daley's deft control, he could, as in 'When London Calls', create verse of some real refinement and penetration. 'When London Calls', furthermore, succeeds in transforming into literature a theme which fuelled our programmatic culture for at least 150 years, and, in some measure, still does. But at perhaps no other period in our history than in the few years around the turn of the century was the need to define and defend one's self against English culture so pressing as to become the stuff of imaginative literature.

Where Barcroft Boake had been haunted by his image of an Eden become Hell, and Victor Daley had rested content in the easier suburbs of secular existence, 'Banjo' Paterson disported himself in the surrounding parklands of Paradise we call Arcadia. Paterson's Arcadia had, naturally, an Australian décor – selected on the basis of both his own rural experience and his contact with two significant forces in the cultural traditions of late nineteenth century Australia. The fact that he edited, in 1905, the first important collection of Australian folksongs is sufficient reminder of Paterson's debt to the popular culture of his time. Yet it is also worth remembering that the Prelude to his *Selected Poems* is little more than an abbreviated plagiarism of Adam Lindsay Gordon's dedication to *Bush Ballads and Galloping Rhymes*. The cultural genesis of 'The Man from Snowy River' is a mating of the bush ballad with that mode of self-conscious verse which enjoyed the greatest prestige amongst Paterson's Australian contemporaries.

In one sense, Paterson's unique achievement was to so remodel Arcadia that it could find a place for horsemen and cattle as well as shepherds and sheep. His other achievement, alongside the gusty, galloping freedom of 'The Man from Snowy River' is the salty, larger-than-life-size comedy of 'Saltbush Bill'. Bill fuses the attributes of the high class confidence trickster (by repute, an archetypal Australian product), the brawny frontiersman, and the identity-seeking antipodean who expresses himself so differently in Daley's 'When London Calls'. Along with the general allegiance to the ballad form, it is the possibilities of the exaggerated comic verse narrative which has been Paterson's principal bequest to his latter-day inheritors. The spirit of Paterson can still be discerned in a good deal of the verse of Douglas Stewart or Ronald McCuaig, J. S. Manifold or Colin Thiele.

Lawson and Paterson are coupled in the history of Australian literature as the twin bright stars of the Nineties constellation. Yet the verse of each is notoriously distinct. They saw outback Australia through different eyes – Paterson had something of the cavalier view of the man on horseback, while Lawson employed the harsher perspectives of the traveller humping his swag. They find their point of contact, perhaps, in a common devotion to the popular ballad. For my own part, I have to confess to finding very little from the great mass of Lawson's verse, including the balladry, which sets it off from the general level of achievement of his contemporaries. His special contributions to our poetry, it seems to me, are comparatively few and fairly represented by the three poems I have included here.

'Middleton's Rouseabout', one of the very few short-line poems that Lawson attempted, is, for all its simplistic appearance, a remarkably succinct portrait of a national type, the ironical repetition in the final stanza in particular carrying some sharp judgements on the dynamics of Australian society. 'The Song of Old Joe Swallow' retains interest for its attempt at solving the problem manifested in 'The Sick Stockrider'. Where Paterson had taken over Gordon's nostalgia, Lawson addresses himself to the more difficult task of dramatizing a poetic personality. With its assured hold on a vernacular diction, 'The Song of Old Joe Swallow' goes halfway towards success, defeated at last only by the obstinate refusal of the metre to shift out of the familiar grooves of balladry into the authentic rhythms of a living personality. By contrast, it is the rhythm of 'One-Hundred-and-Three' which gives that poem its very real distinction. The importance of egalitarian social protest in the Australian literary tradition is one of the *clichés* of historical interpretation; yet there is singularly little important verse in that vein to attest to its actuality. 'One-Hundred-and-Three' is a major success in the kind, and the success depends basically on the passion and indignation with which the protest is registered on the metrical pulse of the poem.

'One-Hundred-and-Three' has its successors in the twentieth century, notably Dorothy Hewett's 'Clancy and Dooley and Don McLeod' (a piece omitted from this selection with some regret). More often, however, the best of our latter-day radical verse has relied on cagier, more sophisticated strategies than the unremitting march of Lawson's piece; one thinks, in this connection, of Wilma Hedley's 'Isaac'.

Had Lawson and Paterson been born into any other culture than that of late nineteenth century Australia, their poetic reputations would probably have been negligible (which is not to deny their continued power and right to touch Australians). On the other hand, it would be difficult for any national literature to ignore Chris Brennan. The complex and often esoteric nature of his verse makes any short-hand judgement of it inappropriate and foolish. All that can perhaps be said here of its level of achievement is that even its most spirited detractors have sensed an opus worthy of the best criticism can bring against it. By way of description, however, one can confidently assert that the more we come to understand the full orchestration of *Poems 1913*, the more it will reveal itself not so much as a Europeanized freak as an achievement wrought out of themes and motifs endemic in the Australian tradition. The idea of Eden, impressed on our poetry by Charles Harpur, is notoriously central to Brennan's imagination; the style of *Poems 1913*, for all its indisputed *symboliste* connections, has equally important epic qualities; the whole structure of this *livre composé* is that of an oblique and prismatically fragmented heroic narrative. In matters both great and small, the essential genesis of *Poems 1913* in its Australian matrix is the quality which must increasingly impress us in Brennan's major work.

Of the total achievement of *Poems 1913*, 'The Wanderer' and 'Epilogue' can give only the barest hints. The thematic, intellectual, and emotional ramifications of the book reveal themselves only to sustained inspection. Yet the two pieces printed here both have a kind of self-sufficiency and go some way towards revealing Brennan's central concerns and his mode of dealing with them. In 'The Wanderer' the literal journeying of the poet soon gives way to a symbolic account of his spiritual quest, which brings him in the end to a quietist state of mind wherein consciousness triumphs in spite of the world's defeat. 'Epilogue' exhibits at a very high level of visibility the most urgent executive problem Brennan posed for himself: that of finding a language appropriate and adequate to the unique range of tasks he demanded of it. The 'Epilogue', in essence a summary statement of the themes and structure of *Poems 1913*, swings between two stylistic poles: the language of the actual with which it commences (a tram moving westwards down Sydney's George Street to Sydney University) and the doctrinal language of the emotions with which it concludes.

If, as he is for many, Brennan is a great poet *manqué*, the critical measure of his failure is probably to be found in his inability to integrate these two modes of language. Viewed from the poet's own standpoint, however, Brennan's failure might appear in a different light. One of his difficulties in bringing his art to its full realization seems to have been that it was posited on the idea of an Eden of the spirit to which all men might aspire and of which some might obtain privileged glimpses. The reality of such glimpses, presumably very close to mystical illumination, is essential to Brennan's conception of man and of poetry, but he never knew it directly himself. The over-writing of at least parts of *Poems 1913* is probably a stylistic over-compensation for what Brennan construed as a crucial lack in the felt emotion of his verse.

Curiously enough, Brennan's close friend, John Le Gay Brereton, was apparently gifted with precisely that kind of insight which would have perfected Brennan's imaginative apparatus for composing his own work. Brereton's father, as well as introducing the delights of the Turkish bath to the antipodes, was also a leading member of Sydney's Swedenborgian community. The younger Brereton's whole youthful environment, coupled with the early manifested bent of his own spirit, made him much more apt for privileged glimpses into the heart of things than the Jesuit-trained, classics-oriented Brennan. Certainly, 'The Silver Gull' realizes the experience of a consciousness which, in the act of observing Nature, is carried out of itself towards union with the Nature it observes. One of the few genuine attempts in all our poetry at recording, at first hand, the mystical perception of creation, 'The Silver Gull' is also one of the extreme extensions of that reflexive fascination with the observing self which stems from Harpur's 'A Midsummer Noon in the Australian Forest'.

The obvious 'influence' on 'The Silver Gull' is, to be sure, Walt Whitman. We know that *Leaves of Grass* was the only book Brereton took on the walking tour which was later transformed into the delightful prose idyll, *Landlopers*, and he often stated his enthusiasm for the American poet. Certainly, the ecstatic dissolution of man into nature with which 'The Silver Gull' concludes recalls and not unsuccessfully challenges the ending of 'Song of Myself'. There is to my mind far more of the real spirit of Whitman in Brereton's poem than in all of the heavily marching quatrains of Bernard O'Dowd – in spite of the Melbourne poet's brief correspondence with the ageing sage of Camden.

One of O'Dowd's major works, 'The Bush', is a somewhat unhappy attempt to assimilate Australian landscape into a kind of universal mythology. Had I been able to find any sufficiently self-contained sequence, I was tempted to include a sequence of 'The Bush' in this anthology – if only for its historical importance. The piece I have included, the well-known sonnet, 'Australia', earns its place for the same reason, and especially by virtue of its imagery. The unresolved images of Eden and Sargasso illuminate in retrospect the central dilemma with which virtually all our nineteenth century poetry was wrestling. The need to find metaphors to realize the poet's idea of Australia has continued into the poetry of our own time, as witness Hope's 'Australia', McAuley's 'Terra Australis', or Stewart's poem of the same name. Its form, too, gives O'Dowd's poem a representative status. As long ago as 1926, Louis Lavater had drawn our attention to the Australian fondness for the sonnet. That it answers a deep need in our culture is indicated by the continuing fidelity of our poets to the form – most notably, perhaps, in that otherwise idiosyncratic poet of the sea's edge, John Blight.

Living, as he did, from 1866 to 1953, O'Dowd was, in crude historical terms, a man of two centuries. But the unwavering moral earnestness of his verse bears no trace of modernity about it. If we are to look for a pivot other than Brennan on which Australian poetry swung from the nineteenth into the twentieth century, we may well find it in the career of Dame Mary Gilmore. In subject, her poems often look back nostalgically to material which, in her own generation, was just beginning to be converted into history: Eureka, or the untouched life of the abori-

gines. The manner in which, from Mary Gilmore's genera-
tion on, their own history became a possible subject for
Australian poets, is nowhere better displayed than in the
well-known 'Botany Bay'.

Yet other preoccupations also find their way into her
poems, notably passionate love between men and women.
While her love poems admit only a very indirect sexuality,
they nevertheless liberated adult passion into the real
world of secular humanity from the artificial Paradises
within which it had been captive for most of the preced-
ing hundred years. In general, Mary Gilmore realized the
optimistic elements in Australian Romanticism more ade-
quately than any previous poet. She was able to move our
verse this step forward by virtue of what it seems fair to
describe as the Romantic idealism of her technique and
attitudes. The aphoristic utterance, the singing metres and
chiming rhymes, cast over the emotions of her poetry a
subdued lyric glamour which in no way destroys the
scrupulous honesty of her perceptions. In perfecting her
own manner, Mary Gilmore was at the same time building
a model which was to command the adherence of a major
stream of our verse-making, declaring itself notably in the
work of poets like Judith Wright, Douglas Stewart, Geof-
frey Dutton and Rosemary Dobson.

The bridging role that Mary Gilmore was able to play
in the history of our verse may in part have been due to
the happy accident of her long life (1865-1962). Certainly,
her presence helps to give substance to a period, roughly
between Federation and the end of the First World War,
which would otherwise look singularly thin in achievement.
It is a period which, in this anthology, is represented
through such figures as Shaw Neilson, Hugh McCrae, and
'Furnley Maurice' (Frank Wilmot). Because of their asso-
ciation with one of the generally agreed upon 'troughs'
of our literary history, it is easy to under-rate these
writers, or to dismiss them with far too coarse a descrip-
tion of their achievement.

Easy remarks can, thus, be made about Neilson's 'Celtic'

spirit; discussion of McCrae's verse can resolve itself into debate about the propriety of peopling the Australian bush with satyrs and centaurs; Furnley Maurice's work may be made the occasion for anecdotes about Coles' Book Arcade. Such superficialities do very little to illuminate the actual quality of their work or their relations to both predecessors and successors.

It would, for instance, in the case of Shaw Neilson be much more useful to 'place' him by reference to the poetry of Emily Dickinson. Both writers nurtured a singular and idiosyncratic talent in circumstances of remarkable cultural seclusion. And the Australian labourer and the American spinster shared one great talent – the capacity to catch in a single line, a single image, a feeling, an *aperçu*, which arouses in the reader what Emily Dickinson called the sense of 'zero at the bone'. His control of the uniquely emotive image is at once Neilson's great legacy to the future of Australian poetry and the warrant of his inheritance from the past. Almost every line he wrote is concerned to make actual the quality of an observing consciousness concentrated to the focal point of a unique sensibility.

For my own taste, McCrae, while quite as idiosyncratic a poet as Neilson, is a lesser one. But as with Neilson, his idiosyncrasy generated at least one quality which would permanently enlarge the possibilities of Australian poetry. It has only shallow connections with satyrs and the centaurs (though it can be felt in pieces like 'Ambuscade' and 'I Blow My Pipes'). As cultural history, it has been identified (by, for instance, Vincent Buckley in *Essays in Poetry, Mainly Australian*) as a chief exhibit of that Nietzschean vitalism which was imported into Australia by, among others, Norman Lindsay. I would prefer to express the quality in terms of the self-regarding delight which McCrae's verse almost invariably displays. The sprightly elegant play of words becomes an end in itself. And to include among the delights of poetry the very shape and pattern of language as much as any feeling or thought it transmits seems to me McCrae's great historical contribution to our verse.

Where Neilson brought to our poetry a sharp new savour in the use of the image, and McCrae a self-regarding delight in words, Furnley Maurice, it may be argued, acclimatized ideas as viable components of Australian poetry. Not that all of our earlier poets had lacked ideas or had been unintelligent – patently, some had deeply pondered the themes of their work. Rather, Maurice was the first to treat thoughts not as the product of composition but as among its basic building blocks. In effect he did for ideas what Neilson had done for the image. He was not, of course, an antipodean Metaphysical (he had neither the intensity nor the wit). But, in some of his poems, because of his willingness to entertain ideas, to juggle with them in a deliberately 'anti-poetical' diction, he was distinctly among the first of the 'Moderns'. Such a judgement will, I believe, be immediately confirmed by a reading of pieces like 'The Agricultural Show, Flemington' or 'Apples in the Moon'.

By the end of the First World War, certain stirrings in the inner life of Australian poetry indicated that it was ready to undergo a major metamorphosis, to advance to a new stage of maturity. The alien and terrible shock of the War (registered here in the poems of Leon Gellert and Vance Palmer) was, in a way, irrelevant to that metamorphosis. Seemingly in response to the peremptory commands of historical necessity, there appeared in the early 1920s two young poets who would work a permanent change in Australian poetry – in the range of themes it could successfully address, in the level of professionalism at which it would conduct itself. There is little doubt that Kenneth Slessor and R. D. FitzGerald thrust Australian verse forward with an imperious force unknown since its foundations in the lines of Charles Harpur.

They did not, of course, work their transformation overnight; starting to write in the 1920s, both FitzGerald and Slessor produced their first indisputably major work in the middle to late 1930s. 'Five Bells' was first published in 1939, FitzGerald's 'Essay on Memory' won the 1938 sesqui-centenary prize. Slessor's creativity seems to have exhausted itself by the end of the Second World War; FitzGerald's imagination, happily, continues to ripen with the passing years (for whatever reason, contemporary Australian society encourages long and fruitful poetic careers). 'The Wind at Your Door', appearing as late as 1959, seems to me to rank among the finest of modern poems of its kind (just as 'Five Bells' is one of the great modern elegies).

To link the achievement of Slessor and FitzGerald may seem a matter of historical convenience, so little, at first sight, does the work of each man resemble that of the other. Slessor's elegant dandyism, the *élan* of even his most deeply felt poetry, seems far removed from the subdued Yeatsian timbre of FitzGerald's characteristic lines. Yet the connection must in the long run be allowed to prevail. Their joint triumph was to seize on the central preoccupations of the Australian poetic imagination, and, for the first time, to realize them in a language of complete adequacy and assurance. Not even excepting the work of Brennan, their poems more thoroughly than ever before fused aspiration and execution.

Slessor's poetry, in particular, fastened on the nexus between the observing sensibility and the phenomenal world. The sensibility itself was a tonic mixture of traditional and modern. Early criticism of Slessor was quick to assert the similarity to T. S. Eliot; but Slessor himself has acknowledged Tennyson as an important source of inspiration and technique. And, indeed, his poems may well dazzle us with their rare commingling of Eliot's edgy toughness with Tennyson's tender fantasy and feeling. But one cannot read Slessor's work very long without realizing that it is packed with a greater assemblage of solid objects (however exotic) than that of almost any other Australian poet. The world is real to Slessor, and in the end it is impervious to consciousness. Impervious to human need, Slessor's physical world is also totally resistant to time. The separate pieces of his *oeuvre* are characteristically set in the absolute present, both past and future almost unknowable. His articulation of such an idiosyncratic sense of time, is at once Slessor's great personal insight and his major contribution to the advancement of our verse. An imaginative tradition posited on a quest for Eden within a secular world must sooner or later have annexed to itself the dimension of time; Slessor was a principal agent of annexation.

Contemporaneously, however, FitzGerald was listening to his own clock ticking away behind the data that Australia offered him. Where Slessor virtually obliterates time from his verse, FitzGerald measures human activity against the long chronology of cosmic process. Time becomes for FitzGerald the index of a history in which the human span is an important but only tiny part of the whole. In poem after poem FitzGerald is able to write out of a sense of the past at last wholly liberated from that artificiality with which Harpur, at the nation's beginnings, was forced to conceive of history: 'There was a settler in the olden times went forth'.

For Australian poetry, Slessor and FitzGerald brought the idea of time within the boundaries of what can be known and used. Their other great act of liberation concerned the representation of the self. No national literature can disregard for too long the primary responsibility of imagining the human self, the personality, in all its range of expression. In the nineteenth century Gordon and others had accepted – without success or real commitment – the well-tried convention of direct dramatization. When Slessor wrote of his Captain Dobbin, or FitzGerald his Abel Tasman, each poet adopted a curiously oblique relation to the personality he wished to release into his lines. There is apparently a slight mistrust of absolute dramatization, a reliance on a peculiar kind of obliquity – which had its successes for Slessor and FitzGerald and continues to do so in, say, the work of Rodney Hall or Geoffrey Lehmann.

47

To prolong this contentious history beyond the water-shed achievement of Slessor and FitzGerald is to risk bringing it onto that dangerous ground where historical interpretation may pass, unnoticed, into critical directives as to the proper reading of contemporary poets or poems. The risk, however, must be accepted, if only for the sake of sketching in the main channels through which Australian poetry has flowed on the near side of the water-shed. Oddly, an immediate sequel to the integrated achievement of Slessor and FitzGerald was a fragmentation of poetic effort into a number of seemingly contra-dictory directions. Yet the competing schools, the argu-ments, the disunity of the 1940s can already be seen as marks of health rather than of decay. What, as a result of Slessor and FitzGerald, happened to our poetry may be stated something like this: for the first hundred years or so of our history, Australian poets struggled fretfully with the lumpy data that time, place and cultural circum-stance had offered to their imaginations. Since Slessor and FitzGerald, they have been freed from their limiting, because unsolved, fixations. The Eden theme, the chal-lenge of the secular, the qualities of the contemplative mind – these matters still lie at the centre of many of the best poems written in this country, but they are appre-hended less as monolithic concepts than as diverse actuali-ties of behaviour. Our modern poets take the materials of their verse where they find them, but surprisingly often they find them within the territory staked out by their nineteenth century forebears.

Thus the poetic generation immediately following Sles-sor and FitzGerald included a number of writers who made use of the new self-confidence to manoeuvre Aus-tralian poetry into a series of new and individual variations on the older themes: Kenneth Mackenzie introducing sexuality into poems of Romantic passion, James Picot discovering a kind of Impressionism as a mode of the sensibility, J. A. R. Mackellar wringing historical nostalgia out of the life of the youngest continent, Harry Hooton finding in the profane world forms of freedom only now beginning to find their way into the main line of our poetic development.

Even the passing alliances, movements and schools of the late 1930s and 40s can be seen as working out their 'modernist' or Europe-oriented slogans within a native tradition which exerted its powerful if not always acknowledged influence. The whole rich ferment was hastened, of course, and intensified by the imminence and then the reality of war. Yet, even without that catalytic influence or the stimulus of overseas connections, it seems likely that the inner growth of Australian poetry would have moved towards the fruitful fragmentation of those years. The Jindyworobaks, the Angry Penguins, the Ern Malley hoax – all were part of a shaking up of our poetic culture towards which its whole history had been tending. The Jindyworobak cult of the aboriginal has, thus, its antetype in Harpur's 'The Aboriginal Mother's Lament' and Kendall's 'The Last of His Tribe'. Ideas about 'conditional culture' had been adumbrated in the work of Mary Gilmore, if not earlier. The almost mystical intensity of feeling about Australian nature expressed by Roland Robinson or Ian Mudie had its earlier counterpart in Brereton's 'The Silver Gull'. The popular nationalism of Mudie's 'They'll Tell You About Me' or the social criticism of J. S. Manifold manifests a plain debt to Paterson, Daley, Lawson.

Even the Angry Penguins – the most international, deliberately 'modernist' group of the early 1940s – were playing out, in the minute particulars of the new professionalism, gestures of the imagination first traced in the nineteenth century. The very title of Max Harris's novel, 'The Vegetative Eye', suggests affinities with the author of 'A Midsummer Noon in the Australian Forest'. The whole irrationalist stress of the movement was an extension and more extreme re-statement of themes which long before had found their way into the heart of the Australian literary imagination.

49

The most celebrated response to Max Harris's theories and practice was the Ern Malley hoax, one of the truly focal episodes in the sociology of our literature. The counter-aesthetic endorsed by James McAuley and Harold Stewart in 'Malley's' poems appeared not only to challenge that of the Angry Penguins but to introduce an entirely new element to our poetry – a deliberated classicism. Yet for all the novelty of McAuley's position (and it did possess some real novelty), it seems to me not entirely unlike that of Charles Harpur – both men were confronting the problem of subduing local experience to the communicable forms of an inherited poetry. McAuley, like Harpur in some of his verse, chose a strict, rigorous, and deliberately imitative convention. But, where Harpur was too close to Milton and the eighteenth century for his efforts to appear to be anything but enfeebled pastiche, when McAuley came to write, say, 'A Letter to John Dryden', he was so far away from the author of 'Absalom and Achitophel' that his borrowing of the closed couplet could much more easily be accepted as a virtuoso reworking of a personal model.

After the Ern Malley episode, with Stewart deciding to move permanently to Japan and McAuley grappling with his conversion to Catholicism, the two men drifted apart (at least as figures in the community of literature). Instead, the currents of time and taste swept McAuley forward in the 1950s to what must have appeared to the world as a new alliance – with A. D. Hope. During that decade, indeed, a long-range observer might well have been pardoned for believing that our literary landscape was dominated by a strange two-headed beast rampaging under the protection of the academy, carrying the banner of 'classicism', and bearing the name of Hope-and-McAuley.

To be sure, it was during the 1950s that Hope and McAuley consolidated their reputations as two of our leading modern poets and seemed to exercise a powerful influence over a considerable band of younger poets, mostly located in universities: Vincent Buckley, Chris Wallace-Crabbe, Evan Jones, to list some representative names. Quite clearly the universities, during this period, did come to occupy a place in the polity of Australian literature which they are unlikely to vacate for some time to come, but it becomes increasingly clear that it was not the temporary overthrow of a virile egalitarian tradition by a band of aloof young academics which gave the 1950s their special quality. Chris Wallace-Crabbe came nearer to defining what was the actual case of the inner life of our poetry in an article contributed to *Meanjin Quarterly*, 1961/2, 'The Habit of Irony? Australian Poetry in the Fifties'. Without a doubt, Wallace-Crabbe put his finger on one of the definitive qualities (technical and imaginative) of much of the best verse of the decade. What he perhaps missed, in associating the practice of irony with the movements of poetry overseas, was the native tradition of scepticism going back at least to Barcroft Boake. Wallace-Crabbe and his contemporaries are much more suave in both the emotions they express and the way they express them than any of their nineteenth century predecessors; but in exploring the contrarieties and dangers of human experience in the secular world, they are extending a pattern of the imagination already, in its major outlines, laid out for them.

That the fascination of the secular had not totally effaced the ambivalent attraction of Eden from the minds of our modern poets is suggested by the continuing strength of a line of verse development quite distinct from that represented by Wallace-Crabbe. Tracing its ancestry back to Mary Gilmore, powerfully tinged by the views and personality of Norman Lindsay, its contemporary prominence can fairly be dated from the early work of Douglas Stewart and Judith Wright. It is hospitable to almost every variety of Romantic feeling from the cool to the most spontaneously intense, from Geoffrey Dutton's emotional sophistication to David Campbell's pastoral subtleties. It can even absorb, as in much of Stewart's work, something of the

Paterson tradition of comic narrative. And, as Les Murray's wide-ranging power makes abundantly clear, it must retain its force and prestige for at least some years yet.

In spite of what I believe to be its very real power to revitalize itself at the sources of its mainstream development, Australian poetry, like any other, cannot rely on that process alone for its continuing health. During the past twenty or so years it has found in at least two other phenomena further means of renewing itself. The first one belongs almost to the sociology of literature: a two-way, cosmopolitan traffic with the northern world. In these latter days, it seems as if a modern version of Daley's 'When London Calls' is neither necessary nor possible. Temporary or permanent expatriates like Peter Porter, Alan Riddell or Rosemary Dobson have their work recognized and welcomed on their native grounds. In reverse, migrant poets who have made Australia their home have, in recent years, made invaluable contributions to the range and quality of verse written in this country. One thinks of poets like David Martin, Norman Talbot, Hari Jones, John Couper, Charles Higham. At its best, this international traffic has enabled Australian poetry to range itself alongside the poetries of, say, England and the United States with much greater ease and assurance than ever before, to learn from the worldwide community of letters without abrogating its indigenous commitments.

Within its own borders, Australian poetry has, in several significant instances, found new strength by absorbing back into the centre of its development lessons from local poets who appear to have defined themselves as on the periphery. A necessary condition of health for any poetry is probably the presence of at least a few poets who defy cultural pigeon-holing. Australian names that spring to mind are John Blight, William Hart-Smith, Eric Rolls. But occasionally, such a figure is suddenly seen to re-define himself at the centre and to generate a whole new output of mainstream poetry. It seems possible that in the 1970s Harry Hooton will be re-located in this way, moving in from idiosyncratic isolation to the formative centre. It is almost certain that in the 1960s such a process happened to Francis Webb. His work in the late Forties and early Fifties – *A Drum for Ben Boyd* and *Leichhardt in Theatre* – seemed to set him apart in a lonely circle of unrepeatable success. There seemed no real hope of the rest of Australian poetry breaking through the imaginative quarantine within which he worked out the painful needs of his private experience. If Webb's verse had any point of contact in modern writing, it appeared to be what A. Alvarez has called the poetry of extremity, expressed for Alvarez by poets such as Robert Lowell and Sylvia Plath.

Yet in the 1960s this hopelessly private poet began to become a usable reference point for some of the newer Australian writers. Bruce Beaver, for instance, in 'Letters to Live Poets' links Webb's corrosive self-insight with the crafty discipline of Lowell's *Life Studies* to make a new and original contribution to Australian poetry. The debt to Webb is, one suspects, also to be found in the verse of Craig Powell or Robert Adamson. The prime agents, however, through whom the former idiosyncrasies of Francis Webb may be converted into the norms of the future, are Rodney Hall and Thomas Shapcott – both of them in their middle thirties, both of them widely published, both of them self-conscious spokesmen for what they represent as a new generation of poets taking over from the outworn orthodoxies of Hope and McAuley. The introduction to their anthology, *New Impulses in Australian Poetry* (1968), makes their polemical purposes quite clear. Whether their manifesto will define current Australian poetry in the way that Wallace-Crabbe's essay defined the verse of the Fifties is still, in my view, open to question. But whatever direction Australian verse may take in the future, this much is sure: there is already a corpus of Australian poems which both imply a native tradition of some solidity and complexity, and offer delight and enrichment to discerning readers anywhere.

HARRY HESELTINE

CHARLES HARPUR

1813-68

The Creek of the Four Graves

I

A settler in the olden times went forth
With four of his most bold and trusted men
Into the wilderness – went forth to seek
New streams and wider pastures for his fast
Increasing flocks and herds. O'er mountain routes
And over wild wolds clouded up with brush,
And cut with marshes perilously deep, –
So went they forth at dawn; at eve the sun,
That rose behind them as they journeyed out,
Was firing with his nether rim a range
Of unknown mountains, that like ramparts towered
Full in their front; and his last glances fell
Into the gloomy forest's eastern glades
In golden gleams, like to the Angel's sword,
And flashed upon the windings of a creek
That noiseless ran betwixt the pioneers
And those new Apennines – ran, shaded o'er
With boughs of the wild willow, hanging mixed
From either bank, or duskily befringed
With upward tapering feathery swamp-oaks,
The sylvan eyelash always of remote
Australian waters, whether gleaming still
In lake or pool, or bickering along
Between the marges of some eager stream.

Before them, thus extended, wilder grew
The scene each moment and more beautiful;
For when the sun was all but sunk below
Those barrier mountains, in the breeze that o'er
Their rough enormous backs deep-fleeced with wood
Came whispering down, the wide up-slanting sea
Of fanning leaves in the descending rays

Danced dazzlingly, tingling as if the trees
Thrilled to the roots for very happiness.

But when the sun had wholly disappeared
Behind those mountains – O what words, what hues
Might paint the wild magnificence of view
That opened westward! Out extending, lo!
The heights rose crowding, with their summits all
Dissolving as it seemed, and partly lost
In the exceeding radiancy aloft;
And thus transfigured, for awhile they stood
Like a great company of archaeons, crowned
With burning diadems, and tented o'er
With canopies of purple and of gold.

Here halting wearied now the sun was set,
Our travellers kindled for their first night's camp
A brisk and crackling fire, which seemed to them
A wilder creature than 'twas elsewhere wont,
Because of the surrounding savageness.
And as they supped, birds of new shape and plume
And wild strange voice came by; and up the steep
Between the climbing forest growths they saw
Perched on the bare abutments of the hills,
Where haply yet some lingering gleam fell through,
The wallaroo* look forth. Eastward at last
The glow was wasted into formless gloom,
Night's front; then westward the high massing woods
Steeped in a swart but mellow Indian hue,
A deep dusk loveliness, lay ridged and heaped,
Only the more distinctly for their shade,
Against the twilight heaven – a cloudless depth,
Yet luminous with sunset's fading glow;
And thus awhile in the lit dusk they seemed
To hang like mighty pictures of themselves
In the still chambers of some vaster world.

---

* A large kangaroo, peculiar to the higher and more difficult
mountains.

At last, the business of the supper done,
The echoes of the solitary place
Came as in sylvan wonder wide about
To hear and imitate the voices strange,
Within the pleasant purlieus of the fire
Lifted in glee; but to be hushed erelong,
 As with the darkness of the night there came
O'er the adventurers, each and all, some sense
Of danger lurking in its forest lairs.

But, nerved by habit, they all gathered round
About the well built fire, whose nimble tongues
Sent up continually a strenuous roar
Of fierce delight, and from their fuming pipes
Drawing rude comfort, round the pleasant light
With grave discourse they planned their next day's deeds.
Wearied at length, their couches they prepared
Of rushes, and the long green tresses pulled
From the bent boughs of the wild willows near;
Then the four men stretched out their tired limbs
Under the dark arms of the forest trees
That mixed aloft, high in the starry air,
In arcs and leafy domes whose crossing curves,
Blended with denser intergrowth of sprays,
Were seen in mass traced out against the clear
Wide gaze of heaven; and trustful of the watch
Kept near them by their master, soon they slept,
Forgetful of the perilous wilderness
That lay around them like a spectral world;
And all things slept; the circling forest trees,
Their foremost boles carved from a crowded mass
Less visible by the watch-fire's bladed gleams
That ran far out in the umbrageous dark
Beyond the broad red ring of constant light;
And even the shaded mountains darkly seen,
Their bluff brows looming through the stirless air,
Looked in their stillness solemnly asleep:
Yea, thence surveyed, the universe might have seemed

Coiled in vast rest; – only that one dark cloud,
Diffused and shapen like a spider huge,
Crept as with scrawling legs along the sky;
And that the stars in their bright orders, still
Cluster by cluster glowingly revealed,
As this slow cloud moved on, high over all,
Peaceful and wakeful, watched the world below.

II

Meanwhile the cloudless eastern heaven had grown
More luminous, and now the moon arose
Above the hill, when lo! that giant cone
Erewhile so dark, seemed inwardly aglow
With her instilled irradiance, while the trees
That fringed its outline, their huge statures dwarfed
By distance into brambles and yet all
Clearly defined against her ample orb,
Out of its very disc appeared to swell
In shadowy relief, as they had been
All sculptured from its surface as she rose.
Then her full light in silvery sequence still
Cascading forth from ridgy slope to slope,
Chased mass by mass the broken darkness down
Into the dense-brushed valleys, where it crouched,
And shrank, and struggled, like a dragon-doubt
Glooming a lonely spirit.

His lone watch
The master kept, and wakeful looked abroad
On all the solemn beauty of the world;
And by some sweet and subtle tie that joins
The loved and cherished, absent from our side,
With all that is serene and beautiful
In Nature, thoughts of home began to steal
Into his musings – when, on a sudden, hark!
A bough cracks loudly in a neighbouring brake!
Against the shade-side of a bending gum.

With a strange horror gathering to his heart,
As if his blood were charged with insect life
And writhed along in clots, he stilled himself
And listened heedfully, till his held breath
Became a pang. Nought heard he: silence there
Had recomposed her ruffled wings, and now
Deep brooded in the darkness; so that he
Again mused on, quiet and reassured.

But there again – crack upon crack! Awake!
O heaven! have hell's worst fiends burst howling up
Into the death-doomed world? Or whence, if not
From diabolic rage, could surge a yell
So horrible as that which now affrights
The shuddering dark! Beings as fell are near!
Yea, beings in their dread inherited hate
Awful, vengeful as hell's worst fiends, are come
In vengeance! For behold from the long grass
And nearer brakes arise the bounding forms
Of painted savages, full in the light
Thrown outward by the fire, that roused and lapped
The rounding darkness with its ruddy tongues
More fiercely than before, as though even it
Had felt the sudden shock the air received
From those terrific cries.

On then they came
And rushed upon the sleepers, three of whom
But started, and then weltered prone beneath
The first fell blow dealt down on each by three
Of the most stalwart of their pitiless foes;
But one again, and yet again, rose up,
Rose to his knees, under the crushing strokes
Of huge clubbed nulla-nullas, till his own
Warm blood was blinding him. For he was one
Who had with misery nearly all his days
Lived lonely, and who therefore in his soul
Did hunger after hope, and thirst for what

Hope still had promised him, some taste at least
Of human good however long deferred;
And now he could not, even in dying, loose
His hold on life's poor chances still to come,
Could not but so dispute the terrible fact
Of death, e'en in death's presence. Strange it is,
Yet oft 'tis seen, that fortune's pampered child
Consents to death's untimely power with less
Reluctance, less despair, than does the wretch
Who hath been ever blown about the world,
The straw-like sport of fate's most bitter blasts;
So though the shadows of untimely death,
Inevitably under every stroke
But thickened more and more, against them still
The poor wretch struggled, nor would cease until
One last great blow, dealt down upon his head
As if in mercy, gave him to the dust,
With all his many woes and frustrate hopes.

The master, chilled with horror, saw it all;
From instinct more than conscious thought he raised
His death-charged tube, and at that murderous crew
Firing, saw one fall ox-like to the earth,
Then turned and fled. Fast fled he, but as fast
His deadly foes went thronging on his track.
Fast! for in full pursuit behind him yelled
Men whose wild speech no word for mercy hath!
And as he fled the forest beasts as well
In general terror through the brakes ahead
Crashed scattering, or with maddening speed athwart
His course came frequent. On, still on, he flies –
Flies for dear life, and still behind him hears
Nearer and nearer, the light rapid dig
Of many feet – nearer and nearer still.

III

So went the chase. Now at a sudden turn
Before him lay the steep-banked mountain creek;

Still on he kept perforce, and from a rock
That beaked the bank, a promontory bare,
Plunging right forth and shooting feet-first down,
Sunk to his middle in the flashing stream,
In which the imaged stars seemed all at once
To burst like rockets into one wide blaze.
Then wading through the ruffled waters, forth
He sprang, and seized a snake-like root that from
The opponent bank protruded, clenching there
His cold hand like a clamp of steel; and thence
He swung his dripping form aloft, the blind
And breathless haste of one who flies for life
Urging him on; up the dark ledge he climbed,
When in its face – O verily our God
Hath those in His peculiar care, for whom
The daily prayers of spotless womanhood
And helpless infancy are offered up! –
There in its face a cavity he felt,
The upper earth of which in one rude mass
Was held fast bound by the enwoven roots
Of two old trees, and which, beneath the mould,
Over the dark and clammy cave below,
Twisted like knotted snakes. 'Neath these he crept,
Just as the dark forms of his hunters thronged
The steep bold rock whence he before had plunged.

Duskily visible beneath the moon
They paused a space, to mark what bent his course
Might take beyond the stream. But now no form
Amongst the moveless fringe of fern was seen
To shoot up from its outline, 'mid the boles
And mixing shadows of the taller trees,
All standing now in the keen radiance there
So ghostly still as in a solemn trance;
But nothing in the silent prospect stirred:
Therefore they augured that their prey was yet
Within the nearer distance, and they all
Plunged forward till the fretted current boiled

Amongst their crowding forms from bank to bank;
And searching thus the stream across, and then
Along the ledges, combing down each clump
Of long-flagged swamp-grass where it flourished high,
The whole dark line passed slowly, man by man,
Athwart the cave!

        Keen was their search but vain,
There grouped in dark knots standing in the stream
That glimmered past them moaning as it went,
They marvelled; passing strange to them it seemed;
Some old mysterious fable of their race,
That brooded o'er the valley and the creek,
Returned upon their minds, and fear-struck all
And silent, they withdrew. And when the sound
Of their retreating steps had died away,
As back they hurried to despoil the dead
In the stormed camp, then rose the fugitive,
Renewed his flight, nor rested from it, till
He gained the shelter of his longed-for home.
And in that glade, far in the doomful wild,
In sorrowing record of an awful hour
Of human agony and loss extreme,
Untimely spousals with a desert death,
Four grassy mounds are there beside the creek,
Bestrewn with sprays and leaves from the old trees
Which moan the ancient dirges that have caught
The heed of dying ages, and for long
The traveller passing then in safety there
Would call the place – The Creek of the Four Graves.

A Midsummer Noon in the Australian Forest

    Not a sound disturbs the air,
    There is quiet everywhere;
    Over plains and over woods
    What a mighty stillness broods!

All the birds and insects keep
Where the coolest shadows sleep;
Even the busy ants are found
Resting in their pebbled mound;
Even the locust clingeth now
Silent to the barky bough:
Over hills and over plains
Quiet, vast and slumbrous, reigns.

Only there's a drowsy humming
From yon warm lagoon slow coming:
'Tis the dragon-hornet – see!
All bedaubed resplendently,
Yellow on a tawny ground –
Each rich spot nor square nor round,
Rudely heart-shaped, as it were
The blurred and hasty impress there

Of a vermeil-crusted seal
Dusted o'er with golden meal.
Only there's a droning where
Yon bright beetle shines in air,
Tracks it in its gleaming flight
With a slanting beam of light,
Rising in the sunshine higher,
Till its shards flame out like fire.

Every other thing is still,
Save the ever-wakeful rill,
Whose cool murmur only throws
Cooler comfort round repose;
Or some ripple in the sea
Of leafy boughs, where, lazily,
Tired summer, in her bower
Turning with the noontide hour,
Heaves a slumbrous breath ere she
Once more slumbers peacefully.

O 'tis easeful here to lie
Hidden from noon's scorching eye,
In this grassy cool recess
Musing thus of quietness.

ADAM LINDSAY GORDON

1833-70

The Sick Stockrider

Hold hard, Ned! Lift me down once more, and lay me in
    the shade.
  Old man, you've had your work cut out to guide
Both horses, and to hold me in the saddle when I sway'd,
  All through the hot, slow, sleepy, silent ride.
The dawn at 'Moorabinda' was a mist rack dull and dense,
  The sunrise was a sullen, sluggish lamp;
I was dozing in the gateway at Arbuthnot's bound'ry fence,
  I was dreaming on the Limestone cattle camp.
We crossed the creek at Carricksford, and sharply through
    the haze,
  And suddenly the sun shot flaming forth;
To southward lay 'Katâwa', with the sandpeaks all ablaze,
  And the flush'd fields of Glen Lomond lay to north.
Now westward winds the bridle path that leads to
    Lindisfarm,
  And yonder looms the double-headed Bluff;
From the far side of the first hill, when the skies are clear
    and calm,
  You can see Sylvester's woolshed fair enough.
Five miles we used to call it from our homestead to the
    place
  Where the big tree spans the roadway like an arch;
'Twas here we ran the dingo down that gave us such a
    chase
  Eight years ago – or was it nine? – last March.

'Twas merry in the glowing morn, among the gleaming
    grass,
  To wander as we've wandered many a mile,
And blow the cool tobacco cloud, and watch the white
    wreaths pass,
  Sitting loosely in the saddle all the while.

'Twas merry 'mid the blackwoods, when we spied the
    station roofs,
  To wheel the wild scrub cattle at the yard,
With a running fire of stockwhips and a fiery run of hoofs;
  Oh! the hardest day was never then too hard!

Aye! we had a glorious gallop after 'Starlight' and his
    gang,
  When they bolted from Sylvester's on the flat;
How the sun-dried reed-beds crackled, how the flint-strewn
    ranges rang
  To the strokes of 'Mountaineer' and 'Acrobat'.
Hard behind them in the timber, harder still across the
    heath,
  Close beside them through the tea-tree scrub we dash'd;
And the golden-tinted fern leaves, how they rustled
    underneath!
  And the honeysuckle osiers, how they crash'd!

We led the hunt throughout, Ned, on the chestnut and the
    grey,
  And the troopers were three hundred yards behind,
While we emptied our six-shooters on the bushrangers at
    bay,
  In the creek with stunted box-tree for a blind!
There you grappled with the leader, man to man and
    horse to horse,
  And you roll'd together when the chestnut rear'd;
He blazed away and missed you in that shallow water-
    course –
  A narrow shave – his powder singed your beard!
In these hours when life is ebbing, how those days when
    life was young
  Come back to us; how clearly I recall
Even the yarns Jack Hall invented, and the songs Jem
    Roper sung;
  And where are now Jem Roper and Jack Hall?

Aye! nearly all our comrades of the old colonial school,
    Our ancient boon companions, Ned, are gone;
Hard livers for the most part, somewhat reckless as a rule,
    It seems that you and I are left alone.

There was Hughes, who got in trouble through that
      business with the cards,
    It matters little what became of him;
But a steer ripp'd up MacPherson in the Cooraminta
      yards,
    And Sullivan was drown'd at Sink-or-swim.

And Mostyn – poor Frank Mostyn – died at last a fearful
      wreck,
    In 'the horrors', at the Upper Wandinong;
And Carisbrooke, the rider, at the Horsefall broke his neck,
    Faith! the wonder was he saved his neck so long!
Ah! those days and nights we squandered at the Logans'
      in the glen –
    The Logans, man and wife, have long been dead.
Elsie's tallest girl seems taller than your little Elsie then;
    And Ethel is a woman grown and wed.

I've had my share of pastime, and I've done my share of
      toil,
    And life is short – the longest life a span;
I care not now to tarry for the corn or for the oil,
    Or for the wine that maketh glad the heart of man.
For good undone and gifts misspent and resolutions vain,
    'Tis somewhat late to trouble. This I know –
I should live the same life over, if I had to live again;
    And the chances are I go where most men go.

The deep blue skies wax dusky, and the tall green trees
      grow dim,
    The sward beneath me seems to heave and fall;
And sickly, smoky shadows through the sleepy sunlight
      swim,
    And on the very sun's face weave their pall.

Let me slumber in the hollow where the wattle blossoms
    wave,
  With never stone or rail to fence my bed;
Should the sturdy station children pull the bush flowers on
    my grave,
  I may chance to hear them romping overhead.

HENRY KENDALL

1839-82

Bell-Birds

By channels of coolness the echoes are calling,
And down the dim gorges I hear the creek falling:
It lives in the mountain where moss and the sedges
Touch with their beauty the banks and the ledges.
Through breaks of the cedar and sycamore bowers
Struggles the light that is love to the flowers;
And, softer than slumber and sweeter than singing,
The notes of the bell-birds are running and ringing.

The silver-voiced bell-birds, the darlings of daytime!
They sing in September their songs of the May-time;
When shadows wax strong, and the thunder-bolts hurtle,
They hide with their fear in the leaves of the myrtle;
When rain and the sunbeams shine mingled together,
They start up like fairies that follow fair weather;
And straightway the hues of their feathers unfolden
Are the green and the purple, the blue and the golden.

October, the maiden of bright yellow tresses,
Loiters for love in these cool wildernesses;
Loiters, knee-deep, in the grasses, to listen,
Where dripping rocks gleam and the leafy pools glisten:
Then is the time when the water-moons splendid
Break with their gold, and are scattered or blended
Over the creeks, till the woodlands have warning
Of songs of the bell-bird and wings of the Morning.

Welcome as waters unkissed by the summers
Are the voices of bell-birds to thirsty far-comers.
When fiery December sets foot in the forest,
And the need of the wayfarer presses the sorest,

Pent in the ridges for ever and ever
The bell-birds direct him to spring and to river,
With ring and with ripple, like runnels whose torrents
Are toned by the pebbles and leaves in the currents.

Often I sit, looking back to a childhood,
Mixt with the sights and the sounds of the wildwood,
Longing for power and the sweetness to fashion,
Lyrics with beats like the heart-beats of Passion; –
Songs interwoven of lights and of laughters
Borrowed from bell-birds in far forest-rafters;
So I might keep in the city and alleys
The beauty and strength of the deep mountain valleys;
Charming to slumber the pain of my losses
With glimpses of creeks and a vision of mosses.

The Last of His Tribe

He crouches, and buries his face on his knees,
    And hides in the dark of his hair;
For he cannot look up to the storm-smitten trees,
    Or think of the loneliness there:
        Of the loss and the loneliness there.

The wallaroos grope through the tufts of the grass,
    And turn to their covers for fear;
But he sits in the ashes and lets them pass
    Where the boomerangs sleep with the spear:
        With the nullah, the sling, and the spear.

Uloola, behold him! The thunder that breaks
    On the tops of the rocks with the rain,
And the wind which drives up with the salt of the lakes,
    Have made him a hunter again:
        A hunter and fisher again.

For his eyes have been full with a smouldering thought;
   But he dreams of the hunts of yore,
And of foes that he sought, and of fights that he fought
   With those who will battle no more:
     Who will go to the battle no more.

It is well that the water which tumbles and fills
   Goes moaning and moaning along;
For an echo rolls out from the sides of the hills,
   And he starts at a wonderful song:
     At the sounds of a wonderful song.

And he sees, through the rents of the scattering fogs,
   The corroboree warlike and grim,
And the lubra who sat by the fire on the logs,
   To watch, like a mourner, for him:
     Like a mother and mourner, for him.

Will he go in his sleep from these desolate lands,
   Like a chief, to the rest of his race,
With the honey-voiced woman who beckons, and stands,
   And gleams like a Dream in his face –
     Like a marvellous Dream in his face?

The Song of Ninian Melville

Sing the song of noisy Ninny – hang the Muses – spit it
    out!
(Tuneful Nine ye needn't help me – poet knows his way
    about!)
Sling me here a penny whistle – look alive, and let me slip
Into Ninny like a father – Ninny with the nimble lip.
Mister Melville, straight descendant from Professor
    Huxley's ape,
Started life a mute for daddy – pulling faces, sporting
    crape;

But, alas, he didn't like it – lots of work and little pay.
Nature whispered, 'you're a windbag – play your cards
    another way.'

Mister Melville picked the hint up – pitched the coffin
    'biz' to pot;
Paid his bills, or didn't pay them – doesn't matter now a
    jot!
Twigging how the bread was buttered, he commenced a
    'waiting game':
Pulled the strings upon the quiet – no one 'tumbled' to his
    aim.
Paine, he purchased, Strauss, he borrowed – read a page
    or two of each;
Posed before his father's porkers – made to them his
    maiden speech.
Then he spluttered, *'Ninny has it! Nin* will keep himself
    in clothes,
Like the gutter Tully, Bradlaugh, leading noodles by the
    nose!'

In the fly-blown village pothouse, where a dribbling bag of
    beer,
Passes for a human being, Nin commenced his new career –
Talked about the 'Christian swindle' – cut the Bible into
    bits –
Shook his fist at Mark and Matthew – gave the twelve
    Apostles fits:
Slipped into the priests and parsons – hammered at the
    British Court –
Boozy boobies were astonished: lubbers of the Lambton
    sort!
Yards of ear were cocked to listen – yards of mouth began
    to shout,
*'Here's a cove as is long-headed – Ninny knows his way
    about.'*

Mister Melville was delighted – game in hand was paying
    well:
Fools and coin don't hang together – Nin became a
    howling swell!
Took to 'stumping' on the Racecourse – cut the old
    debating club:
Wouldn't do for mighty Ninny now to mount a local tub!
Thornton's Column was his platform: here our orator
    began
Hitting at the yellow heathen – cracking up the 'working
    man' –
Spitting out at Immigration: roaring, like a worried bull,
At the lucre made from tallow – at the profit raised on
    wool.

Said our Ninny to our Ninny, 'I have not the slightest
    doubt
Soaping down the " 'orny 'anded" is the safest "bizness"
    out!
Little work for spanking wages – this is just the thing they
    like,
So I'll prop the eight hour swindle – be the boss in every
    strike.
In the end, I'll pull a pot off – what I'm at is bound to
    take:
Ninny sees a bit before him – Ninny's eyes are wide awake!
When the boobies make me member, Parkes, of course,
    will offer tip –
I will take the first fat billet – then my frouzy friends may
    rip.'

So it came to pass that Melville, *Mister* Melville, I should
    say –
Dodged about with deputations, half a dozen times a day!
Started strikes and bossed the strikers – damned employers,
    every one,
On the Column – off the Column – in the shanty – in the
    sun!

'Down with masters – up with wages! keep the "pigtail"
    out of this!'
This is what our Ninny shouted – game, you see, of hit or
    miss!
World, of course, is full of noodles – some who bray at
    Wallsend sent
Thing we know to be a windbag bouncing into
    Parliament!

Common story, this of Ninny! many fellows of his breed
Prowl about to bone the guinea, up to dirty tricks indeed!
Haven't now the time to tan them: but, by Jove, I'd like
    to tan
Back of that immense imposter that they call the 'working
    man'!
Drag upon our just employers – sponger on a worn-out
    wife
Boozing in some alley pothouse every evening of his life!
Type he is of Nin's supporters: tot him up and tot him
    down,
He would back old Nick to-morrow for the sake of half a
    crown!

House with high, august traditions – Chamber where the
    voice of Lowe,
And the lordly words of Wentworth sounded thirty years
    ago –
Hall familiar to our fathers, where, in days exalted, rang
All the tones of all the feeling which ennobled Bland and
    Lang –
We in ashes – we in sack cloth, sorrow for the insult cast
By a crowd of bitter boobies on the grandeur of the past!
Take again your penny whistle – boy, it is no good to me:
Last invention is a bladder with the title of M.P.!

VICTOR DALEY

1858-1905

Dreams

I have been dreaming all a summer day
Of rare and dainty poems I would write;
Love-lyrics delicate as lilac-scent,
Soft idylls woven of wind, and flower, and stream,
And songs and sonnets carven in fine gold.

The day is fading and the dusk is cold;
Out of the skies has gone the opal gleam,
Out of my heart has passed the high intent
Into the shadow of the falling night –
Must all my dreams in darkness pass away?

I have been dreaming all a summer day:
Shall I go dreaming so until Life's light
Fades in Death's dusk, and all my days are spent?
Ah, what am I the dreamer but a dream!
The day is fading and the dusk is cold.

My songs and sonnets carven in fine gold
Have faded from me with the last day-beam
That purple lustre to the sea-line lent,
And flushed the clouds with rose and chrysolite,
So days and dreams in darkness pass away.

I have been dreaming all a summer day
Of songs and sonnets carven in fine gold;
But all my dreams in darkness pass away;
The day is fading, and the dusk is cold.

When London Calls

They leave us – artists, singers, all –
  When London calls aloud,
Commanding to her Festival
  The gifted crowd.

She sits beside the ship-choked Thames,
  Sad, weary, cruel, grand;
Her crown imperial gleams with gems
  From many a land.

From overseas, and far away,
  Come crowded ships and ships –
Grim-faced she gazes on them; yea,
  With scornful lips.

The garden of the earth is wide;
  Its rarest blooms she picks
To deck her board, this haggard-eyed
  Imperatrix.

Sad, sad is she, and yearns for mirth;
  With voice of golden guile
She lures men from the ends of earth
  To make her smile.

The student of wild human ways
  In wild new lands; the sage
With new great thoughts; the bard whose lays
  Bring youth to age;

The painter young whose pictures shine
  With colours magical;
The singer with the voice divine –
  She lures them all.

But all their new is old to her
   Who bore the Anakim;
She gives them gold or Charon's fare
   As suits her whim.

Crowned Ogress – old, and sad, and wise –
   She sits with painted face
And hard, imperious, cruel eyes
   In her high place.

To him who for her pleasure lives,
   And makes her wish his goal,
A rich Tarpeian gift she gives –
   That slays his soul.

The story-teller from the Isles
   Upon the Empire's rim,
With smiles she welcomes – and her smiles
   Are death to him.

For Her, whose pleasure is her law,
   In vain the shy heart bleeds –
The Genius with the Iron Jaw
   Alone succeeds.

And when the Poet's lays grow bland,
   And urbanised, and prim –
She stretches forth a jewelled hand
   And strangles him.

She sits beside the ship-choked Thames
   With Sphinx-like lips apart –
Mistress of many diadems –
   Death in her heart!

A. B. 'BANJO' PATERSON

1864-1941

The Man from Snowy River

There was movement at the station, for the word had
    passed around
  That the colt from old Regret had got away,
And had joined the wild bush horses – he was worth a
    thousand pound,
  So all the cracks had gathered to the fray.
All the tried and noted riders from the stations near and
    far
  Had mustered at the homestead overnight,
For the bushmen love hard riding where the wild bush
    horses are,
  And the stock-horse snuffs the battle with delight.

There was Harrison, who made his pile when Pardon won
    the cup,
  The old man with his hair as white as snow;
But few could ride beside him when his blood was fairly
    up –
  He would go wherever horse and man could go.
And Clancy of the Overflow came down to lend a hand,
  No better horseman ever held the reins;
For never horse could throw him while the saddle-girths
    would stand –
  He learnt to ride while droving on the plains.

And one was there, a stripling on a small and weedy beast;
  He was something like a racehorse undersized,
With a touch of Timor pony – three parts thoroughbred
    at least –
  And such as are by mountain horsemen prized.
He was hard and tough and wiry – just the sort that won't
    say die –
  There was courage in his quick impatient tread;

And he bore the badge of gameness in his bright and fiery
    eye,
    And the proud and lofty carriage of his head.

But still so slight and weedy, one would doubt his power
    to stay,
    And the old man said, 'That horse will never do
For a long and tiring gallop – lad, you'd better stop away,
    Those hills are far too rough for such as you.'
So he waited, sad and wistful – only Clancy stood his
    friend –
    'I think we ought to let him come,' he said;
'I warrant he'll be with us when he's wanted at the end,
    For both his horse and he are mountain bred.

'He hails from Snowy River, up by Kosciusko's side,
    Where the hills are twice as steep and twice as rough;
Where a horse's hoofs strike firelight from the flint stones
    every stride,
    The man that holds his own is good enough.
And the Snowy River riders on the mountains make their
    home,
    Where the river runs those giant hills between;
I have seen full many horsemen since I first commenced to
    roam,
    But nowhere yet such horsemen have I seen.'

So he went; they found the horses by the big mimosa
    clump,
    They raced away towards the mountain's brow,
And the old man gave his orders, 'Boys, go at them from
    the jump,
    No use to try for fancy riding now.
And, Clancy, you must wheel them, try and wheel them to
    the right.
    Ride boldly, lad, and never fear the spills,
For never yet was rider that could keep the mob in sight,
    If once they gain the shelter of those hills.'

So Clancy rode to wheel them – he was racing on the
    wing
  Where the best and boldest riders take their place,
And he raced his stock-horse past them, and he made the
    ranges ring
  With the stockwhip, as he met them face to face.
Then they halted for a moment, while he swung the
    dreaded lash,
  But they saw their well-loved mountain full in view,
And they charged beneath the stockwhip with a sharp and
    sudden dash,
  And off into the mountain scrub they flew.

Then fast the horsemen followed, where the gorges deep
    and black
  Resounded to the thunder of their tread,
And the stockwhips woke the echoes, and they fiercely
    answered back
  From cliffs and crags that beetled overhead.
And upward, ever upward, the wild horses held their way,
  Where mountain ash and kurrajong grew wide;
And the old man muttered fiercely, 'We may bid the mob
    good day,
  No man can hold them down the other side.'

When they reached the mountain's summit, even Clancy
    took a pull –
  It well might make the boldest hold their breath;
The wild hop scrub grew thickly, and the hidden ground
    was full
  Of wombat holes, and any slip was death.
But the man from Snowy River let the pony have his head,
  And he swung his stockwhip round and gave a cheer,
And he raced him down the mountain like a torrent down
    its bed,
  While the others stood and watched in very fear.

He sent the flint-stones flying, but the pony kept his feet,
   He cleared the fallen timber in his stride,
And the man from Snowy River never shifted in his seat –
   It was grand to see that mountain horseman ride.
Through the stringy barks and saplings, on the rough and
      broken ground,
   Down the hillside at a racing pace he went;
And he never drew the bridle till he landed safe and sound
   At the bottom of that terrible descent.

He was right among the horses as they climbed the farther
      hill,
   And the watchers on the mountain, standing mute,
Saw him ply the stockwhip fiercely; he was right among
      them still,
   As he raced across the clearing in pursuit.
Then they lost him for a moment, where two mountain
      gullies met
   In the ranges – but a final glimpse reveals
On a dim and distant hillside the wild horses racing yet,
   With the man from Snowy River at their heels.

And he ran them single-handed till their sides were white
      with foam;
   He followed like a bloodhound on their track,
Till they halted, cowed and beaten; then he turned their
      heads for home,
   And alone and unassisted brought them back.
But his hardy mountain pony he could scarcely raise a trot,
   He was blood from hip to shoulder from the spur;
But his pluck was still undaunted, and his courage fiery
      hot,
   For never yet was mountain horse a cur.

And down by Kosciusko, where the pine-clad ridges raise
   Their torn and rugged battlements on high,
Where the air is clear as crystal, and the white stars fairly
      blaze

At midnight in the cold and frosty sky,
And where around the Overflow the reed-beds sweep and
sway
To the breezes, and the rolling plains are wide,
The Man from Snowy River is a household word today,
And the stockmen tell the story of his ride.

Saltbush Bill

Now this is the law of the Overland that all in the West
obey –
A man must cover with travelling sheep a six-mile stage a
day;
But this is the law which the drovers make, right easily
understood,
They travel their stage where the grass is bad, but they
camp where the grass is good;
They camp, and they ravage the squatter's grass till never
a blade remains,
Then they drift away as the white clouds drift on the edge
of the saltbush plains;
From camp to camp and from run to run they battle it
hand to hand
For a blade of grass and the right to pass on the track of
the Overland.
For this is the law of the Great Stock Routes, 'tis written
in white and black –
The man that goes with a travelling mob must keep to a
half-mile track;
And the drovers keep to a half-mile track on the runs
where the grass is dead,
But they spread their sheep on a well-grassed run till they
go with a two-mile spread.
So the squatters hurry the drovers on from dawn till the
fall of night,
And the squatters' dogs and the drovers' dogs get mixed in
a deadly fight.

Yet the squatters' men, though they hunt the mob, are
    willing the peace to keep,
For the drovers learn how to use their hands when they go
    with the travelling sheep;
But this is the tale of a Jackaroo that came from a foreign
    strand,
And the fight that he fought with Saltbush Bill, the King
    of the Overland.

Now Saltbush Bill was a drover tough as ever the country
    knew,
He had fought his way on the Great Stock Routes from the
    sea to the big Barcoo;
He could tell when he came to a friendly run that gave
    him a chance to spread,
And he knew where the hungry owners were that hurried
    his sheep ahead;
He was drifting down in the Eighty drought with a mob
    that could scarcely creep
(When the kangaroos by the thousand starve, it is rough
    on the travelling sheep),
And he camped one night at the crossing-place on the
    edge of the Wilga run;
'We must manage a feed for them here,' he said, 'or half
    of the mob are done!'
So he spread them out when they left the camp wherever
    they liked to go,
Till he grew aware of a Jackaroo with a station-hand in
    tow.
They set to work on the straggling sheep, and with many a
    stockwhip crack
They forced them in where the grass was dead in the
    space of the half-mile track;
And William prayed that the hand of Fate might suddenly
    strike him blue
But he'd get some grass for his starving sheep in the teeth
    of that Jackaroo.

So he turned and he cursed the Jackaroo; he cursed him,
    alive or dead,
From the soles of his great unwieldly feet to the crown of
    his ugly head,
With an extra curse on the moke he rode and the cur at
    his heels that ran,
Till the Jackaroo from his horse got down and went for
    the drover-man;
With the station-hand for his picker-up, though the sheep
    ran loose the while,
They battled it out on the well-grassed plain in the regular
    prize-ring style.

Now, the new chum fought for his honour's sake and the
    pride of the English race,
But the drover fought for his daily bread with a smile on
    his bearded face;
So he shifted ground, and he sparred for wind, and he
    made it a lengthy mill,
And from time to time as his scouts came in they whispered
    to Saltbush Bill –
'We have spread the sheep with a two-mile spread, and
    the grass it is something grand;
You must stick to him, Bill, for another round for the pride
    of the Overland.'
The new chum made it a rushing fight, though never a
    blow got home,
Till the sun rode high in the cloudless sky and glared on
    the brick-red loam,
Till the sheep drew in to the shelter-trees and settled them
    down to rest;
Then the drover said he would fight no more, and gave his
    opponent best.

So the new chum rode to the homestead straight, and told
    them a story grand
Of the desperate fight that he fought that day with the
    King of the Overland;

And the tale went home to the Public Schools of the pluck
    of the English swell –
How the drover fought for his very life, but blood in the
    end must tell.
But the travelling sheep and the Wilga sheep were boxed
    on the Old Man Plain;
'Twas a full week's work ere they drafted out and hunted
    them off again;
A week's good grass in their wretched hides, with a curse
    and a stockwhip crack
They hunted them off on the road once more to starve on
    the half-mile track.
And Saltbush Bill, on the Overland, will many a time
    recite
How the best day's work that he ever did was the day that
    he lost the fight.

MARY GILMORE

1865-1962

Eve-Song

I span and Eve span
A thread to bind the heart of man;
But the heart of man was a wandering thing
That came and went with little to bring:
Nothing he minded what we made,
As here he loitered, and there he stayed.

I span and Eve span
A thread to bind the heart of man;
But the more we span the more we found
It wasn't his heart but ours we bound.
For children gathered about our knees:
The thread was a chain that stole our ease.
And one of us learned in our children's eyes
That more than man was love and prize.
But deep in the heart of one of us lay
A root of loss and hidden dismay.

He said he was strong. He had no strength
But that which comes of breadth and length.
He said he was fond. But his fondness proved
The flame of an hour when he was moved.
He said he was true. His truth was but
A door that winds could open and shut.

And yet, and yet, as he came back,
Wandering in from the outward track,
We held our arms, and gave him our breast,
As a pillowing place for his head to rest.
I span and Eve span,
A thread to bind the heart of man!

86

Never Admit the Pain

Never admit the pain,
    Bury it deep;
Only the weak complain,
    Complaint is cheap.

Cover thy wound, fold down
    Its curtained place;
Silence is still a crown,
    Courage a grace.

The Men of Eureka

(A Recollection)

They have gone out, the men of Eureka,
One by one they have passed. Now there is none
Of them left to sit by the fire and talk;
For them, life's journey is over and done.
    Digger by digger they marched,
        Each man in his order;
    As digger by digger they went,
        Over the border.

I was a child while still we talked of them,
And, when there came one walking lame, I ran
To my father, and, my hand in his, cried,
Eager for stories, 'Here comes a Eureka man!'
    Digger by digger they marched,
        All named in their order,
    As digger by digger they went,
        Over the border.

And the men who had been at Eureka
Made me a flag of stars, and gave me
A name, and the name they gave was *Eureka*:
'For the child,' they said, 'is one of our kin.'

Digger by digger they marched,
   Each numbered in order,
Who digger by digger are gone,
   Over the border.

And many a time, with a wooden sword,
I stood, my father's kinsman, Ross, and laced
Upon the air with glancing strokes, while cried
They there, '*Well placed! Well struck, Eureka!*'
   Digger by digger they marched,
     Each man in his order,
   Who digger by digger are gone,
     Over the border.

Now shall I weep them, even as the tribes
Wept those they deemed illustrious, who passed
From them forever, or, far-journeying,
Moved outward from their ken, the seen no more.

It is said that the last lone survivor of the Eureka Stockade
died in 1931. His name, I believe, was Potter, and his grave is
in New Zealand. That grave should be in Australia, and with an
Australian monument over it.

The Yarran-Tree

The Lady of the Yarran-tree,
   She built herself a house,
And, happy in it, there she lived
   As tidy as a mouse;
She set a stool against the fire,
   And hung the broom beside,
And yet, although she sat alone,
   The door was open wide.

And she beside the Yarran-tree
   Was busy as could be;
She kept her sheep, she carded wool,
   Her bleach was white to see;

She baked her bread from wheat she grew,
   She tanned the good ox-hide;
And still, for all she sat alone,
   Her door was open wide.

The Lady of the Yarran-tree
   Looked out, one night, and saw
The dark hand of a stranger reach
   To lay on her his law;
She rose and drew the curtain close,
   Her little lamp to hide –
And yet, for all she was alone,
   The door stood open wide.

I asked her if she didn't know
   The fears of woman-kind,
That, though by day they come and go,
   Are still within the mind.
She looked at me and slowly said,
   'Such fears in me abide!'
And yet I knew she sat alone,
   The door left open wide.

The Yarran-tree against the spring
   Put out its amber green,
Like golden berries, on each twig,
   Its blossoms all were seen;
I saw the stranger watch the tree,
   The woman there inside –
And still, although she sat alone,
   The door was open wide.

To her beside the Yarran-tree,
   I said, 'Go buy a ring,
A ring of silver laced with steel,
   Through which a shot may sing;

Then, when the stranger hears the song,
  As winds shall bear it wide,
It will be safe to sit alone,
  The house-door open wide.'

Then she beside the Yarran-tree,
  She turned and looked at me,
She laid the spinning from her hand,
  And spake as still could be;
'Go you,' she said, 'and make the ring
  And make of it your pride;
That I may safely sit alone,
  The door set open wide.'

I took the woman at her word,
  And straitly there I made
A ring of silver laced with steel,
  That sang as trumpets played;
I set it down against the step,
  And though the door is wide,
The Lady of the Yarran-tree
  Dwells ever safe inside.

An Aboriginal Simile

There was no stir among the trees,
No pulse in the earth,
No movement in the void;
The grass was a dry white fire.
Then in the distance rose a cloud,
And a swift rain came:
Like a woman running,
The wind in her hair.

Old Botany Bay

'I'm old
Botany Bay;
Stiff in the joints,
Little to say.

I am he
Who paved the way,
That you might walk
At your ease to-day;

I was the conscript
Sent to hell
To make in the desert
The living well;

I bore the heat,
I blazed the track –
Furrowed and bloody
Upon by back.

I split the rock;
I felled the tree:
The nation was –
Because of me!'

Old Botany Bay
Taking the sun
From day to day . . .
Shame on the mouth
That would deny
The knotted hands
That set us high!

BARCROFT BOAKE

1866-92

Where the Dead Men Lie

Out on the wastes of the Never Never –
  That's where the dead men lie!
There where the heat-waves dance for ever –
  That's where the dead men lie!
That's where the Earth's loved sons are keeping
Endless tryst: not the west wind sweeping
Feverish pinions can wake their sleeping –
  Out where the dead men lie!

Where brown Summer and Death have mated –
  That's where the dead men lie!
Loving with fiery lust unsated –
  That's where the dead men lie!
Out where the grinning skulls bleach whitely
Under the saltbush sparkling brightly;
Out where the wild dogs chorus nightly –
  That's where the dead men lie!

Deep in the yellow, flowing river –
  That's where the dead men lie!
Under the banks where the shadows quiver –
  That's where the dead men lie!
Where the platypus twists and doubles,
Leaving a train of tiny bubbles;
Rid at last of their earthly troubles –
  That's where the dead men lie!

East and backward pale faces turning –
  That's how the dead men lie!
Gaunt arms stretched with a voiceless yearning –
  That's how the dead men lie!

Oft in the fragment hush of nooning
Hearing again their mother's crooning,
Wrapt for aye in a dreamful swooning –
 That's how the dead men lie!

Only the hand of Night can free them –
 That's when the dead men fly!
Only the frightened cattle see them –
 See the dead men go by!
Cloven hoofs beating out one measure,
Bidding the stockman know no leisure –
That's when the dead men take their pleasure!
 That's when the dead men fly!

Ask, too, the never-sleeping drover:
 He sees the dead pass by;
Hearing them call to their friends – the plover,
 Hearing the dead men cry;
Seeing their faces stealing, stealing,
Hearing their laughter pealing, pealing,
Watching their grey forms wheeling, wheeling
 Round where the cattle lie!

Strangled by thirst and fierce privation –
 That's how the dead men die!
Out on Moneygrub's farthest station –
 That's how the dead men die!
Hardfaced greybeards, youngsters callow;
Some mounds cared for, some left fallow;
Some deep down, yet others shallow;
 Some having but the sky.

Moneygrub, as he sips his claret,
 Looks with complacent eye
Down at his watch-chain, eighteen-carat –
 There, in his club, hard by:

Recks not that every link is stamped with
Names of the men whose limbs are cramped with
Too long lying in grave mould, camped with
    Death where the dead men lie.

An Allegory

The fight was over, and the battle won
A soldier, who beneath his chieftain's eye
Had done a mighty deed and done it well,
And done it as the world will have it done –
A stab, a curse, some quick play of the butt,
Two skulls cracked crosswise, *but the colours saved* –
Proud of his wounds, proud of the promised cross,
Turned to his rear-rank man, who on his gun
Leant heavily apart. 'Ho, friend!' he called,
'You did not fight then: were you left behind?
I saw you not.' The other turned and showed
A gaping, red-lipped wound upon his breast.
'Ah,' said he sadly, 'I was in the smoke!'
Threw up his arms, shivered, and fell and died.

BERNARD O'DOWD

1866-1953

Australia

Last sea-thing dredged by sailor Time from Space,
Are you a drift Sargasso, where the West
In halcyon calm rebuilds her fatal nest?
Or Delos of a coming Sun-God's race?
Are you for Light, and trimmed, with oil in place,
Or but a Will o' Wisp on marshy quest?
A new demesne for Mammon to infest?
Or lurks millennial Eden 'neath your face?

The cenotaphs of species dead elsewhere
That in your limits leap and swim and fly,
Or trail uncanny harp-strings from your trees,
Mix omens with the auguries that dare
To plant the Cross upon your forehead sky,
A virgin helpmate Ocean at your knees.

HENRY LAWSON

1867-1922

Middleton's Rouseabout

Tall and freckled and sandy,
  Face of a country lout;
This was the picture of Andy,
  Middleton's Rouseabout.

Type of a coming nation,
  In the land of cattle and sheep,
Worked on Middleton's station,
  'Pound a week and his keep'.

On Middleton's wide dominions
  Plied the stockwhip and shears;
Hadn't any opinions,
  Hadn't any 'idears'.

Swiftly the years went over,
  Liquor and drought prevailed;
Middleton went as a drover
  After his station had failed.

Type of a careless nation,
  Men who are soon played out,
Middleton was: – and his station
  Was bought by the Rouseabout.

Flourishing beard and sandy,
  Tall and solid and stout:
This is the picture of Andy,
  Middleton's Rouseabout.

Now on his own dominions
  Works with his overseers;
Hasn't any opinions,
  Hasn't any idears.

The Song of Old Joe Swallow

When I was up the country in the rough and early days,
I used to work along ov Jimmy Nowlett's bullick-drays;
Then the reelroad wasn't heered on, an' the bush was wild
an' strange,
An' we useter draw the timber from the saw-pits in the
range –
Load provisions for the stations, an' we'd travel far and
slow
Through the plains an' 'cross the ranges in the days of long
ago.

Then it's yoke up the bullicks and tramp beside 'em slow,
An' saddle up yer horses an' a-ridin' we will go,
To the bullick-drivin', cattle-drovin',
Nigger, digger, roarin', rovin'
Days o' long ago.

Once me and Jimmy Nowlett loaded timber for the town,
But we hadn't gone a dozen mile before the rain come
down,
An' me an' Jimmy Nowlett an' the bullicks an' the dray
Was cut off on some risin' ground while floods around us
lay;
An' we soon run short of tucker an' terbaccer, which was
bad,
An' pertaters dipped in honey was the only tuck we had.

An' half our bullicks perished when the drought was on
the land,
An' the burnin' heat that dazzles as it dances on the sand;
When the sun-baked clay an' gravel paves for miles the
burnin' creeks,
An' at ev'ry step yer travel there a rottin' carcase reeks –
But we pulled ourselves together, for we never used ter
know
What a feather bed was good for in those days o' long ago.

97

But in spite ov barren ridges an' in spite ov mud an' heat,
An' the dust that browned the bushes when it rose from
    bullicks' feet,
An' in spite ov cold and chilblains when the bush was
    white with frost,
An' in spite of muddy water where the burnin' plain was
    crossed,
An' in spite of modern progress, and in spite of all their
    blow,
'Twas a better land to live in, in the days o' long ago.

When the frosty moon was shinin' o'er the ranges like a
    lamp,
An' a lot of bullick-drivers was a-campin' on the camp,
When the fire was blazin' cheery an' the pipes was drawin'
    well,
Then our songs we useter chorus an' our yarns we useter
    tell;
An' we'd talk ov lands we come from, and ov chaps we
    useter know,
For there always was behind us *other* days o' long ago.

Ah, them early days was ended when the reelroad crossed
    the plain,
But in dreams I often tramp beside the bullick-team again:
Still we pauses at the shanty just to have a drop er cheer,
Still I feels a kind ov pleasure when the campin'-ground is
    near;
Still I smells the old tarpaulin me an' Jimmy useter throw
'Cross the timber-truck for shelter in the days ov long ago.

I have been a-driftin' back'ards with the changes ov the
    land,
An' if I spoke ter bullicks now they wouldn't understand,
But when Mary wakes me sudden in the night I'll often
    say:
'Come here, Spot, an' stan' up, Bally, blank an' blank an'
    come-eer-way.'

An' she says that, when I'm sleepin', oft my elerquince 'ill
    flow
In the bullick-drivin' language ov the days o' long ago.

Well, the pub will soon be closin', so I'll give the thing a
    rest;
But if you should drop on Nowlett in the far an' distant
    west –
An' if Jimmy uses doubleyou instead of ar an' vee,
An' if he drops his aitches, then you're sure to know it's he.
An' yer won't forgit to arsk him if he still remembers Joe
As knowed him up the country in the days o' long ago.

Then it's yoke up the bullicks and tramp beside 'em slow,
An' saddle up yer horses an' a-ridin' we will go,
To the bullick-drivin', cattle drovin',
Nigger, digger, roarin', rovin'
Days o' long ago.

One-Hundred-and-Three

With the frame of a man and the face of a boy, and a
    manner strangely wild,
And the great, wide, wondering, innocent eyes of a silent-
    suffering child;
With his hideous dress and his heavy boots, he drags to
    Eternity –
And the Warder says, in a softened tone: 'Catch step,
    One-Hundred-and-Three.'

'Tis a ghastly travesty of drill – or a shameful farce of
    work –
But One-Hundred-and-Three he catches step with a start,
    a shuffle and jerk.
He is silenced and starved and 'drilled' in gaol – and a
    waster's son was he:
His sins were written before he was born – (Keep step!
    One-Hundred-and-Three.)

They shut a man in the four-by-eight, with a six-inch slit
    for air,
Twenty-three hours of the twenty-four, to brood on his
    virtues there.
The dead stone walls and the iron door close in like iron
    bands
On eyes that had followed the distant haze out there on
    the Level Lands.

Bread and water and hominy, and a scrag of meat and a
    spud,
A Bible and thin flat book of rules, to cool a strong man's
    blood;
They take the spoon from the cell at night – and a
    stranger would think it odd;
But a man might sharpen it on the floor, and go to his own
    Great God.

One-Hundred-and-Three, it is hard to believe that you
    saddled your horse at dawn,
And strolled through the bush with a girl at eve, or lolled
    with her on the lawn.
There were picnic parties in sunny bays, and ships on the
    shining sea;
There were foreign ports in the glorious days – (Hold up,
    One-Hundred-and-Three!)

A man came out at exercise time from one of the cells
    to-day:
'Twas the ghastly spectre of one I knew, and I thought he
    was far away;
We dared not speak, but he signed 'Farewell – fare – well',
    and I knew by this
And the number *stamped* on his clothes (not *sewn*) that a
    heavy sentence was his.

Where five men do the work of a boy, with warders *not* to
    see –

It is sad and bad and uselessly mad, it is ugly as it can be,
From the flower-beds shaped to fit the gaol, in circle and
    line absurd,
To the gilded weathercock on the church, agape like a
    strangled bird –

Agape like a strangled bird in the sun, and I wonder what
    he could see?
The Fleet come in, and the Fleet go out? (Hold up, One-
    Hundred-and-Three!)
The glorious sea, and the bays and Bush, and the distant
    mountains blue –
(Keep step, keep step, One-Hundred-and-Three, for my
    heart is halting too.)

The great, round church with its volume of sound, where
    we dare not turn our eyes –
They take us there from our separate hells to sing of
    Paradise;
The High Church service swells and swells where the
    tinted Christs look down –
It is easy to see who is weary and faint and weareth the
    thorny crown.

Every creed hath its Certain Hope, but here, in Hopeless
    Doubt,
Despairing prisoners faint in church, and the warders
    carry them out.
There are swift-made signs that are not to God as they
    march us hellward then;
It is hard to believe that we knelt as boys to 'For ever and
    ever, Amen'.

They double-lock at four o'clock; the warders leave their
    keys,
And the Governor walks with a friend at eve through his
    stone conservatories;

Their window-slits are like idiot mouths, with square
    stone chins adrop –
The weatherstains for the dribble, and the flat stone
    foreheads atop.

Rules, regulations – Red Tape and rules; all and alike they
    bind:
Under separate treatment place the deaf; in the dark cell
    shut the blind!
And somewhere down in his sandstone tomb, with never a
    word to save,
One-Hundred-and-Three is keeping step, as he'll keep it
    to his grave.

The press is printing its smug, smug lies, and paying its
    shameful debt –
It speaks of the comforts that prisoners have, and 'holidays'
    prisoners get.
The visitors come with their smug, smug smiles through
    the gaol on a working day,
And the Public hears with its large, large ears what
    Authorities have to say.

They lay their fingers on well-hosed walls, and they tread
    on the polished floors;
They peep in the generous, shining cans with their Ration
    Number Four.
And the visitors go with their smug, smug smiles; the
    reporters' work is done;
Stand up! my men, who have done your time on Ration
    Number One!

He shall be buried alive without meat, for a day and a
    night unheard,
If he speak to a fellow-prisoner, though he die for want of
    a word.
He shall be punished, and he shall be starved, and he shall
    in darkness rot.

He shall be murdered, body and soul – and God saith:
    'Thou shalt not.'

I've seen the remand-yard men go out, by the subway out
    of the yard –
And I've seen them come in with a foolish grin and a
    sentence of Three Years Hard.
They send a half-starved man to the Court, where the
    hearts of men they carve –
Then feed him up in the hospital to give him the
    strength to starve.

You get the gaol-dust in your throat, in your skin the dead
    gaol-white;
You get the gaol-whine in your voice and in every letter
    you write.
And in your eyes comes the bright gaol-light – not the glare
    of the world's distraught,
Not the hunted look, nor the guilty look, but the awful
    look of the Caught.

We crave for sunlight, we crave for meat, we crave for the
    Might-have-Been,
But the cruellest thing in the walls of a gaol is the craving
    for nicotine.
Yet the spirit of Christ is everywhere where the heart of a
    man can dwell –
It comes like tobacco in prison, or like news to the separate
    cell.

The brute is a brute, and a kind man kind, and the strong
    heart does not fail –
A crawler's a crawler everywhere, but a man is a man in
    gaol;
For the kindness of man to man is great when penned in a
    sandstone pen –
The public call us the 'criminal class', but the warders call
    us 'the men'.

The champagne lady comes home from the course in
    charge of the criminal swell –
They carry her in from the motor car to the lift in the
    Grand Hotel;
But armed with the savage Habituals Act they are waiting
    for you and me –
And drunkards in judgment on drunkards sit (Keep step,
    One-Hundred-and-Three!).

The clever scoundrels are all outside, and the moneyless
    mugs in gaol –
Men do twelve months for a mad wife's lies or Life for a
    strumpet's tale.
If the people knew what the warders know, and felt as the
    prisoners feel –
If the people knew, they would storm their gaols as they
    stormed the old Bastille.

Warders and prisoners, all alike, in a dead rot dry and
    slow –
The author must not write for his own, and the tailor must
    not sew.
The billet-bound officers dare not speak, and discharged
    men dare not tell,
Though many and many an innocent man must brood in
    this barren hell.

Ay! clang the spoon on the iron floor, and shove in the
    bread with your toe,
And shut with a bang the iron door, and clank the bolt –
    just so;
But One-Hundred-and-Three is near the end when the
    clonking gaol-bell sounds –
He cannot swallow the milk they send when the doctor has
    gone his rounds.

They have smuggled him out to the hospital, with no one
    to tell the tale,

But it's little that doctors or nurses can do for the patient
    from Starvinghurst Gaol.
The blanket and screen are ready to draw. . . . There are
    footsteps light and free –
And the angels are whispering over his bed: 'Keep step –
    One-Hundred-and-Three.'

CHRISTOPHER BRENNAN

1870-1932

The Wanderer

1902 –

Quoniam cor secretum concupivi
factus sum vagus inter stellas huius revelationis:
Atque annus peregrinationis meae
quasi annus ventorum invisibilium.

When window-lamps had dwindled, then I rose
and left the town behind me; and on my way
passing a certain door I stopt, remembering
how once I stood on its threshold, and my life
was offer'd to me, a road how different
from that of the years since gone! and I had but
to rejoin an olden path, once dear, since left.
All night I have walk'd and my heart was deep awake,
remembering ways I dream'd and that I chose,
remembering lucidly, and was not sad,
being brimm'd with all the liquid and clear dark
of the night that was not stirr'd with any tide;
for leaves were silent and the road gleam'd pale,
following the ridge, and I was alone with night.
But now I am come among the rougher hills
and grow aware of the sea that somewhere near
is restless; and the flood of night is thinn'd
and stars are whitening. O, what horrible dawn
will bare me the way and crude lumps of the hills
and the homeless concave of the day, and bare
the ever-restless, ever-complaining sea?

*

Each day I see the long ships coming into port
and the people crowding to their rail, glad of the shore:
because to have been alone with the sea and not to have
        known
of anything happening in any crowded way,

and to have heard no other voice than the crooning sea's
has charmed away the old rancours, and the great winds
have search'd and swept their hearts of the old irksome
    thoughts:
so, to their freshen'd gaze, each land smiles a good home.
Why envy I, seeing them made gay to greet the shore?
Surely I do not foolishly desire to go
hither and thither upon the earth and grow weary
with seeing many lands and peoples and the sea:
but if I might, some day, landing I reck not where
have heart to find a welcome and perchance a rest,
I would spread the sail to any wandering wind of the air
this night, when waves are hard and rain blots out the
    land.

*

I am driven everywhere from a clinging home,
O autumn eves! and I ween'd that you would yet
have made, when your smouldering dwindled to odorous
    fume,
close room for my heart, where I might crouch and dream
of days and ways I had trod, and look with regret
on the darkening homes of men and the window-gleam,
and forget the morrows that threat and the unknown way.
But a bitter wind came out of the yellow-pale west
and my heart is shaken and fill'd with its triumphing cry:
You shall find neither home nor rest: for ever you roam
with stars as they drift and wilful fates of the sky!

*

O tame heart, and why are you weary and cannot rest?
here is the hearth with its glow and the roof that forbids
    the rain,
a swept and a garnish'd quiet, a peace: and were you not
    fain
to be gather'd in dusk and comfort and barter away the
    rest?

And is your dream now of riding away from a stricken
    field
on a lost and baleful eve, when the world went out in rain,
one of some few that rode evermore by the bridle-rein
of a great beloved chief, with high heart never to yield?

Was that you? and you ween you are back in your life of
    old
when you dealt as your pride allow'd and reck'd not of
    other rein?
Nay, tame heart, be not idle: it is but the ancient rain
that minds you of manhood foregone and the perilous joy
    of the bold.

*

Once I could sit by the fire hourlong when the dripping
    eaves
sang cheer to the shelter'd, and listen, and know that the
    woods drank full,
and think of the morn that was coming and how the
    freshen'd leaves
would glint in the sun and the dusk beneath would be
    bright and cool.

Now, when I hear, I am cold within: for my mind drifts
    wide
where the blessing is shed for naught on the salt waste of
    the sea,
on the valleys that hold no rest and the hills that may not
    abide:
and the fire loses its warmth and my home is far from me.

*

How old is my heart, how old, how old is my heart,
and did I ever go forth with song when the morn was new?
I seem to have trod on many ways: I seem to have left
I know not how many homes; and to leave each
was still to leave a portion of mine own heart,

108

of my old heart whose life I had spent to make that home
and all I had was regret, and a memory.
So I sit and muse in this wayside harbour and wait
till I hear the gathering cry of the ancient winds and again
I must up and out and leave the embers of the hearth
to crumble silently into white ash and dust,
and see the road stretch bare and pale before me: again
my garment and my home shall be the enveloping winds
and my heart be fill'd wholly with their old pitiless cry.

*

I sorrow for youth – ah, not for its wildness (would that
    were dead!)
but for those soft nests of time that enticed the maiden
    bloom
of delight and tenderness to break in delicate air
– O her eyes in the rosy face that bent over our first babe!
but all that was, and is gone, and shall be all forgotten;
it fades and wanes even now: and who is there cares but I?
and I grieve for my heart that is old and cannot cease from
    regret.
Ay, might our harms be haven'd in some deathless heart:
but where have I felt its over-brooding luminous tent
save in those eyes of delight (and ah! that they must
    change)
and of yore in her eyes to whom we ran with our childish
    joy?
O brother! if such there were and each of us might lead
    each
to lean above the little pools where all our heart
lies spilt and clear and shining along the dusky way,
and dream of one that could save it all and salve our ache!

*

You, at whose table I have sat, some distant eve
beside the road, and eaten and you pitied me
to be driven an aimless way before the pitiless winds,
how much ye have given and knew not, pitying foolishly!

For not alone the bread I broke, but I tasted too
all your unwitting lives and knew the narrow soul
that bodies it in the landmarks of your fields,
and broods dumbly within your little seasons' round,
where, after sowing, comes the short-lived summer's mirth,
and, after harvesting, the winter's lingering dream,
half memory and regret, half hope, crouching beside
the hearth that is your only centre of life and dream.
And knowing the world how limitless and the way how
    long,
and the home of man how feeble and builded on the
    winds,
I have lived your life, that eve, as you might never live
knowing, and pity you, if you should come to know.

*

I cry to you as I pass your windows in the dusk;

Ye have built you unmysterious homes and ways in the
    wood
where of old ye went with sudden eyes to the right and
    left;
and your going was now made safe and your staying
    comforted,
for the forest edge itself, holding old savagery
in unsearch'd glooms, was your houses' friendly barrier.
And now that the year goes winterward, ye thought to hide
behind your gleaming panes, and where the hearth sings
    merrily
make cheer with meat and wine, and sleep in the long
    night,
and the uncared wastes might be a crying unhappiness.
But I, who have come from the outer night, I say to you
the winds are up and terribly will they shake the dry
    wood:
the woods shall awake, hearing them, shall awake to be
    toss'd and riven,
and make a cry and a parting in your sleep all night

as the wither'd leaves go whirling all night along all ways.
And when ye come forth at dawn, uncomforted by sleep,
ye shall stand at amaze, beholding all the ways overhidden
with worthless drift of the dead and all your broken world:
and ye shall not know whence the winds have come, nor
    shall ye know
whither the yesterdays have fled, or if they were.

*

Come out, come out, ye souls that serve, why will ye die?
or will ye sit and stifle in your prison-homes
dreaming of some master that holds the winds in leash
and the waves of darkness yonder in the gaunt hollow of
    night?
nay, there is none that rules: all is a strife of the winds
and the night shall billow in storm full oft ere all be done.
For this is the hard doom that is laid on all of you,
to be that whereof ye dream, dreaming against your will.
But first ye must travel the many ways, and your close-
    wrapt souls
must be blown thro' with the rain that comes from the
    homeless dark:
for until ye have had care of the wastes there shall be no
    truce
for them nor you, nor home, but ever the ancient feud;
and the soul of man must house the cry of the darkling
    waves
as he follows the ridge above the waters shuddering
    towards night,
and the rains and the winds that roam anhunger'd for
    some heart's warmth.
Go: tho' ye find it bitter, yet must ye be bare
to the wind and the sea and the night and the wail of
    birds in the sky;
go: tho' the going be hard and the goal blinded with rain
yet the staying is a death that is never soften'd with sleep.

*

Dawns of the world, how I have known you all,
so many, and so varied, and the same!
dawns o'er the timid plains, or in the folds
of the arm'd hills, or by the unsleeping shore;
a chill touch on the chill flesh of the dark
that, shuddering, shrinks from its couch, and leaves
a homeless light, staring, disconsolate,
on the drear world it knows too well, the world
it fled and finds again, its wistful hope
unmet by any miracle of night,
that mocks it rather, with its shreds that hang
about the woods and huddled bulks of gloom
that crouch, malicious, in the broken combes,
witness to foulnesses else unreveal'd
that visit earth and violate her dreams
in the lone hours when only evil wakes.

*

What is there with you and me, that I may not forget
but your white shapes come crowding noiselessly in my
    nights,
making my sleep a flight from a thousand beckoning
    hands?
Was it not enough that your cry dwelt in my waking ears
that now, seeking oblivion, I must yet be haunted
by each black maw of hunger that yawns despairingly
a moment ere its whitening frenzy bury it?
O waves of all the seas, would I could give you peace
and find my peace again: for all my peace is fled
and broken and blown along your white delirious crests!

*

O desolate eves along the way, how oft,
despite your bitterness, was I warm at heart!
not with the glow of remember'd hearths, but warm
with the solitary unquenchable fire that burns
a flameless heat deep in his heart who has come
where the formless winds plunge and exult for aye

among the naked spaces of the world,
far past the circle of the ruddy hearths
and all their memories. Desperate eves,
when the wind-bitten hills turn'd violet
along their rims, and the earth huddled her heat
within her niggard bosom, and the dead stones
lay battle-strewn before the iron wind
that, blowing from the chill west, made all its way
a loneliness to yield its triumph room;
yet in that wind a clamour of trumpets rang,
old trumpets, resolute, stark, undauntable,
singing to battle against the eternal foe,
the wronger of this world, and all his powers
in some last fight, foredoom'd disastrous,
upon the final ridges of the world:
a war-worn note, stern fire in the stricken eve,
and fire thro' all my ancient heart, that sprang
towards that last hope of a glory won in defeat,
whence, knowing not sure if such high grace befall
at the end, yet I draw courage to front the way.

*

The land I came thro' last was dumb with night,
a limbo of defeated glory, a ghost:
for wreck of constellations flicker'd perishing
scarce sustain'd in the mortuary air,
and on the ground and out of livid pools
wreck of old swords and crowns glimmer'd at whiles;
I seem'd at home in some old dream of kingship:
now it is clear grey day and the road is plain,
I am the wanderer of many years
who cannot tell if ever he was king
or if ever kingdoms were: I know I am
the wanderer of the ways of all the worlds,
to whom the sunshine and the rain are one
and one to stay or hasten, because he knows

no ending of the way, no home, no goal,
and phantom night and the grey day alike
withhold the heart where all my dreams and days
might faint in soft fire and delicious death:
and saying this to myself as a simple thing
I feel a peace fall in the heart of the winds
and a clear dusk settle, somewhere, far in me.

Epilogue

1908

The droning tram swings westward: shrill
the wire sings overhead, and chill
midwinter draughts rattle the glass
that shows the dusking way I pass
to yon four-turreted square tower
that still exalts the golden hour
where youth, initiate once, endears
a treasure richer with the years.

Dim-seen, the upper stories fleet
along the twisting shabby street;
beneath, the shop-fronts' cover'd ways
bask in their lampions' orange blaze,
or stare phantasmal, weirdly new,
in the electrics' ghastly blue:
and, up and down, I see them go,
along the windows pleas'd and slow
but hurrying where the darkness falls,
the city's drift of pavement thralls
whom the poor pleasures of the street
lure from their niggard homes, to meet
and mix, unknown, and feel the bright
banality 'twixt them and night:
so, in my youth, I saw them flit
where their delusive dream was lit;

so now I see them, and can read
the urge of their unwitting need
one with my own, however dark,
and questing towards one mother-ark.
But, past the gin-shop's ochrous flare,
sudden, a gap of quiet air
and gather'd dark, where, set a pace
beyond the pavement's coiling race
and mask'd by bulk of sober leaves,
the plain obtruncate chancel heaves,
whose lancet-windows faintly show
suffusion of a ruddy glow,
the lamp of adoration, dim
and rich with unction kept for Him
whom Bethlehem's manger first made warm,
the sweetest god in human form,
love's prisoner in the Eucharist,
man's pleading, patient amorist:
and there the sacring laver stands
where I was brought in pious hands,
a chrisom-child, that I might be
accepted of that company
who, thro' their journeying, behold
beyond the apparent heavens, controll'd
to likeness of a candid rose,
ascending where the gold heart glows,
cirque within cirque, the blessed host,
their kin, their comfort, and their boast.

With them I walk'd in love and awe
till I was ware of that grim maw
and lazar-pit that reek'd beneath:
what outcast howlings these? what teeth
gnashing in vain? and was that bliss
whose counter-hemisphere was this?
and could it be, when times fulfill'd
had made the tally of either guild,
that this mid-world, dredg'd clean in both,

should no more bar their gruesome troth?
So from beneath that choiring tent
I stepp'd, and tho' my spirit's bent
was dark to me as yet, I sought
a sphere appeas'd and undistraught;
and found viaticum and goal
in that hard atom of the soul,
that final grain of deathless mind,
which Satan's watch-fiends shall not find
nor the seven mills of darkness bruise,
for all permission to abuse;
stubborn, yet, if one seek aright,
translucent all within and bright
with sheen that hath no paradigm,
not where our proud Golcondas brim,
tho' sky and sea and leaf and flower,
in each rare mood of virtual power,
sleep in their gems' excepted day:
and so, nor long, the guarded ray
broke on my eagerness, who brought
the lucid diamond-probe of thought
and, driving it behind, the extreme
blind vehemence of travailing dream
against the inhibitory shell:
and found, no grim eternal cell
and presence of the shrouded Norn,
but Eden, clad in nuptial morn,
young, fair, and radiant with delight
remorse nor sickness shall requite.

Yes, Eden was my own, my bride;
whatever malices denied,
faithful and found again, nor long
absent from aura of wooing song:
but promis'd only, while the sun
must travel yet thro' times undone;
and life must guard the prize of youth,
and thought must steward into truth

the mines of magian ore divined
in rich Cipangos of the mind:
and I, that made my high attempt
no bliss whence any were exempt,
their fellow-pilgrim, I must greet
these listless captives of the street,
these fragments of an orphan'd drift
whose dower was our mother's thrift,
and, tho' they know it not, have care
of what would be their loving prayer
if skill bestow'd might help them heed
their craving for the simple meed
to be together in the light
when loneliness and dark incite:
long is the way till we are met
where Eden pays her hoarded debt
and we are orb'd in her, and she
hath still'd her hungering to be,
with plentitude beyond impeach,
single, distinct, and whole in each:
and many an evening hour shall bring
the dark crowd's dreary loitering
to me who pass and see the tale
of all my striving, bliss or bale,
dated from either spire that strives
clear of the shoal of shiftless lives,
and promise, in all years' despite,
fidelity to old delight.

J. LE GAY BRERETON
1871-1933

The Silver Gull

With strong slow stroke
Oaring her way against the breeze
Above the blustering waves that shoulder and smoke
The silver gull moves on with strenuous ease;
Then sidelong shoots on high
With sudden cry
Of rapture in the wind's imperious will
And that sweet whirling dream
Of blending purpose;
Poised a moment, still,
She glides, a fancied shape of air, down that invisible
    stream.

I lie on the warm sea-beach
And out to the wandering heart
Of feathered life in the beating air I reach
Arms that beseech
– Arms of my soul that in the living air
As answer to my prayer
Are wings of ecstasy;
And on the fierce quest silently I start
Above the envious crowding of the sea.

Delirium of delight!
Caught by the wind, I strain
In glorious throes of fight.
Finding the uttermost pleasure
That love can force from pain,
Naked I strive, and take
From poverty all her treasure,
Living for life's own sake.

O sister seabird, hearken, I call to thee!
Sister! my life and thine
Still intertwine,
And not till side by side
Equal and glad and free
Down the invisible stream we twain may glide,
Shall you or I seek rest
On weathered ledge or reef or feathered nest.

Wider the shelter of my grand wings outspread
Encloses earth and sea
And thee, unconscious wandering heart – and thee.
I am forgotten: but thou art still my care
Who have known thy life and know thy way is mine,
For over the waves thou lovest I too have sped
Where now at my heart they shine;
For I am the world-encircling eddying vast of air.

In me is the manifold urge,
The shedding of leaves, the upward push of the seed,
Of all the life upon earth
The scramble and fury and fret,
The ceaseless monotonous chant of eternal surge,
The pangs of change and of triumph in death and birth,
The ache of unending need
Lest we should have peace and forget.

And mine is the torrent of hate,
Growling black flood with a seething foam of red,
And the insolent pomp of the ape in a robe of state,
And the sliding silence of guile;
And mine is the eager meeting of souls that are newly wed
– Throb, throb, O passionate heart!
Heed not the impotent hands that would fain defile
The shrine of the god who for sake of the One still moulds
    the many apart.

I am the spirit of joy set free,
Knowing no limits, for further than thought can reach
And as far as love can bless
I hold exultant reign.
I am I, unbodied, supreme,
The spirit of joy.

O sister, warm wind-wrestling bird, we two
Are there like flying flakes against the blue.

J. SHAW NEILSON

1872-1942

The Orange Tree

The young girl stood beside me. I
    Saw not what her young eyes could see:
– A light, she said, not of the sky
    Lives somewhere in the Orange Tree.

– Is it, I said, of east or west?
    The heartbeat of a luminous boy
Who with his faltering flute confessed
    Only the edges of his joy?

Was he, I said, borne to the blue
    In a mad escapade of Spring
Ere he could make a fond adieu
    To his love in the blossoming?

– Listen! the young girl said. There calls
    No voice, no music beats on me;
But it is almost sound: it falls
    This evening on the Orange Tree.

– Does he, I said, so fear the Spring
    Ere the white sap too far can climb?
See in the full gold evening
    All happenings of the olden time?

Is he so goaded by the green?
    Does the compulsion of the dew
Make him unknowable but keen
    Asking with beauty of the blue?

– Listen! the young girl said. For all
    Your hapless talk you fail to see
There is a light, a step, a call
    This evening on the Orange Tree.

– Is it, I said, a waste of love
   Imperishably old in pain,
Moving as an affrighted dove
   Under the sunlight or the rain?

Is it a fluttering heart that gave
   Too willingly and was reviled?
Is it the stammering at a grave,
   The last word of a little child?

– Silence! the young girl said. Oh, why,
   Why will you talk to weary me?
Plague me no longer now, for I
   Am listening like the Orange Tree.

Song Be Delicate

Let your song be delicate.
   The skies declare
No war – the eyes of lovers
   Wake everywhere.

Let your voice be delicate.
   How faint a thing
Is Love, little Love crying
   Under the Spring.

Let your song be delicate.
   The flowers can hear:
Too well they know the tremble
   Of the hollow year.

Let your voice be delicate.
   The bees are home:
All their day's love is sunken
   Safe in the comb.

Let your song be delicate.
  Sing no loud hymn:
Death is abroad. . . . Oh, the black season!
  The deep – the dim!

May

Shyly the silver-hatted mushrooms make
  Soft entrance through,
And undelivered lovers, half awake,
  Hear noises in the dew.

Yellow in all the earth and in the skies,
  The world would seem
Faint as a widow mourning with soft eyes
  And falling into dream.

Up the long hill I see the slow plough leave
  Furrows of brown;
Dim is the day and beautiful; I grieve
  To see the sun go down.

But there are suns a many for mine eyes
  Day after day:
Delightsome in grave greenery they rise,
  Red oranges in May.

Schoolgirls Hastening

Fear it has faded and the night:
  The bells all peal the hour of nine:
The schoolgirls hastening through the light
  Touch the unknowable Divine.

What leavening in my heart would bide!
  Full dreams a thousand deep are there:
All luminants succumb beside
  The unbound melody of hair.

Joy the long timorous takes the flute:
  Valiant with colour songs are born:
Love the impatient absolute
  Lives as a Saviour in the morn.

Get thou behind me Shadow-Death!
  Oh ye Eternities delay!
Morning is with me and the breath
  Of schoolgirls hastening down the way.

Native Companions Dancing

On the blue plains in wintry days
  These stately birds move in the dance.
Keen eyes have they, and quaint old ways
On the blue plains in wintry days.
The Wind, their unseen Piper, plays,
  They strut, salute, retreat, advance;
On the blue plains, in wintry days,
  These stately birds move in the dance.

Beauty Imposes

Beauty imposes reverence in the Spring,
Grave as the urge within the honeybuds,
It wounds us as we sing.

Beauty is joy that stays not overlong.
Clad in the magic of sincerities,
It rides up in a song.

Beauty imposes chastenings on the heart,
Grave as the birds in last solemnities
Assembling to depart.

HUGH McCRAE

1876-1958

I Blow My Pipes

I blow my pipes, the glad birds sing,
The fat young nymphs about me spring,
The sweaty centaur leaps the trees
And bites his dryad's splendid knees;
The sky, the water, and the earth
Repeat aloud our noisy mirth . . .
Anon, tight-bellied bacchanals,
With ivy from the vineyard walls,
Lead out and crown with shining glass
The wine's red baby on the grass.

*

I blow my pipes, the glad birds sing,
The fat young nymphs about me spring,
I am the lord,
I am the lord,
I am the lord of everything!

Ambuscade

Or the black centaurs, statuesquely still,
 Whose moving eyes devour the snuffling mares,
And watch with baneful rage their nervous strides
 Whip the dark river white, lest, unawares,
Some danger seize them . . . Statuesquely still,
 Behind the waving trellises of cane,
The centaurs feel their hearts – besieged with blood –
 Stagger like anvils when the sled-blows rain
Shower on shower in persistent flood . . .

Now Cornus, he, the oldest of the group,
   With many wounds, strong arms, and clay-rolled hair,
Coughs for a signal to his dreadful troop
   And springs, wide-fingered, from the crackling lair.
Loudly the victims neigh, they thrash the stream,
   They tear their foemen's beards with frothy teeth,
And fill the banks with sparkling spires of steam
   That heavenward roll in one tumultuous wreath.

Within the branches of an ancient oak,
   A mother-satyr, sleeping with her young,
Smit by a sudden stone, upbraids the stroke;
   Then turns to see from whence it has been flung.
Scarce does she mark the cursed centaur pack,
   Than, standing clear, she blows a whistle shrill,
Which, like an echo, straight comes flying back
   Louder and louder down the empty hill.

A roar of hooves, a lightning view of eyes
   Redder than fire, of long straight whistling manes,
Stiff crests, and tails drawn out against the skies,
   Of angry nostrils, webbed with leaping veins,
The stallions come!

Fantasy

I love to lie under the lemon
   That grows by the fountain;
To see the stars flutter and open
   Along the blue mountain.

To hear the last wonderful piping
   That rises to heaven, –
Six quavers to sum up delight in,
   And sorrow in seven –

To dream that the mythic wood-women,
   Each brown as the honey
The bees took their toll of from Hybla,
   On days that were sunny,

Come parting the hedge of my garden
   To dance a light measure
With soft little feet on the greensward,
   Peak-pointed for pleasure.

While Pan, on a leopard reclining,
   And birds on his shoulder,
Gives breath to a flute's wanton sighing
   Until their eyes smoulder.

Then, lo, in the pool of the valley
   Cries centaur to centaur,
As, plashing, they leap the white moonbuds
   The goddess had leant o'er.

They climb the steep sides of the chasm
   With hollowy thunder –
Whole cliffs at the stroke of their hoof-beats
   Split tumbling asunder!

They climb the steep sides of the chasm,
   And rush through the thicket
That chokes up the pathways that lead to
   My green garden-wicket.

They seize on the dancing wood-women,
   And kick poor Pan over
The back of his fat spotted leopard
   Amid the lush clover.

So I wake, and eagerly listen –
   But only the fountain,
Still sleeping and sobbing, complains at
   The foot of the mountain.

Enigma

I watch her fingers while they prance
Like little naked women, tango-mad,
Along the keys, a cup-shot dance –
Music, who'll say, more joyous or more sad?

A mystery . . . but not so strange
As she, Enigma is her pretty name;
And, though she smiles, her veiled eyes range
Through tears of melancholy and shame.

She laughs and weeps . . . Is it because
Only tonight she gave herself to me?
The new bud frightened to be glad . . .
The child's first vision of the insatiate sea.

FURNLEY MAURICE

1881-1942

Plunder

The fisherman leans backward on his cord;
    The shallows wash his footprints clean away.
His beard is stuck with scales; without a word
    He hauls and hauls, dreaming upon his prey.

No thought of coffers' jewelled band and latch,
    Nor of white, bleeding mermaidens that sprawl
Gasping in suffocation 'midst the catch
    Disturbs his thrifty brooding on the haul.

Spill out your netted hoard, your toll of scales,
    The snared amazement that your gullery pulls
From the drowned gardens where slow water-gales
    Wash unknown jungles and world-weary hulls!

Fishes moustached, spotted and spikey-finned,
    Flash terror-struck and burst upon the sands!
Now, from your slippery mass, toll of the wind,
    Sort the slim pike with eager, callused hands!

Apples in the Moon

We came round by the little dark pond;
    Apples, bunched in the moon,
Had lifted our bodies, proud and fond
    To a gentleness, coming soon.
Is it coming soon? Is it something to speak?
    Something to fold our mood?
There goes a long white ray across the creek
    Coiling, unsummoned, unwooed!

Something to think, lad, something to praise?
    Some magnificence to do?
But it's a deep slime that is over the gaze;
    Maybe their lies are true.
So moons and apples mean little to us
    When all's so rotten for sure;
Teeth and bones and boys shall the harvests truss
    And only filth endure.

The screaming rocs come lower than low
    Shedding black blasts from steeple to station
And under the ruinous thunders timidly flow
    The dark unwaking silences of desolation.
Pyres of smouldering love and law!
    Plato to Christ ashes, all ashes!
And the great bloody tongue of the world's awe
    Licking its bloody gashes!

Something to think, lad, to say or to do;
    Their fires die down, die dark;
In the pyres of the beautiful things and true
    Is there some living spark?

Only the wind is free,
A wind that spreads no dust;
Nothing but caking mud
Made from the blood
Of the poor world's agony
And the spittle of its disgust.

Wide, wide the shroud,
Way down south,
Down back,
Down Lenah Valley track
Red, red as a harlot's mouth,
Red, bunched apples are rotting against a cloud.

Coming round the small dark pond,
    To a vision of apples high in the moon;
A flash of grace, one heart-beat of something fond,
    An instant flash of approaching boon
        Dead in its speck!
        Fondness is wreck,
        Boon is shame,
        Pity a sunken stone
        And the name
        Of Beauty a blasphemy grown.
We must be blinder, lad, when apples glow,
Eyes are only to weep with now.

The Agricultural Show, Flemington, Victoria

I

The lumbering tractor rolls its panting round,
The windmills fan the blue; feet crush the sand;
The pumps spurt muddy water to the sound,
The muffled thud and blare of a circus band.

II

    For this is the other life I know so little of,
A life of fevered effort, of wool and tortured love!
Why didn't somebody tell me ere 'twas too late to learn
This life with its fire and vigour, by brake and anguished
    burn,
Gorgeous and ghastly and rare,
Flourished out there, out there?
But I just sit in a tram and pay my fare;
Me, an important man in the job I hold.
But there, there are the roots of the hills of gold
That my clawed fingers tell.
Why didn't somebody say before I was old

That there were brumbies to break and these store mobs to
    muster
When I was bred to the clang of a tram bell,
Answered an 'ad' and took up a shopman's duster?

III

Here is a world that stands upon sun and rain
In a humid odour of wool where the sheafing grain
Falls like pay in the palm.
I but rode out the calm
In a regular job and felt the years fall by
To a pension and senile golf; that's the whole tale;
But there's another world in the white of a bullock's eye
Strained as he horns a rail.

I, with an unshod outlaw between my knees
Dream, but awake to the old 'Fares please, fares please.'
The long low bellowing of yarded herds,
The song of sweating horsemen on the plains,
The outlaw's mating scream,
Drought and the offal-birds,
Yellowing lemons and longed-for rains –
That was the dream.

IV

Here Science like a helpful angel lifts
The drag, straightens the backs and shortens shifts;
While in the town
Men are the engine's slaves
And, drunk with Science, pull the lever down
And stagger into fragmentary graves.

The tractors pant their tract,
The combs of the reapers thrust
Their yielding paths and the stooks are stacked
While clumsy thumbs adjust

The flayer's beating thongs
And evening with tired songs
Sinks down upon the dust.
What load do the geldings carry?
What load do the bullocks drag
Worse than the loads of fear that harry
The city salesman with his bag?
Salesmen and bullocks stagger in the chains
And their red nostrils snuffle at the dust,
Lashed through life and death in the frightful lust
Of urgency that coils in men's mad brains.

V

For there are many worlds to taunt our faith;
The fabled cattle-hills, the green wool-plains;
But fair or fabulous, fact or thin as a wraith
All drift into feverish sums of losses and gains.

Man's god is what he gets his living by;
No doubt this nuzzling litter of auburn swine
Came like an old Venetian argosy
Laden with all the elegant stuffs
For shining hose and scented ruffs,
Its bellying topsails gleaming in the sun
Along the horizon line –
To some bush-whiskered father of a run.

This lustful stallion, Pegasus without wings,
Is a feather-legged temple in a desert place;
This sleek ring-nostrilled bull is King of Kings,
And doe-eyed Jerseys mumble Heaven's grace.

The cloying odour of the milking sheds,
The docking days, the branding days, perchance
The springing pasterns of the thoroughbreds
Are all mere counters of deliverance.

133

VI

Many the urgent calls of the cocky's day;
What of his play?
'Within,' the Mongolian Giant is on sight –
And here's his boot to whet the appetite.
The spruiker with his flowery talk enjoins
Me and my likes to view the abortive things
That nestle under the marquee's greasy wings –
A patient, worn-out woman collects the coins.
Not tired snakes nor dancing dogs,
Nor green and human frogs,
Nor ladies bearded or fat,
Nor shark nor seven-teated cow,
Nor feat of horsemanship
Could stir a calm like that,
Put a white tremor on her lip
Or raise the cynically disillusioned brow.
Worn out no doubt is she
With the joy of looking, free,
Too long at each inane monstrosity
Till there's no more wonder
On earth or under
The sea.
But wayback Dan closes a week's carouse
With one long, sixpenny look at a three-tailed mouse.

VII

I've heard the waggon-wheels grinding by ruts and stumps
Scouring the black night for a possible camp;
I've watched the breeching flop on the horses' rumps
In the green light of a wavering bottle-lamp.
And I have come at last on a sweet home and a bed
And woke to see through the broken blind a munching cow
        at the bail,
To hear, while the magpies yodelled in the slow dawn's
        searching spread,
The sharp spurt of the milk into the pail.

VIII

The things of the body pass,
And these are of the day;
The things that nourish
The body flourish
In weather and sun
But soon, like flowers, they're done
And leave no husk.
But the mind's things pass
Not readily away;
The mind goes like a camel in the dusk
Nibbling the grass
Between the stones of the tombs
Or gorging among the sheaves
Of blotted leaves
That fall from the housèd looms.
So while the æons run
Hearts leap and brains contrive;
Honey is of the sun
But there's no sun in the hive.

IX

The morning pastures of the spirit spread
Their dewy carpets for anointed feet,
But the lashed herd and the shearing shed,
These are man's clothes and meat.
For there are many worlds to plague our hopes,
Crumbling owl-haunted belfries of 'perhaps,'
And lantern-lighted alleys whence the stranger gropes
His way to the Andean slopes,
And the old stone stairs of faith scooped out by a myriad
      feet,
Green at the base, where timeless water laps.
Though there are many worlds, none is complete.

X

For all the yellowing melons of marvellous size,
And dogs that pen their sheep from the drover's eyes,

And the hew and thew
Of the beanstalk axemen climbing to the blue,
We all turn homeward dusty and overcast
By a sense of cattle-hills without a name;
Carrying bags of samples of the vast
Uncomprehended regions whence they came.
Drenched with the colour of unexperienced days
We go our different ways;
Stallions loose on the plains; apples of Hesperides;
Quiet lakes and milking sheds; 'Fares please, fares please.'

BRIAN VREPONT

1882-1955

The Net-Menders

I came upon them by a strip of sea,
In a drizzle of rain mending their fishing-net,
Four swift brown hands, and lean with industry,
Shuttling the thin twine skilfully in-out, repairing the fret
Of rock-jag, shark-tooth and thresh;
He, tense as a mackerel, strong and agile,
Sea-eyed and grim as a rock, turned, and his smile
Was as the wonder of sunshine on sea-rock,
His fingers harping the net-mesh;
She on the sea-side, facing the land, took stock
Of me leisurely nearing, through half-shut eyes.
'Defence,' I thought; but her mouth relaxed, went sweet
And soft as a sea-flower, her hands' enterprise
On the sea-side of the breaks in the net
Rippling the strings of the two-sided harp o' the sea,
And I thought, 'Here is where sea-melodies meet,
Mending the breakage of earth-and-sea-fret,'
And the strange great grace of simplicity came on me.

If they had angers in them, these two by the sea,
Not in the two days dwelt with them,
Watching the shuttle flying, the flat corks tied,
And the strong boat pitch-caulked for battle with the sea,
Was flaw apparent in the gem;
Their poverty, too real for pride to hide,
Gave them no envy, not even in the lamp-light
And shadows of our talk,
Not when the net was trailed and netted nought
Save weed, nor when I spoke, that unforgettable night
We fought the tide, and drifted home star-caught,

And I spoke of the hawk
Now in the dark vanished, that all day long
Circled and soared and plunged on innocence; 'Cruel life!'
    I cried;
But my cry crossed over the woman's song,
Over the zither of the boat cutting the brine, and died,
And the man said, 'It is life,'
And the boat gritted the waiting sand
With sound of a cleansing knife,
And we slept, at life's command.

WILLIAM BAYLEBRIDGE

1883-1942

On Moral Laws

Why, tell, should moral laws in time have length
Past their relation, purpose, strength?
Let those, now, to the past related
With that past be waived, o'er-dated.
As man amends the law that's spent –
Though once expedient – in his Parliament,
So must he mend those laws whose larger scope,
Beyond our breathing day, more serves his hope.
Since knowledge knows no absolute,
The laws it prompts are a concurrent fruit;
And the whole tree must wither with its root.
New knowledge breaks to flower – a new election;
And life to law moves of a new complexion.

The force of these successive codes
Springs, runs, and fails, with their confirming god's;
But, 'Ours have an Earth-outsoaring nature,'
Some say. 'Look! this is their feature –
These laws of faultless Heaven were ordained.'
Shall this dull mystery longer be maintained –
That Man's Earth-hallowing strength is bowed
To flatter some intrigue in void or cloud?
Our codes, the purpose high that each fulfils,
Shall be as Man's occasion wills.

Be brief, ye strong, with this pretence –
This chatterer's sham, this stripped Omnipotence!
Mortality hath there a wakeful god
On these, our spirit-driven, to lay the rod:
Man's thrust to life (so runs the vow) shall cease –
It is not ease, it is not peace.
What! shirking dust, ev'n such are we –
For these to barter all that sets Man free?

Morals, a stuff of time, might make pretence,
But how ineptly! to omniscience;
And use (where vital this) in moral law
No dead Dictation on its lapse shall draw –
The law that lives must oft re-rendered be,
Not absolute, but for the ascent yet free.
If laws, occasion-called, Earth's Man
Remit to a removed plan,
To Heaven or such, him our revisions rule
A dullard plucked in his own school.

O wealth of wit! too artless in its span –
That God, Space, Nature, were made for Man –
That this forlorn mote in the Universe
Their functions, to exalt him, may coerce!
Dupes! while we play this mock-sublime,
We lose the step, or haply mark but time.

Morals, that may his shaping ne'er transcend,
Man, who moulded, now shall re-amend.
If final were each such decreeing,
Its fact had fallen from Man's truceless being.
Self-liable, refuse that death;
Look onward still; use louder breath
For relevant codes, for raisèd laws
Conceived in terms of Man's Effect and Cause!

Man, by will and choice, shall now
His state with its due increment endow –
Shall use ideals vowed to this,
Whose ends high practice only can release –
Exalt the part he takes in being
By canons of his own unblurred decreeing –
And so defeat that old abortion,
Man, in moral torment and distortion.
Such morals shall he find in that assay,
Ev'n Heaven, to envy moved, would tremble with dismay.

VANCE PALMER

1885-1959

The Farmer Remembers the Somme

Will they never fade or pass!
The mud, and the misty figures endlessly coming
In file through the foul morass,
And the grey flood-water lipping the reeds and grass,
And the steel wings drumming.

The hills are bright in the sun:
There's nothing changed or marred in the well-known
    places;
When work for the day is done
There's talk, and quiet laughter, and gleams of fun
On the old folks' faces.

I have returned to these:
The farm, and the kindly Bush, and the young calves
    lowing;
But all that my mind sees
Is a quaking bog in a mist – stark, snapped trees,
And the dark Somme flowing.

PETER HOPEGOOD

1891-1967

Snake's-Eye View of a Serial Story

Once, on my cyclic boundary-creep,
   Across our garden fence I saw
Man's first invention taking shape
   And heard professed Man's primal law . . .
   Devised to hobble fang and claw.
      A youth was whittling pensively
         An arm's length section of a bough.
      He trimmed it quite extensively . . .
         Intensively as well . . . and now
      He paused to swing it to and fro.
I marvelled at his industry
   And certainly such skill demanded
Appreciative signs from me.
   Had but sufficient time been granted
   His patient zeal I must have vaunted.
      Just then, intoning from the bush,
         Our erstwhile gardener's accents sighed,
      '*Now* who is it you aim to bash?
         By rights a man should tan your hide
         Then send you packing far and wide.'
His upward-glancing eye betraying
   Solely glad innocence and pride
In work that needs no justifying,
   The craftsman laid his flint aside
   And therewith candidly replied:
      'Well, Dad, to straighten out my kinks
         And ease my natural urge to fidget,
      Whilst you were snatching forty winks,
         I sort of figured out this gadget
         Which, rightly pushed, could swell our budget.
'It exercises limbs and trunk
   Far better than a croquet mallet

Developing both speed and spunk.
   The "Indian Club" I thought to call it.
   Gymnasiums could well install it.
      'And, Sir, for peaceful purposes
        Alone of course, it's warrantable.
     It never, never would be used,
        Loomed circumstance however sable,
        To straighten out my brother, Abel.'

And . . . do you know? I must admit . . .
   Of course I cannot speak for others . . .
The lad's shrewd honesty and wit
   Seemed to eclipse his dad's and mother's
   And even *at that time* his brother's.

These souvenirs of long ago
   Could seem but fictional narrations . . .
So faultily one's memories flow
   Confusing deeds and creeds and nations,
And Summit Talks, *and* Action Stations?

LEON GELLERT

b. 1892

These Men

Men moving in a trench, in the clear noon,
    Whetting their steel within the crumbling earth;
Men, moving in a trench 'neath a new moon
    That smiles with a slit mouth and has no mirth;
Men moving in a trench in the grey morn,
    Lifting bodies on their clotted frames;
Men with narrow mouths thin-carved in scorn
    That twist and fumble strangely at dead names.

*

These men know life – know death a little more.
    These men see paths and ends, and see
Beyond some swinging open door
    Into eternity.

TOM INGLIS MOORE

b. 1901

Align Your Act

Chessmen, dreams, and peacock feathers
   Delight in an ivory tower;
With no Ariadne, we voyagers wander
Threadless the maze of time's agenda,
   Yet strive to arrive at the ease of a flower.

These pilgrims here, the portulacas,
   Soon reach their Meccas in form
Of the sun's gold, but where is our guiding
Faith as we climb, with the peaks clouding
   And hatred hiding the track with storm?

Take a focus on yellow Arcturus,
   Who heard Job cry in the night!
Turn from the tower, the solved equation
Of petals, the rancours of revolution,
   To the clear flame of the spirit's light.

In birth, in desire, in the grave's ending
   We are one in the brotherhood
Of human bonding – shall hope not summon
The peoples' yearning for peace in common
   To the morning unfearing, the way understood?

Align your act with the sun and Arcturus.
   Ascend with the iris to span
Self and the world, earth and heaven.
Explore the heart till we find the haven,
   Core of the maze, the integral man.

KENNETH SLESSOR

1901-71

Thieves' Kitchen

Good roaring pistol-boys, brave lads of gold,
Good roistering easy maids, blown cock-a-hoop
On floods of tavern-steam, I greet you! Drunk
With wild Canary, drowned in wines of old,
I'll swear your round, red faces dive and swim
Like clouds of fire-fish in a waxen tide,
    And these are seas of smoke we thieves behold.

Yet I've a mind I know what arms enchain
With flesh my shoulders . . . aye, and what warm legs
Wind quickly into mine . . . 'tis no pale mermaid,
No water-wench that floats in a smoky main
Betwixt the tankard and my knees . . . in faith,
I know thee, Joan, and by the beard of God,
    I'll prove to-night thy mortal parts again!

Leap, leap, fair vagabonds, your lives are short . . .
Dance firelit in your cauldron-fumes, O thieves,
Ram full your bellies with spiced food, gulp deep
Those goblets of thick ale – yea, feast and sport,
Ye Cyprian maids – lie with great, drunken rogues,
Jump by the fire – soon, soon your flesh must crawl
    And Tyburn flap with birds, long-necked and swart!

Fixed Ideas

Ranks of electroplated cubes, dwindling to glitters,
Like the other pasture, the trigonometry of marble,
Death's candy-bed. Stone caked on stone,
Dry pyramids and racks of iron balls.

Life is observed, a precipitate of pellets,
Or grammarians freeze it into spar,
Their rhomboids, as for instance, the finest crystal
Fixing a snowfall under glass. Gods are laid out
In alabaster, with horny cartilage
And zinc ribs; or systems of ecstasy
Baked into bricks. There is a gallery of sculpture,
Bleached bones of heroes, Gorgon masks of bushrangers;
But the quarries are of more use than this,
Filled with the rolling of huge granite dice,
Ideas and judgments: vivisection, the Baptist Church,
Good men and bad men, polygamy, birth-control. . . .

Frail tinkling rush
Water-hair streaming
Prickles and glitters
Cloudy with bristles
River of thought
Swimming the pebbles –
Undo, loosen your bubbles!

Metempsychosis

Suddenly to become John Benbow, walking down William
    Street
With a tin trunk and a five-pound note, looking for a place
    to eat,
And a peajacket the colour of a shark's behind
That a Jew might buy in the morning. . . .

To fry potatoes (God save us!) if you feel inclined,
Or to kiss the landlady's daughter, and no one mind,
In a peel-papered bedroom with a whistling jet
And a picture of the Holy Virgin. . . .

Wake in a shaggy bale of blankets with a fished-up
    cigarette,

Picking over 'Turfbird's Tattle' for a Saturday morning
    bet,
With a bottle in the wardrobe easy to reach
And a blast of onions from the landing. . . .

Tattooed with foreign ladies' tokens, a heart and dagger
    each,
In places that make the delicate female inquirer screech,
And over a chest smoky with gunpowder-blue –
Behold! – a mermaid piping through a coach-horn!

Banjo-playing, firing off guns, and other momentous things
    to do,
Such as blowing through peashooters at hawkers to
    improve the view –

Suddenly paid-off and forgotten in Woolloomooloo. . . .

Suddenly to become John Benbow. . . .

Sensuality

Feeling hunger and cold, feeling
Food, feeling fire, feeling
Pity and pain, tasting
Time in a kiss, tasting
Anger and tears, touching
Eyelids with lips, touching
Plague, touching flesh, knowing
Blood in the mouth, knowing
Laughter like flame, holding
Pickaxe and pen, holding
Death in the hand, hearing
Boilers and bells, hearing
Birds, hearing hail, smelling
Cedar and sweat, smelling

Petrol and sea, feeling
Hunger and cold, feeling
Food, feeling fire. . . .

Feeling.

South Country

After the whey-faced anonymity
Of river-gums and scribbly-gums and bush,
After the rubbing and the hit of brush,
You come to the South Country

As if the argument of trees were done,
The doubts and quarrelling, the plots and pains,
All ended by these clear and gliding planes
Like an abrupt solution.

And over the flat earth of empty farms
The monstrous continent of air floats back
Coloured with rotting sunlight and the black,
Bruised flesh of thunderstorms:

Air arched, enormous, pounding the bony ridge,
Ditches and hutches, with a drench of light,
So huge, from such infinities of height,
You walk on the sky's beach

While even the dwindled hills are small and bare,
As if, rebellious, buried, pitiful,
Something below pushed up a knob of skull,
Feeling its way to air.

Captain Dobbin

Captain Dobbin, having retired from the South Seas
In the dumb tides of 1900, with a handful of shells,
A few poisoned arrows, a cask of pearls,
And five thousand pounds in the colonial funds,
Now sails the street in a brick villa, 'Laburnum Villa',
In whose blank windows the harbour hangs
Like a fog against the glass,
Golden and smoky, or stoned with a white glitter,
And boats go by, suspended in the pane,
Blue Funnel, Red Funnel, Messageries Maritimes,
Lugged down the port like sea-beasts taken alive
That scrape their bellies on sharp sands,
Of which particulars Captain Dobbin keeps
A ledger sticky with ink,
Entries of time and weather, state of the moon,
Nature of cargo and captain's name,
For some mysterious and awful purpose
Never divulged.
For at night, when the stars mock themselves with lanterns,
So late the chimes blow loud and faint
Like a hand shutting and unshutting over the bells,
Captain Dobbin, having observed from bed
The lights, like a great fiery snake, of the *Comorin*
Going to sea, will note the hour
For subsequent recording in his gazette.

But the sea is really closer to him than this,
Closer to him than a dead, lovely woman,
For he keeps bits of it, like old letters,
Salt tied up in bundles
Or pressed flat,
What you might call a lock of the sea's hair,
So Captain Dobbin keeps his dwarfed memento,
His urn-burial, a chest of mummied waves,
Gales fixed in print, and the sweet dangerous countries
Of shark and casuarina-tree,

Stolen and put in coloured maps,
Like a flask of seawater, or a bottled ship,
A schooner caught in a glass bottle;
But Captain Dobbin keeps them in books,
Crags of varnished leather
Pimply with gilt, by learned mariners
And masters of hydrostatics, or the childish tales
Of simple heroes, taken by Turks or dropsy.
So nightly he sails from shelf to shelf
Or to the quadrants, dangling with rusty screws,
Or the hanging-gardens of old charts,
So old they bear the authentic protractor-lines,
Traced in faint ink, as fine as Chinese hairs.

Over the flat and painted atlas-leaves
His reading-glass would tremble,
Over the fathoms, pricked in tiny rows,
Water shelving to the coast.
Quietly the bone-rimmed lens would float
Till, through the glass, he felt the barbéd rush
Of bubbles foaming, spied the albicores,
The blue-finned admirals, heard the wind-swallowed cries
Of planters running on the beach
Who filched their swags of yams and ambergris,
Birds' nests and sandalwood, from pastures numbed
By the sun's yellow, too meek for honest theft;
But he, less delicate robber, climbed the walls,
Broke into dozing houses
Crammed with black bottles, marish wine
Crusty and salt-corroded, fading prints,
Sparkle-daubed almanacs and playing cards,
With rusty cannon, left by the French outside,
Half-buried in sand,
Even to the castle of Queen Pomaree
In the Yankee's footsteps, and found her throne-room piled
With golden candelabras, mildewed swords,
Guitars and fowling-pieces, tossed in heaps
With greasy cakes and flung-down calabashes.

Then Captain Dobbin's eye,
That eye of wild and wispy scudding blue,
Voluptuously prying, would light up
Like mica scratched by gully-suns,
And he would be fearful to look upon
And shattering in his conversation;
Nor would he tolerate the harmless chanty,
No *Shenandoah*, or the dainty mew
That landsmen offer in a silver dish
To Neptune, sung to pianos in candlelight.
Of these he spoke in scorn,
For there was but one way of singing *Stormalong*,
He said, and that was not really singing,
But howling, rather – shrieked in the wind's jaws
By furious men; not tinkled in drawing-rooms
By lap-dogs in clean shirts.
And, at these words,
The galleries of photographs, men with rich beards,
Pea-jackets and brass buttons, with folded arms,
Would scowl approval, for they were shipmates, too,
Companions of no cruise by reading-glass,
But fellows of storm and honey from the past –
'The Charlotte, Java, '93',
'Knuckle and Fred at Port au Prince',
'William in his New Rig',
Even that notorious scoundrel, Captain Baggs,
Who, as all knew, owed Dobbin Twenty Pounds
Lost at fair cribbage, but he never paid,
Or paid 'with the slack of the tops'l sheets'
As Captain Dobbin frequently expressed it.

There were their faces, grilled a trifle now,
Cigar-hued in various spots
By the brown breath of sodium-eating years,
On quarter-decks long burnt to the water's edge,
A resurrection of the dead by chemicals.
And the voyages they had made,
Their labours in a country of water,

Were they not marked by inadequate lines
On charts tied up like skins in a rack?
Or his own Odysseys, his lonely travels,
His trading days, an autobiography
Of angles and triangles and lozenges
Ruled tack by tack across the sheet,
That with a single scratch expressed the stars,
Merak and Alamak and Alpherat,
The wind, the moon, the sun, the clambering sea,
Sails bleached with light, salt in the eyes,
Bamboos and Tahiti oranges,
From some forgotten countless day,
One foundered day from a forgotten month,
A year sucked quietly from the blood,
Dead with the rest, remembered by no more
Than a scratch on a dry chart –
Or when the return grew too choking bitter-sweet
And laburnum-berries manifestly tossed
Beyond the window, not the fabulous leaves
Of Hotoo or canoe-tree or palmetto,
There were the wanderings of other keels,
Magellan, Bougainville and Cook,
Who found no greater a memorial
Than footprints over a lithograph.

For Cook he worshipped, that captain with the sad
And fine white face, who never lost a man
Or flinched a peril; and of Bougainville
He spoke with graceful courtesy, as a rival
To whom the honours of the hunting-field
Must be accorded. Not so with the Spaniard,
Sebastian Juan del Cano, at whom he sneered
Openly, calling him a fool of fortune
Blown to a sailors' abbey by chance winds
And blindfold currents, who slept in a fine cabin,
Blundered through five degrees of latitude,
Was bullied by mutineers a hundred more,
And woke and found himself across the world.

Coldly in the window,
Like a fog rubbed up and down the glass
The harbour, bony with mist
And ropes of water, glittered; and the blind tide
That crawls it knows not where, nor for what gain,
Pushed its drowned shoulders against the wheel,
Against the wheel of the mill.
Flowers rocked far down
And white, dead bodies that were anchored there
In marshes of spent light.
Blue Funnel, Red Funnel,
The ships went over them, and bells in engine-rooms
Cried to their bowels of flaring oil,
And stokers groaned and sweated with burnt skins,
Clawed to their shovels.
But quietly in his room,
In his little cemetery of sweet essences
With fond memorial-stones and lines of grace,
Captain Dobbin went on reading about the sea.

Elegy in a Botanic Gardens

The smell of birds' nests faintly burning
Is autumn. In the autumn I came
Where spring had used me better,
To the clear red pebbles and the men of stone
And foundered beetles, to the broken Meleager
And thousands of white circles drifting past,
Cold suns in water; even to the dead grove
Where we had kissed, to the Tristania tree
Where we had kissed so awkwardly,
Noted by swans with damp, accusing eyes,
All gone to-day; only the leaves remain,
Gaunt paddles ribbed with herringbones
Of watermelon-pink. Never before
Had I assented to the hateful name
Meryta Macrophylla, on a tin tag.

That was no time for botany. But now the schools,
The horticulturists, come forth
Triumphantly with Latin. So be it now,
Meryta Macrophylla, and the old house,
Ringed with black stone, no Georgian Headlong Hall
With glass-eye windows winking candles forth,
Stuffed with French horns, globes, air-pumps, telescopes
And Cupid in a wig, playing the flute,
But truly, and without escape,
THE NATIONAL HERBARIUM,
Repeated dryly in Roman capitals,
THE NATIONAL HERBARIUM.

The Night-Ride

Gas flaring on the yellow platform; voices running up and
    down;
Milk-tins in cold dented silver; half-awake I stare,
Pull up the blind, blink out – all sounds are drugged;
The slow blowing of passengers asleep;
Engines yawning; water in heavy drips;
Black, sinister travellers, lumbering up the station,
One moment in the window, hooked over bags;
Hurrying, unknown faces – boxes with strange labels –
All groping clumsily to mysterious ends,
Out of the gaslight, dragged by private Fates.
Their echoes die. The dark train shakes and plunges;
Bells cry out; the night-ride starts again.
Soon I shall look out into nothing but blackness,
Pale, windy fields. The old roar and knock of the rails
Melts in dull fury. Pull down the blind. Sleep. Sleep.
Nothing but grey, rushing rivers of bush outside.
Gaslight and milk-cans. Of Rapptown I recall nothing else.

Five Bells

Time that is moved by little fidget wheels
Is not my Time, the flood that does not flow.
Between the double and the single bell
Of a ship's hour, between a round of bells
From the dark warship riding there below,
I have lived many lives, and this one life
Of Joe, long dead, who lives between five bells.

Deep and dissolving verticals of light
Ferry the falls of moonshine down. Five bells
Coldly rung out in a machine's voice. Night and water
Pour to one rip of darkness, the Harbour floats
In air, the Cross hangs upside-down in water.

Why do I think of you, dead man, why thieve
These profitless lodgings from the flukes of thought
Anchored in Time? You have gone from earth,
Gone even from the meaning of a name;
Yet something's there, yet something forms its lips
And hits and cries against the ports of space,
Beating their sides to make its fury heard.

Are you shouting at me, dead man, squeezing your face
In agonies of speech on speechless panes?
Cry louder, beat the windows, bawl your name!

But I hear nothing, nothing . . . only bells,
Five bells, the bumpkin calculus of Time.
Your echoes die, your voice is dowsed by Life,
There's not a mouth can fly the pygmy strait –
Nothing except the memory of some bones
Long shoved away, and sucked away, in mud;
And unimportant things you might have done,
Or once I thought you did; but you forgot,
And all have now forgotten – looks and words
And slops of beer; your coat with buttons off,

Your gaunt chin and pricked eye, and raging tales
Of Irish kings and English perfidy,
And dirtier perfidy of publicans
Groaning to God from Darlinghurst.

Five bells

Then I saw the road, I heard the thunder
Tumble, and felt the talons of the rain
The night we came to Moorebank in slab-dark,
So dark you bore no body, had no face,
But a sheer voice that rattled out of air
(As now you'd cry if I could break the glass),
A voice that spoke beside me in the bush,
Loud for a breath or bitten off by wind,
Of Milton, melons, and the Rights of Man,
And blowing flutes, and how Tahitian girls
Are brown and angry-tongued, and Sydney girls
Are white and angry-tongued, or so you'd found.
But all I heard was words that didn't join
So Milton became melons, melons girls,
And fifty mouths, it seemed, were out that night,
And in each tree an Ear was bending down,
Or something had just run, gone behind grass,
When, blank and bone-white, like a maniac's thought,
The naphtha-flash of lightning slit the sky,
Knifing the dark with deathly photographs.
There's not so many with so poor a purse
Or fierce a need, must fare by night like that,
Five miles in darkness on a country track,
But when you do, that's what you think.

Five bells

In Melbourne, your appetite had gone,
Your angers too; they had been leeched away
By the soft archery of summer rains
And the sponge-paws of wetness, the slow damp
That stuck the leaves of living, snailed the mind,

And showed your bones, that had been sharp with rage,
The sodden ecstasies of rectitude.
I thought of what you'd written in faint ink,
Your journal with the sawn-off lock, that stayed behind
With other things you left, all without use,
All without meaning now, except a sign
That someone had been living who now was dead:
'At Labassa. Room 6 x 8
On top of the tower; because of this, very dark
And cold in winter. Everything has been stowed
Into this room – 500 books all shapes
And colours, dealt across the floor
And over sills and on the laps of chairs;
Guns, photoes of many different things
And differant curioes that I obtained. . . .'

In Sydney, by the spent aquarium-flare
Of penny gaslight on pink wallpaper,
We argued about blowing up the world,
But you were living backward, so each night
You crept a moment closer to the breast,
And they were living, all of them, those frames
And shapes of flesh that had perplexed your youth,
And most your father, the old man gone blind,
With fingers always round a fiddle's neck,
That graveyard mason whose fair monuments
And tablets cut with dreams of piety
Rest on the bosoms of a thousand men
Staked bone by bone, in quiet astonishment
At cargoes they had never thought to bear,
These funeral-cakes of sweet and sculptured stone.

Where have you gone? The tide is over you,
The turn of midnight water's over you,
As Time is over you, and mystery,
And memory, the flood that does not flow.
You have no suburb, like those easier dead
In private berths of dissolution laid –

The tide goes over, the waves ride over you
And let their shadows down like shining hair,
But they are Water; and the sea-pinks bend
Like lilies in your teeth, but they are Weed;
And you are only part of an Idea.
I felt the wet push its black thumb-balls in,
The night you died, I felt your eardrums crack,
And the short agony, the longer dream,
The Nothing that was neither long nor short;
But I was bound, and could not go that way,
But I was blind, and could not feel your hand.
If I could find an answer, could only find
Your meaning, or could say why you were here
Who now are gone, what purpose gave you breath
Or seized it back, might I not hear your voice?

I looked out of my window in the dark
At waves with diamond quills and combs of light
That arched their mackerel-backs and smacked the sand
In the moon's drench, that straight enormous glaze,
And ships far off asleep, and Harbour-buoys
Tossing their fireballs wearily each to each,
And tried to hear your voice, but all I heard
Was a boat's whistle, and the scraping squeal
Of seabirds' voices far away, and bells,
Five bells. Five bells coldly ringing out.   *Five bells*

Beach Burial

Softly and humbly to the Gulf of Arabs
The convoys of dead sailors come;
At night they sway and wander in the waters far under,
But morning rolls them in the foam.

Between the sob and clubbing of the gunfire
Someone, it seems, has time for this,
To pluck them from the shallows and bury them in burrows
And tread the sand upon their nakedness;

And each cross, the driven stake of tidewood,
Bears the last signature of men,
Written with such perplexity, with such bewildered pity,
The words choke as they begin –

'*Unknown seaman*' – the ghostly pencil
Wavers and fades, the purple drips,
The breath of the wet season has washed their inscriptions
As blue as drowned men's lips,

Dead seamen, gone in search of the same landfall,
Whether as enemies they fought,
Or fought with us, or neither; the sand joins them together,
Enlisted on the other front.

El Alamein

R. D. FITZGERALD

b. 1902

The Hidden Bole

You will not find, though cannas flame for you
and garlanded earth threads tiptoe round her stage,
not wearily trudging as on pilgrimage
but gay in the pelting floodlight of the sun;
though flickering swifts, patterned against their blue,
volley down slanting planes and close and form,
massed at the fringe of storm,
and through their intricate figure curve as one;
though the four seasons, linked and intertwined
with turning stars, wheel measures for a skilled
Pavlova's solving – nowhere will you find
her feet that dazzled death and now are stilled.

So question further the deep gulfs of space
retreating beyond boundaries past the shed
light of old suns long given to the dead –
cast shells of radiance drifting out and on.
Ask, what of time? which footlessly they pace,
a swung void with no bottom and no mark
to measure against the dark
or split hours going sharply from hours gone.
Ask of this maze of tangled interplay
and tensions locked obscurely, shifting lines,
how shall new morning seize from yesterday
the flowers it traced in fugitive designs?

Renewal and spring might answer, show what gap
the hand can pierce through change's barrier-fence,
closing upon us, secret and immense
and yet but kin of our own life, a crossed
lattice of counterpoise and overlap
and moments hooked on moments that ever expand.

161

Dare reach then with that hand
what yonder endures, if briefly, still embossed
on earth's old thought . . . which is all thought, conjoint,
flung out like spirals from that inmost strait,
the Nothing (contracted to some blackened point)
where wakes the dream, the brooding Ultimate.

Beauty, are you some shadow on this dream
which dreams the world, this vision whereunto
our lives grow out, absorbing, beyond view?
We are as fingers for its sense, or eyes,
or focal-centres of its broader beam –
changing, dissolving aspects whose summed whole
spells out the shape, the goal,
not making it some essence from the skies,
ethereal, whose presence clings, pervades,
but granites (fire and law and flesh and dust),
not Cause that topples, Reason that half persuades,
but the full all-that-is, the blinding Must.

Or are you the sweet tinkling of taut strings,
aloof from such bewilderments, immune,
attentive to the enchantment of your tune,
lulled to all else, yourself your own delight?
Are you the quest of our imaginings?
the risen cream upon man's milk of thought?
gem which himself has wrought
of gold and ivory wrested from old night?
Or with the magic of air-twisted spells
have you waylaid us, trapped in ecstasies,
betrayed us to our nerves – sour infidels –
with tricks of scent and sun and silken breeze?

Certain I may not name you nature's child
nature shall call you and that cry reflect
against your home, the cliffs of intellect,
and echo down gorges greenly sensual;

but if that shout stirs elsewhere in the wild
it finds no answer, wandering where it list
till at last gagged in mist –
white silence, choking all things natural.
Savages know you not. You have small being
in the out-world – none, should no mind impress
upon the cell-brought sight its wider seeing:
you woo waked arteries with a trained caress.

Nature is your alembic: you distil
dread magics from the foam of seas; diffuse
colours and clouds through all our senses; use
mountains for talismans; put us in bond
to moonlight, the charmed circle of your will.
Yet, since it is within us that you lurk,
chiefly man's choicest work
you wield against himself, a subtler wand;
for you therein guided his hand and brain,
building the arts in which he dared exult,
blindfold to crafty wiles that thus sustain
your power upon him, ancient as occult.

All perishes; all passes: vampire blooms
that sucked the sunset for deep hues of dusk
are drained by shadow, soon in turn a husk
squeezed brittle and spent for the moon's thirsting
    whiteness.
One above other writhe the wrestling dooms;
and nothing attains some loveliness but mars
century-toil of stars.
What of the apex then, your poising lightness –
is it the fertile force within this mud,
not just the plant that springs there? Beauty, answer!
for all goes under the black viscid flood,
and time will fell the tower as death the dancer.

And when hid workings of commingled tides,
conspiracy of current, wind and swell,

cast on the shores of consciousness some shell
from the unknown, uncomprehended deep;
or chance, or cosmic will, or what besides,
pricks a revealed, mapped atoll on time's chart
upflung as Buonaparte;
these also, struggle spares not. Storms will sweep
reinlessly on – till ripples, feeble, spent,
lap at one grain their might had once far-hurled,
which silts Atlantis a new continent
in the last thundering quarter of the world.

Into whose hands will float the ripe tomorrow?
This drift sets to no beacon, wavers, is vague:
ice brought our dominance; and quake or plague
might well supplant us with the developed bat,
give bees inheritance of our masque of sorrow.
Nor needs it judgement of volcanic hail
to make our weakness fail:
nature could tip her balance with a gnat –
could, for all's strange, even save her elder whelp,
granting, when hordes and famines overrun,
unlikely leads – say, dark infusion of help
from those by-tribes now lagging long in the sun.

We ask no more than let our joy be frail,
since its whole wisdom is its passing hence;
nor would we stamp on you the permanence
which, only, is death. Ay, roots of a new growth
strangle the column in the woods, impale
crevices of old carvings, lion-headed,
which are the moss-embedded
dreams of dead chiseling hands; and out of both –
from the dead hands and that they sought to freeze
static in stone – the contending jungle twines,
through whose thick ferment every fresh dawn sees
your flowers that flourish – to flutter from the vines.

Yet one dropped bud might question bitterly
whither, and what cause served by earth's recalling,
ignorant that no cause need be, its falling
being what spun hours have worked for and last aim
of evolution – old, gnarled, twisted tree.
For that's a very banyan; and who knows
where its true nucleus grows
when every shoot of progress makes the claim?
I see it as mass; even boughs the plan rejects,
shed at the outmost fringe, are of the whole –
sheltering, share the life their loss protects,
the main line of ascent, the hidden bole.

Sports of its growth, the tree spurs tendrils out,
branches of that same life which grew the dawn;
sows in a proton-space like myriad spawn
infinite universes of its dream. . . .
And over all and ever – from new sprout
as from wind-withered pioneering arm –
your wild profusion and charm,
your flowers that visibly crown the cryptic scheme!
Whether you be then purpose to this growing
or 'purpose' have no meaning to be attained,
here looms one landmark near my own small knowing;
fresh fronds, bright berries, score me milestones gained.

You are the light before us, though it dances
and none can follow it far; you are the song
heard between gusts of storm. We shall not long
live with you; but we shape, each to his seeing,
in stone or labour, fragment-like advances
in our pursuits of you whom no hand holds.
You escape even such moulds
as eyes that speak, flung shoulders and feet fleeing,
all art of flesh – which is most true, most proud,
being brief, with colours fading to the grey
of gathered months, such as already cloud
the twirling symbol of what my words would say.

Death lets her dance on always through my mind –
is there a grave could close away Giselle
when music calls her, when lorn flutes impel,
and necromancing strings that cry and quiver?
No curtain falls. Eyes, were you drunk or blind
not knowing her steps although you watched their thief,
the wind's toe-pointing leaf,
not seeing her swiftness chase the pebbled river?
She is the prisoned sunshine that became
delicate contour of escaping fire;
she is the snowflake blown upon the flame –
song and the melting wraith of song's desire.

Only one age could reach her, being stacked
on the thick labour of piled other ages:
only one page among time's handwrit pages
could find right context, turn of phrase, wise word,
to form her sentence, rhyme her into fact.
So does she crown our thought, all thought involve –
as all sweet tones resolve
into the twilight chiming of a bird.
Fade twilight; bird give over: the immense
murmur of night halts at your edge of air –
I praise your triumph for its transience,
that the notes pass and fair dies into fair.

This Night's Orbit

I have walked on moonlit grass before,
back and along outside my house.
And if there is nothing can restore
that time, and little enough to rouse
so much as thought of it here within sound
of a clean sea, beside white dunes,
amid bottle-brush, I would not be bound
in this night's orbit or this moon's.

For all that I know now or have known
is even my life itself, outspread
where still I walk; old scenes are blown
like sand across these hillocks; and my head
could bury in the past. But always I have met,
and shall meet, the fresh hour. And though one migh
read a learnt lesson through and regret
blunders made, chances killed outright,
harms done, and that greatest harm of all –
days wasted, profitless, without joy –
it is not that either. The turn and fall
of living brings me into the employ
of wars, business, events, to run
new errands, hardly or my own will,
along an old time's pathway, one
overgrown but known blindfold still.

Heemskerck Shoals

Fiji, 6 February 1643

Too many councils and committees, too many
making decisions beforehand – that was no way
to run an expedition. Still that catch-penny
assembly in Batavia had last say
and first say too; and there it was all set down
what had to be done; yes, even to the way
you must keep your face, indifferent, lest you betray
the excitement of gold and let its worth be shown
if an Indian brought you gold. How would they like
the faces held on a vessel trapped between wind
and a half-circle reef? Just now to strike
as the ships drove through, shot through, where the lashing
    thinned
a little to calmer water, would have made known
rather death's cast for faces. What one could guess,
however, was faces round the board-room table

growing graver and longer as the report showed less
and chiller prospect of profit. There was not much
gold for them in this trip; and that dear fable
of a rich continent was whittled back
to New Holland, known already, and a pack
of snarling reefs and jagged islands, such
as these to leeward, and that murderous coast
of murderous savages which now could boast
at least a label, States Land; and of course
there was Van Diemen's Land. Shake those from your purse
and count the pieces. He'd tell them in plain Dutch
what Abel Tasman thought of it! The gain
was learning what not to expect: that was the most
a practical man could show them – no New Spain,
no Mexico, no Peru, no treaty struck
with turban'd monarchs who'd take beads and muck
in exchange for pearls and spices. Yet to log
the wind's direction, the sea's rankest mood
in the emptiness of the forties, even to plot
wide, open, landless ocean, was to unfog
the foot of the atlas, fill its amplitude
with better than spouting dolphins. And was not
knowledge, in the end, itself a weightier good
than puffed-up trade? A point not understood
by the company of course! The line to take
with the company was that there was unlatched
an eastern door to America, which could
be pushed whenever they might choose to break
a quick route open through clear seas not watched
by jealous competitors. . . .

                    More could have been done
but for such tight instructions. They should have run,
for example, east from the Three Kings rocks to make
round the last cape cut on the clouds, then on to explore
all States Land, length and breadth. And a proved mistake
was dropping back Van Diemen's Land in the wake,
instead of working to windward when that shore
swinging away to north might well have solved

the problem of New Holland, closed its extent,
and patched a gap or two in the continent
by limits fixed. But northward would have involved
departure from the instructions wanting more
authority than his own hands held. That meant
calling the officers of both ships to council,
talking, persuading; and their bare consent
was hardly enough: it needed written reports
from each of them in overwhelming favour
of such a change of plan; and to win them over
to what they would see as simply making charts,
forsaking business for a cartographer's pencil,
was more than could have been hoped for. In any event
Batavia would have misered anything big
under a pile of archives lest there follow
others to chew what Dutchmen couldn't swallow;
short-sighted though that was while the Portuguese
were still to be reckoned with and there were these
Englishmen everywhere. There would not lag
others too far behind to rediscover,
then claim for themselves. You could not hide in a bag
thousands of miles of trafficable seas.

As a practical man he disliked these dreams – a child's
of gold-roofed castles choked with kings and candies. . . .
It was a long time now since there were left
any forgotten empires lost in the wilds,
with unbelievable treasure to be reft
by right of being well armed – believed some gift
of moral superiority! Nor were Indies
unheard of if they were rich and their hot soil
supported millions of rice-fields, or in toil
at the loom, or carving ivory and such litter
for merchants to gorge bales with. It was unthrift
of the faculties to dazzle them on a glitter
of wishes that dulled the mind; men would do better
to ask of the southern land in sober terms
what could be made of it that they could put

their strength and skill in making. Think of farms
growing into the hills and foot by foot
driving the wastes before them; cities, unbuilt,
only awaiting builders; shipyards bursting
with vessels on the slips about to be spilt
into the stream of trade; and a harbour-mouth
crammed with those vessels bringing home to the south
wealth fairly won, not milkers come from thirsting
ports of the foreign north.

                      No one as yet
had considered settlement; the land was poor –
Pelsart had said so – almost desert, and set
right round the world from home. But should you moor
your destiny in a place, why! home is the door
you enter at night for food and shelter, met
by love and little children; some other spot
is right round the world, and soon what someone forgot
a generation ago. And perhaps the ground
was not all barren; it would be one task
to learn its needs and fill them; good was not found
but by that ache of striving which might ask
too much of ordinary men. Though that
was what the thought in his mind was biting at:
the necessity in men, deep down, close cramped,
not seen in their own hearts, for some attempt
at being more than ordinary men,
rising above themselves. It was an urge
that swung from wars to follies, being the purge
of stagnation from the veins, and violent when
there was little to work it off against; but was
man's only greatness also. Then, because
room hungered there for greatness, gaped in demand,
men could give greatness gladly to that land.

It was strange the love he had for it – for a country
he had not seen; so that its future stood
above his own time's fortunes in a mood
that came on him very often. Little doubt

this love was that old urge thus pressing out
from himself also; which was why an entry
in the ship's log at noon, a day's advance
through blue uncertainty, a desperate chance –
like that these minutes back which taught the feel
of coral running inches under the keel –
and all that was the venture in action, had
(his heart was sure of it) significance
beyond the loss on the ledger. There increased
conviction that the voyage was not to the bad
but notable: the place which lay, unleased,
beneath its empty centuries and stars turning,
was waking under his love and would call those
fired with the same unreasonable yearning
who'd take it for their own. And they must hear
always that call and watch that nothing close
their sons' ears to it. Watchfulness, discerning:
these there must be that year should pass to year
assurance for restless bodies and minds burning
of fields opening before them, crafts to pursue,
aims for them outside servitude. For the rest,
it might not matter who came, his countrymen
or others thinking like them. As one who knew
the millions propagating in Asia's pen,
yet knew the jangling, unsatisfied states were filled
with hate in Europe, where were overtilled
soils and men too, squeezed penury at best –
consoled by wars – his thoughts turned more on race
than national arrogance, that pitiful jest.
And lately he had feared the Atlantic's west,
where much fresh hope was pivoted, could drown
in a black stream it drunkenly gulped down –
slaves who might not stay slaves. There was one place –
only the south was left – where spread clear floors
for feet of the European. He'd have it the test
of southern citizenship how much the need
to preserve it so by battle and vigilant doors
was sacred in men's bone, immutable creed.

Meanwhile his reckoning was disputed, since
Le Maire had traversed this latitude, yet the chart
was dumb on islands hereabouts. Were they part
of the lost Solomons? It was hard to convince
even himself on reckoning – which, truth told,
was guesswork a little refined. He must accept
his pilot-major's view of it: they had crept
westerly – though he doubted – and, over-bold,
run down Espiritu Santo. Was this cluster
Espiritu Santo? Not to his way of thinking,
but that must be set aside. He would have to muster
another precious council after all,
collect opinions on the apparent shrinking
of twenty degrees of Pacific toss and fall,
and discuss and record the course that they must hold
in these new circumstances. It was well
a council hadn't been needed when disaster
boiled all about them – a committee on sinking
the vertical course to coral.

                         Oh, to confound
them and their chart, to prove the reckoning sound,
as yet might show in the outcome! Here could jut
more findings out of waves and ignorance, but
at the slack end of long reckoning. Some new breed
of cross-staff should be thought of (none too soon) ;
though unless you carried time round in your pocket
you still would miss your easting. You might read
a morning height of the sun, like that at noon
for latitude, compound and interlock it
with tabled declination, then oppose
hour-angle to ascension – very close,
and very pretty; but time stayed out to mock it!
How could you carry time? Perhaps a glass
kept under rigid watch and neatly turned
at every run of the sand? No, let it pass:
that wouldn't do; one should not be concerned
with such an insoluble problem. Bad enough
to have populated the southland with the stuff

of fantasy and imagined there old forces
at their old interplay about the sources
of human passion and struggle, all in the span
of a breath and gone in a breath! Such things could be,
though likelier meriting laughter; but if you ran
chasing the rainbow back where it began,
you'd not catch longitude. A big decision
might come for acquisitive settlement, a plan
to establish depots, bases – hardly free
nationhood and endeavour as in that vision;
but no one would take longitudes at sea,
and after all one was a practical man.

The Face of the Waters

Once again the scurry of feet – those myriads
crossing the black granite; and again
laughter cruelly in pursuit; and then
the twang like a harpstring or the spring of a trap,
and the swerve on the polished surface: the soft little pads
sidling and skidding and avoiding; but soon caught up
in the hand of laughter and put back. . . .

There is no release from the rack
of darkness for the unformed shape,
the unexisting thought
stretched half-and-half
in the shadow of beginning and that denser black
under the imminence of huge pylons –
the deeper nought;
but neither is there anything to escape,
or to laugh,
or to twang that string which is not a string but silence
plucked at the heart of silence.

Nor can there be a floor to the bottomless;
except in so far as conjecture must arrive,

lungs cracking, at the depth of its dive;
where downward further is further distress
with no change in it; as if a mile and an inch
are equally squeezed into a pinch,
and retreating limits of cold mind
frozen, smoothed, defined.

Out of the tension of silence (the twanged string);
from the agony of not being (that terrible laughter
tortured by darkness); out of it all
once again the tentative migration; once again
a universe on the edge of being born:
feet running fearfully out of nothing
at the core of nothing:
colour, light, life, fearfully
becoming eyes and understanding: sound becoming ears. . . .

For eternity is not space reaching
on without end to it; not time without end to it,
nor infinity working round in a circle;
but a placeless dot enclosing nothing,
the pre-time pinpoint of impossible beginning,
enclosed by nothing, not even by emptiness –
impossible: so wholly at odds with possibilities
that, always emergent and wrestling and interlinking
they shatter it and return to it, are all of it and part of it.
It is your hand stretched out to touch your neighbour's,
and feet running through the dark, directionless like
        darkness.

Worlds that were spun adrift re-enter
that intolerable centre;
indeed the widest-looping comet
never departed from it;
it alone exists.
And though, opposing it, there persists
the enormous structure of forces, laws,
as background for other coming and going,

that's but a pattern, a phase, no pause,
of ever-being-erected, ever-growing
ideas unphysically alternative
to nothing, which is the quick. You may say hills live,
or life's the imperfect aspect of a flowing
that sorts itself as hills; much as thoughts wind
selectively through mind.

The egg-shell collapses
in the fist of the eternal instant;
all is what it was before.
Yet is that eternal instant
the pinpoint bursting into reality,
the possibilities and perhapses,
the feet scurrying on the floor.
It is the suspense also
with which the outward thrust
holds the inward surrender –
the stresses in the shell before it buckles under:
the struggle to magpie-morning and all life's clamour and
    lust;
the part breaking through the whole;
light and the clear day and so simple a goal.

Song in Autumn

Though we have put
white breath to its brief caper
in the early air,
and have known elsewhere
stiff fingers, frost underfoot,
sun thin as paper;

cold then was a lens
focussing sight, and showed that riggers' gear,
the spider's cables,

anchored between the immense
steel trusses of built grass. The hills were so near
you could pick up pebbles.

It is different at evening: damp rises
not crisp or definite like frost
but seeping into the blood and brain –
the end of enterprises.
And while, out of many things lost,
courage may remain,

this much is certain
from others' experience
and was indeed foretold:
noon's over; the days shorten.
Let there be no pretence;
none here likes the cold.

Bog and Candle

I

At the end of life paralysis or those creeping teeth,
the crab at lung or liver or the rat in the brain,
and flesh become limp rag, and sense tap of a cane –
if you would pray, brother, pray for a clean death.

For when the work you chip from age-hard earth must
     pause,
faced with the dark, unfinished, where day gave love and
     jest,
day and that earth in you shall pit you to their test
of struggle in old bog against the tug of claws.

II

What need had such a one for light at the night's rim?
Yet in the air of evening till the medley of sound –
children and birds and traffic – settled in the profound
meditation of earth, it was the blind man's whim

to set at his wide window the warm gift of flame
and put a match to wick for sight not like his own –
for his blank eyes could pierce that darkness all have known,
the thought: 'What use the light, or to play out the game?'

Yet could disperse also the fog of that queer code
which exalts pain as evidence of some aim or end
finer than strength it tortures, so sees pain as friend –
good in itself and guiding to great ultimate good.

Then he would touch the walls of the cold place where he
    sat
but know the world as wider, since here, beside his hand,
this flame could reach out, out, did touch but under-
    stand. . . .
Life in a man's body perhaps rayed out like that.

So it is body's business and its inborn doom
past will, past hope, past reason and all courage of heart,
still to resist among the roof-beams ripped apart
the putting-out of the candle in the blind man's room.

Macquarie Place

I will go out and hear the strain
of rat-bag orators at large.
There is a battery in my brain
which just that fever might re-charge.

The blends of curious craziness
which crank and anarchist extol
could fill with their electric stress
the run-down fury of my soul.

Whether some economic scheme
to conquer currencies, and spread
over the honeyed earth its dream,
moves them, that all men may be fed;

or whether warnings of the worst
in drink or diet or the boss,
or judgement coming with a burst;
they bring back vision gone as loss.

For nudist, atheist, or pest,
half genius and half distraught,
has in his frenzy of unrest
the drive of some determining thought.

God keep me sane until my last
of breath or knowing; but let faint
fervour still reach me from the vast
madness of prophet and of saint.

I could proclaim the world is flat
with reasonable skill and wit,
but need fanatic zest if that
I would persuade myself of it.

So I will cross Macquarie Place
and covet zeal as crude as loud
in lunch-hour lunatics who face
amused indifference of the crowd.

The Wind at Your Door

(To Mary Gilmore)

My ancestor was called on to go out —
a medical man, and one such must by law
wait in attendance on the pampered knout
and lend his countenance to what he saw,
lest the pet, patting with too bared a claw,
be judged a clumsy pussy. Bitter and hard,
see, as I see him, in that jailhouse yard.

Or see my thought of him: though time may keep
elsewhere tradition or a portrait still,
I would not feel under his cloak of sleep
if beard there or smooth chin, just to fulfil
some canon of precision. Good or ill
his blood's my own; and scratching in his grave
could find me more than I might wish to have.

Let him then be much of the middle style
of height and colouring; let his hair be dark
and his eyes green; and for that slit, the smile
that seemed inhuman, have it cruel and stark,
but grant it could be too the ironic mark
of all caught in the system – who the most,
the doctor or the flesh twined round that post?

There was a high wind blowing on that day;
for one who would not watch, but looked aside,
said that when twice he turned it blew his way
splashes of blood and strips of human hide
shaken out from the lashes that were plied
by one right-handed, one left-handed tough,
sweating at this paid task, and skilled enough.

That wind blows to your door down all these years.
Have you not known it when some breath you drew
tasted of blood? Your comfort is in arrears
of just thanks to a savagery tamed in you
only as subtler fears may serve in lieu
of thong and noose – old savagery which has built
your world and laws out of the lives it spilt.

For what was jailyard widens and takes in
my country. Fifty paces of stamped earth
stretch; and grey walls retreat and grow so thin
that towns show through and clearings – new raw birth
which burst from handcuffs – and free hands go forth
to win tomorrow's harvest from a vast
ploughland – the fifty paces of that past.

But see it through a window barred across,
from cells this side, facing the outer gate
which shuts on freedom, opens on its loss
in a flat wall. Look left now through the grate
at buildings like more walls, roofed with grey slate
or hollowed in the thickness of laid stone
each side the court where the crowd stands this noon.

One there with the officials, thick of build,
not stout, say burly (so this obstinate man
ghosts in the eyes) is he whom enemies killed
(as I was taught) because the monopolist clan
found him a grit in their smooth-turning plan,
too loyally active on behalf of Bligh.
So he got lost; and history passed him by.

But now he buttons his long coat against
the biting gusts, or as a gesture of mind,
habitual; as if to keep him fenced
from stabs of slander sticking him from behind,
sped by the schemers never far to find
in faction, where approval from one source
damns in another clubroom as of course.

This man had Hunter's confidence, King's praise;
and settlers on the starving Hawkesbury banks
recalled through twilight drifting across their days
the doctor's fee of little more than thanks
so often; and how sent by their squeezed ranks
he put their case in London. I find I lack
the hateful paint to daub him wholly black.

Perhaps my life replies to his too much
through veiling generations dropped between.
My weakness here, resentments there, may touch
old motives and explain them, till I lean
to the forgiveness I must hope may clean
my own shortcomings; since no man can live
in his own sight if it will not forgive.

Certainly I must own him whether or not
it be my will. I was made understand
this much when once, marking a freehold lot,
my papers suddenly told me it was land
granted to Martin Mason. I felt his hand
heavily on my shoulder, and knew what coil
binds life to life through bodies, and soul to soil.

There, over to one corner, a bony group
of prisoners waits; and each shall be in turn
tied by his own arms in a human loop
about the post, with his back bared to learn
the price of seeking freedom. So they earn
three hundred rippling stripes apiece, as set
by the law's mathematics against the debt.

These are the Irish batch of Castle Hill,
rebels and mutineers, my countrymen
twice over: first, because of those to till
my birthplace first, hack roads, raise roofs; and then
because their older land time and again
enrolls me through my forebears; and I claim
as origin that threshold whence we came.

One sufferer had my surname, and thereto
'Maurice', which added up to history once;
an ignorant dolt, no doubt, for all that crew
was tenantry. The breed of clod and dunce
makes patriots and true men: could I announce
that Maurice as my kin I say aloud
I'd take his irons as heraldry, and be proud.

Maurice is at the post. Its music lulls,
one hundred lashes done. If backbone shows
then play the tune on buttocks! But feel his pulse;
that's what a doctor's for; and if it goes
lamely, then dose it with these purging blows –
which have not made him moan; though, writhing there,
'Let my neck be,' he says, 'and flog me fair.'

One hundred lashes more, then rest the flail.
What says the doctor now? 'This dog won't yelp;
he'll tire you out before you'll see him fail;
here's strength to spare; go on!' Ay, pound to pulp;
yet when you've done he'll walk without your help,
and knock down guards who'd carry him being bid,
and sing no song of where the pikes are hid.

It would be well if I could find, removed
through generations back – who knows how far? –
more than a surname's thickness as a proved
bridge with that man's foundations. I need some star
of courage from his firmament, a bar
against surrenders: faith. All trials are less
than rain-blacked wind tells of that old distress.

Yet I can live with Mason. What is told
and what my heart knows of his heart, can sort
much truth from falsehood, much there that I hold
good clearly or good clouded by report;
and for things bad, ill grows where ills resort:
they were bad times. None know what in his place
they might have done. I've my own faults to face.

Invocation of Josefa Asasela

Much I have had in mind,
lately, a lonely man,
not of my race or kind,
dying far from his own;
who, in a fickle shift
of Arctic wind, was lost
on pack-ice driven adrift –
reft from his frozen coast;

and have considered much,
bewildered – and with distress

for all caught in the clutch
of the claws of loneliness –
whether this man who sought,
strangely, to live apart,
lived with a mastering thought
or was distraught in his heart.

Certainly there have been
lovers of solitude:
some who have found therein
strength, or a faith renewed,
and so have turned from the street,
the till, the desk or the sword,
not in the hour of defeat
though in retreat from the horde –

men for whom, because
of rich companionships
in books or thoughts, it was
good to achieve eclipse,
and who – after riding the surge
of public affairs – would save
integrity; lest it merge
in the turgid wake of the wave.

But here was a village lad
under a tropic day,
born to its life, and bred
to the old, shared, island way
of laughter and work that blend
with custom and death and birth –
what did he think to find
at the utter end of the earth?

Kandavu men, it is said,
have backs that will only stretch
on a foreign mat for a bed,
and legs with a nagging twitch;

and you'll find Kandavu-born
in trading-craft that ride
from Cancer to Capricorn,
on every turn of the tide.

A digging-stick is the tool
to toughen hands of the young;
and the reef grows fish. A fool
believes a traveller's tongue.
Distance, where it unfurls,
drops hunger; it spills no balms
on the weary, like feasts or girls. . . .
But the sea-wind swirls through the palms.

And Asasela was one
who, much like all the rest,
found communal discipline
little turned to his taste.
So it was up and go
to ships and the world's girth,
desertion in Mexico,
then slow months working north.

Authorities missed or lost
the intruder; for he went
beyond two frontiers (crossed
by stealth or by accident)
and on unhindered, except
as dazed by crowds in a town;
ate if he could; and slept
where he stumbled, dropped, lay down.

So, struggling still, he found
the place and the years that were
to become his life, his mind,
as trapper and craftsman in fur,
skilled at fashioning a glove
or handling dogs in the snow

of the climate he came to love
above the warm long-ago.

Half a life back I heard
of the man's cold death; though then
his name was only a word
and a wonder, forgotten again –
nothing one could attach
to scenes that memory views;
just what an eye might catch
in a corner patch of the news.

But now, impelled by a trick
of conscience, I invoke
this man who turned his back
on his age, his home, his folk –
partly a matter of pride
in the body's powers – and I ask:
Were the calls of his day denied?
Did he step aside from a task?

Yet with this thought like a thorn
in my own skin, I can
still somewhat try to discern
qualities in the man
not wholly cause for reproof
if one had rods to probe
a mind in-turned and aloof
on the ice-clad roof of the globe.

For in space-like loneliness
there can be silence, deep
as the soul's own silences;
nor it is merely escape
to choose to be one with the work
of storm and stars, although
as a life no more than a spark
in the polar dark and the snow.

Asasela I read
as man the seeker, caught
less in the complex need
of the mind to grow into thought
than in the primal appeals
of challenge and daring choice,
like the hunt for the finer seals
far out on the miles of ice.

In his tent on the shore were found
his diary, his bible, his traps.
Beyond in the opening sound
was the running ice in the rips.
And, low in the sky, the sun
in its unsetting path
may have seemed, like a sign, to atone
for the loneliness of his death.

J. A. R. MACKELLAR

1904-32

Football Field: Evening

Cross bars and posts, the echo of distant bells,
The cool and friendly scent of whispering turf;
And in the air a little wind that tells
Of moonlit waves beyond a murmuring surf.

The glittering blue and verdant afternoon
Has locked up all its colours, leaving dearth,
Deserted, underneath a careless moon,
The glory has departed from this earth.

The goals stand up on their appointed lines,
But all their worth has faded with the sun;
Unchallenged now I cross their strict confines;
The ball is gone, the game is lost and won.

I walk again where once I came to grief,
Crashing to earth, yet holding fast the ball,
Symbol of yet another True Belief,
The last but surely not the least of all:

To strain and struggle to the end of strength;
To lean on skill, not ask a gift of chance,
To win, or lose, and recognize at length
The game the thing; the rest, a circumstance.

And now the teams are vanished from the field,
But still an echo of their presence clings;
The moon discovers what the day concealed,
The gracefulness and grief of passing things.

Quick as the ball is thrown from hand to hand
And fleetly as the wing three-quarters run,
Swifter shall Time to his defences stand
And bring the fastest falling one by one,

Until the moon, that looked on Stonehenge ground
Before the stones, will rise and sink and set
Above this field, where also will be found
The relics of a mystery men forget.

Twelve o'Clock Boat

Only the creaking murmur of the wheel,
The trembling of the engines as they turn;
The ferry glides upon an even keel,
And Pinchgut squats in shadow hard astern. . . .

The lips of ocean murmur at delay.
The lovely moon no longer will refuse,
And from the arms of darkness slips away
To tryst with young Ephesians on Vaucluse,

Naked as when some mercenary Greek
The galleys bore to Carthage stared the sky,
Feeling a wind Sicilian on his cheek,
And fell asleep with no more hope than I

Of life eternal, love, or length of days,
Dreaming he saw his Macedonian home;
Awoke, and duly went his ordered ways
To die at Zama, on the swords of Rome.

But what was moon to him, and what was sea
Two thousand years before myself was born,
Are sickle moon and silver yet to me,
Though Scipio should wait upon Cremorne.

JAMES PICOT
1906-44

For It Was Early Summer

Madelaine came running up the stair . . .

Not where the surf breaks,
        not in the glare, but under,
Anemones were warm in their green chamber . . .
Is the leaf a tendril or a finger?

Shades a delicious pool this coolibah . . .
Brown serpents mated in the mown alfalfa.

A jacaranda many jacarandas
Rocked lightly to the asphalt, all in purple.
Cradle-clothes, beside a camphor-laurel.

That Ayrshire in a brown and silver paddock
Ran away, in the grey and russet paddock . . .
When we tried to coax her, did we hoax her?

And birds? Their many notes trouble my spelling
With ecstasy: the dove,
Intolerably mellow;
Call, fall, trill, whistle, water-tumble telling
Love . . . to his fellow.

And Madelaine . . . running up the stair . . .
Racket and dress, brown face, became her hair!

A. D. HOPE

b. 1907

Australia

A Nation of trees, drab green and desolate grey
In the field uniform of modern wars,
Darkens her hills, those endless, outstretched paws
Of Sphinx demolished or stone lion worn away.

They call her a young country, but they lie:
She is the last of lands, the emptiest,
A woman beyond her change of life, a breast
Still tender but within the womb is dry.

Without songs, architecture, history:
The emotions and superstitions of younger lands,
Her rivers of water drown among inland sands,
The river of her immense stupidity

Floods her monotonous tribes from Cairns to Perth.
In them at last the ultimate men arrive
Whose boast is not: 'we live' but 'we survive',
A type who will inhabit the dying earth.

And her five cities, like five teeming sores,
Each drains her: a vast parasite robber-state
Where second-hand Europeans pullulate
Timidly on the edge of alien shores.

Yet there are some like me turn gladly home
From the lush jungle of modern thought, to find
The Arabian desert of the human mind,
Hoping, if still from the deserts the prophets come,

Such savage and scarlet as no green hills dare
Springs in that waste, some spirit which escapes
The learned doubt, the chatter of cultured apes
Which is called civilization over there.

The Wandering Islands

You cannot build bridges between the wandering islands;
The Mind has no neighbours, and the unteachable heart
Announces its armistice time after time, but spends
Its love to draw them closer and closer apart.

They are not on the chart; they turn indifferent shoulders
On the island-hunters; they are not afraid
Of Cook or De Quiros, nor of the empire-builders;
By missionary bishops and the tourist trade

They are not annexed; they claim no fixed position;
They take no pride in a favoured latitude;
The committee of atolls inspires in them no devotion
And the earthquake belt no special attitude.

A refuge only for the shipwrecked sailor;
He sits on the shore and sullenly masturbates,
Dreaming of rescue, the pubs in the ports of call or
The big-hipped harlots at the dockyard gates.

But the wandering islands drift on their own business,
Incurious whether the whales swim round or under,
Investing no fear in ultimate forgiveness.
If they clap together, it is only casual thunder

And yet they are hurt – for the social polyps never
Girdle their bare shores with a moral reef;
When the icebergs grind them they know both beauty and
        terror;
They are not exempt from ordinary grief;

And the sudden ravages of love surprise
Them like acts of God – its irresistible function
They have never treated with convenient lies
As a part of geography or an institution.

An instant of fury, a bursting mountain of spray,
They rush together, their promontories lock,
An instant the castaway hails the castaway,
But the sounds perish in that earthquake shock.

They do not actually gain communication

And then, in the crash of ruined cliffs, the smother
And swirl of foam, the wandering islands part.
But all that one mind ever knows of another,
Or breaks the long isolation of the heart,

Was in that instant. The shipwrecked sailor senses
His own despair in a retreating face.
Around him he hears in the huge monotonous voices
Of wave and wind: 'The Rescue will not take place.'

The Death of the Bird

For every bird there is this last migration:
Once more the cooling year kindles her heart;
With a warm passage to the summer station
Love pricks the course in lights across the chart.

Year after year a speck on the map, divided
By a whole hemisphere, summons her to come;
Season after season, sure and safely guided,
Going away she is also coming home.

And being home, memory becomes a passion
With which she feeds her brood and straws her nest,
Aware of ghosts that haunt the heart's possession
And exiled love mourning within the breast.

The sands are green with a mirage of valleys;
The palm-tree casts a shadow not its own;
Down the long architrave of temple or palace
Blows a cool air from-moorland scarps of stone.

And day by day the whisper of love grows stronger;
That delicate voice, more urgent with despair,
Custom and fear constraining her no longer,
Drives her at last on the waste leagues of air.

A vanishing speck in those inane dominions,
Single and frail, uncertain of her place,
Alone in the bright host of her companions,
Lost in the blue unfriendliness of space,

She feels it close now, the appointed season:
The invisible thread is broken as she flies;
Suddenly, without warning, without reason,
The guiding spark of instinct winks and dies.

Try as she will, the trackless world delivers
No way, the wilderness of light no sign,
The immense and complex map of hills and rivers
Mocks her small wisdom with its vast design.

And darkness rises from the eastern valleys,
And the winds buffet her with their hungry breath,
And the great earth, with neither grief nor malice,
Receives the tiny burden of her death.

Imperial Adam

Imperial Adam, naked in the dew,
Felt his brown flanks and found the rib was gone.
Puzzled he turned and saw where, two and two,
The mighty spoor of Jahweh marked the lawn.

Then he remembered through mysterious sleep
The surgeon fingers probing at the bone,
The voice so far away, so rich and deep:
'It is not good for him to live alone.'

Turning once more he found Man's counterpart
In tender parody breathing at his side.
He knew her at first sight, he knew by heart
Her allegory of sense unsatisfied.

The pawpaw drooped its golden breasts above
Less generous than the honey of her flesh;
The innocent sunlight showed the place of love;
The dew on its dark hairs winked crisp and fresh.

This plump gourd severed from his virile root,
She promised on the turf of Paradise
Delicious pulp of the forbidden fruit;
Sly as the snake she loosed her sinuous thighs,

And waking, smiled up at him from the grass;
Her breasts rose softly and he heard her sigh –
From all the beasts whose pleasant task it was
In Eden to increase and multiply

Adam had learned the jolly deed of kind:
He took her in his arms and there and then,
Like the clean beasts, embracing from behind,
Began in joy to found the breed of men.

Then from the spurt of seed within her broke
Her terrible and triumphant female cry,
Split upward by the sexual lightning stroke.
It was the beasts now who stood watching by:

The gravid elephant, the calving hind,
The breeding bitch, the she-ape big with young
Were the first gentle midwives of mankind;
The teeming lioness rasped her with her tongue;

The proud vicuña nuzzled her as she slept
Lax on the grass; and Adam watching too
Saw how her dumb breasts at their ripening wept,
The great pod of her belly swelled and grew,

And saw its water break, and saw, in fear,
Its quaking muscles in the act of birth,
Between her legs a pigmy face appear,
And the first murderer lay upon the earth.

Pasiphae

There stood the mimic cow; the young bull kept
Fast by the nose-ring, trampling in his pride,
Nuzzled her flanks and snuffed her naked side.
She was a queen: to have her will she crept
In that black box; and when her lover leapt
And fell thundering on his wooden bride,
When straight her fierce, frail body crouched inside
Felt the wet pizzle pierce and plunge, she wept.

She wept for terror, for triumph; she wept to know
Her love unable to embrace its bliss
So long imagined, waking and asleep.
But when within she felt the pulse, the blow,
The burst of copious seed, the burning kiss
Fill her with monstrous life, she did not weep.

Letter from the Line

Island-hopping in the rough, the rumbustious season,
The migratory poet, most solitary of birds,
Having left Los Angeles with a *Kyrie eleison*,
Repacks his baggage of carefully chosen words.

For lucky Jim has given his last lecture,
From the bogus mission his wits emerge alive,
From a land where, despite de Tocqueville's shrewd
    conjecture,
The liberal arts, like living fossils, survive.

Now in mid-Pacific he looks before and after
Astride the equator, surveys each hemisphere;
And his heart on the watershed between tears and laughter
Is glad to be crossing but cross that you are not here.

Glad not to peddle his prestidigitation
Nor to sing for his supper in islands of alien speech;
Though the natives were friendly enough in their own
    fashion,
Rubbed noses, hung him with flowers, danced for him on
    the beach;

Glad, though his mirth is a species of comic horror,
To have seen the salaried Muses display their skill
In the universities of Sodom and Gomorrah:
Blind Homer, Blind Harry treading corn at the mill;

To have seen a land whose living tissues function
Better, they say, with a mechanical heart;
Where the surgeon invites the loblolly boy with unction
To open him up and take his organs apart;

Where the supermarket dictates the range of desire
And the passions are packaged: take the largest pack and
    you save,
But the jumbo-size blonde who is given free to each buyer
May be turned in for cash if that's what you'd rather have.

Glad – but of course such observations are silly:
Travellers' tales are as tall as their comments are snide.
To a visiting comet the cosmos is bound to look chilly
And the whale doesn't look his best when you travel inside.

But now, sweeping back on the outward arc of its passage,
Sadly the comet surveys its luminous tail,
And, nearing Nineveh with his useless message,
Jonah regrets the belly of the whale.

For you, my friends, are still in the monster's belly,
We were warm there for a while, we found it fun
To tickle his ribs inside till he shook like a jelly
And gaped with his gullet to give us a glimpse of the sun.

I may not see you again. As the vessel's motion
Carries me towards my past I review my loss
And the Bear dips down, while glittering from the ocean
Coldly the seven stars dredge up their Cross.

Ode on the Death of Pius the Twelfth

To every season its proper act of joy,
To every age its natural mode of grace,
Each vision its hour, each talent we employ
    Its destined time and place.

I was at Amherst when this great pope died;
The northern year was wearing towards the cold;
The ancient trees were in their autumn pride
    Of russet, flame and gold.

Amherst in Massachusetts in the Fall:
I ranged the college campus to admire
Maple and beech, poplar and ash in all
    Their panoply of fire.

Something that since a child I longed to see,
This miracle of the other hemisphere:
Whole forests in their annual ecstasy
    Waked by the dying year.

Not budding Spring, not Summer's green parade
Clothed in such glory these resplendent trees;
The lilies of the field were not arrayed
    In riches such as these.

Nature evolves their colours as a call,
A lure which serves to fertilize the seed;
How strange then that the splendour of the Fall
    Should serve no natural need

And, having no end in nature, yet can yield
Such exquisite natural pleasure to the eye!
Who could have guessed in summer's green concealed
    The leaf's resolve to die?

Yet from the first spring shoots through all the year,
Masked in the chlorophyll's intenser green,
The feast of crimson was already there,
    These yellows blazed unseen.

Now in the bright October sun the clear
Translucent colours trembled overhead
And as I walked, a voice I chanced to hear
    Announced: The Pope is dead!

A human voice, yet there the place became
Bethel: each bough with pentecost was crowned;
The great trunks rapt in unconsuming flame
    Stood as on holy ground.

I thought of this old man whose life was past,
Who in himself and his great office stood
Against the secular tempest as a vast
    Oak spans the underwood;

Who in the age of Armageddon found
A voice that caused all men to hear it plain,
The blood of Abel crying from the ground
    To stay the hand of Cain;

Who found from that great task small time to spare:
– For him and for mankind the hour was late –
So much to snatch, to save, so much to bear
    That Mary's part must wait,

Until in his last years the change began:
A strange illumination of the heart,
Voices and visions such as mark the man
    Chosen and set apart.

His death, they said, was slow, grotesque and hard,
Yet in that gross decay, until the end
Untroubled in his joy, he saw the Word
    Made spirit and ascend.

Those glorious woods and that triumphant death
Prompted me there to join their mysteries:
This Brother Albert, this great oak of faith,
    Those fire-enchanted trees.

Seven years have passed, and still, at times, I ask
Whether in man, as in those plants, may be
A splendour, which his human virtues mask,
    Not given to us to see?

If to some lives at least comes a stage
When, all the active man now left behind,
They enter on the treasure of old age,
    This autumn of the mind.

Then, while the heart stands still, beyond desire
The dying animal knows a strange serene:
Emerging in its ecstasy of fire
    The burning soul is seen.

Who sees it? Since old age appears to men
Senility, decrepitude, disease,
What Spirit walks among us, past our ken,
    As we among these trees,

Whose unknown nature, blessed with keener sense
Catches its breath in wonder at the sight
And feels its being flood with that immense
    Epiphany of light?

Crossing the Frontier

Crossing the frontier they were stopped in time,
Told, quite politely, they would have to wait:
Passports in order, nothing to declare,
And surely holding hands was not a crime;
Until they saw how, ranged across the gate,
All their most formidable friends were there.
Wearing his conscience like a crucifix,

Her father, rampant, nursed the Family Shame;
And, armed with their old-fashioned dinner-gong,
His aunt, who even when they both were six,
Had just to glance towards a childish game
To make them feel that they were doing wrong.

And both their mothers, simply weeping floods,
Her head-mistress, his boss, the parish priest,
And the bank manager who cashed their cheques;
The man who sold him his first rubber-goods;
Dog Fido, from whose love-life, shameless beast,
She first observed the basic facts of sex.

They looked as though they had stood there for hours;
For years; perhaps for ever. In the trees
Two furtive birds stopped courting and flew off;
While in the grass beside the road the flowers
Kept up their guilty traffic with the bees.
Nobody stirred. Nobody risked a cough.

Nobody spoke. The minutes ticked away;
The dog scratched idly. Then, as parson bent
And whispered to a guard who hurried in,
The customs-house loudspeakers with a bray
Of raucous and triumphant argument
Broke out the wedding march from *Lohengrin*.

He switched the engine off: 'We must turn back.'
She heard his voice break, though he had to shout
Against a din that made their senses reel,
And felt his hand, so tense in hers, go slack.
But suddenly she laughed and said: 'Get out!
Change seats! Be quick!' and slid behind the wheel.

And drove the car straight at them with a harsh,
Dry crunch that showered both with scraps and chips,
Drove through them; barriers rising let them pass;
Drove through and on and on, with Dad's moustache
Beside her twitching still round waxen lips
And Mother's tears still streaming down the glass.

Moschus Moschiferus
A Song for St Cecilia's Day

In the high jungle where Assam meets Tibet
The small Kastura, most archaic of deer,
Were driven in herds to cram the hunters' net
And slaughtered for the musk-pods which they bear;

But in those thickets of rhododendron and birch
The tiny creatures now grow hard to find.
Fewer and fewer survive each year. The search
Employs new means, more exquisite and refined:

The hunters now set out by two or three;
Each carries a bow and one a slender flute.
Deep in the forest the archers choose a tree
And climb; the piper squats against the root.

And there they wait until all trace of man
And rumour of his passage dies away.
They melt into the leaves and, while they scan
The glade below, their comrade starts to play.

Through those vast listening woods a tremulous skein
Of melody wavers, delicate and shrill:
Now dancing and now pensive, now a rain
Of pure, bright drops of sound and now the still,

Sad wailing of lament; from tune to tune
It winds and modulates without a pause;
The hunters hold their breath; the trance of noon
Grows tense; with its full power the music draws

A shadow from a juniper's darker shade;
Bright-eyed, with quivering muzzle and pricked ear,
The little musk-deer slips into the glade
Led by an ecstasy that conquers fear.

A wild enchantment lures him, step by step,
Into its net of crystalline sound, until
The leaves stir overhead, the bowstrings snap
And poisoned shafts bite sharp into the kill.

Then, as the victim shudders, leaps and falls,
The music soars to a delicious peak,
And on and on its silvery piping calls
Fresh spoil for the rewards the hunters seek.

But when the woods are emptied and the dusk
Draws in, the men climb down and count their prey,
Cut out the little glands that hold the musk
And leave the carcasses to rot away.

A hundred thousand or so are killed each year;
Cause and effect are very simply linked:
Rich scents demand the musk, and so the deer,
Its source, must soon, they say, become extinct.

Divine Cecilia, there is no more to say!
Of all who praised the power of music, few
Knew of these things. In honour of your day
Accept this song I too have made for you.

On an Engraving by Casserius
For Dr John Z. Bowers

Set on this bubble of dead stone and sand,
Lapped by its frail balloon of lifeless air,
Alone in the inanimate void, they stand,
These clots of thinking molecules who stare
Into the night of nescience and death,
And, whirled about with their terrestrial ball,
Ask of all being its motion and its frame:
This of all human images takes my breath;
Of all the joys in being a man at all,
This folds my spirits in its quickening flame.

Turning the leaves of this majestic book
My thoughts are with those great cosmographers,
Surgeon adventurers who undertook
To probe and chart time's other universe.
This one engraving holds me with its theme:
More than all maps made in that century
Which set true bearings for each cape and star,
De Quiros' vision or Newton's cosmic dream,
This reaches towards the central mystery
Of whence our being draws and what we are.

It came from that great school in Padua:
Casserio and Spiegel made this page.
Vesalius, who designed the *Fabrica*,
There strove, but burned his book at last in rage;
Fallopius by its discipline laid bare
The elements of this humanity,
Without which none knows that which treats the soul;
Fabricius talked with Galileo there:
Did those rare spirits in their colloquy
Divine in their two skills the single goal?

'One force that moves the atom and the star,'
Says Galileo; 'one basic law beneath

All change!' 'Would light from Achernar
Reveal how embryon forms within its sheath?'
Fabricius asks, and smiles. Talk such as this,
Ranging the bounds of our whole universe,
Could William Harvey once have heard? And once
Hearing, strike out that strange hypothesis,
Which in *De Motu Cordis* twice recurs,
Coupling the heart's impulsion with the sun's?

Did Thomas Browne at Padua, too, in youth
Hear of their talk of universal law
And form that notion of particular truth
Framed to correct a science they foresaw,
That darker science of which he used to speak
In later years and called the Crooked Way
Of Providence? Did *he* foresee perhaps
An age in which all sense of the unique,
And singular dissolves, like ours today,
In diagrams, statistics, tables, maps?

Not here! The graver's tool in this design
Aims still to give not general truth alone,
Blue-print of science or data's formal line:
Here in its singularity he has shown
The image of an individual soul;
Bodied in this one woman, he makes us see
The shadow of his anatomical laws.
An artist's vision animates the whole,
Shines through the scientist's detailed scrutiny
And links the person and the abstract cause.

Such were the charts of those who pressed beyond
Vesalius their master, year by year
Tracing each bone, each muscle, every frond
Of nerve until the whole design lay bare.
Thinking of this dissection, I descry
The tiers of faces, their teacher in his place,
The talk at the cadaver carried in:

'A woman – with child!'; I hear the master's dry
Voice as he lifts a scalpel from its case:
'With each new step in science, we begin.'

Who was she? Though they never knew her name,
Dragged from the river, found in some alley at dawn,
This corpse none cared, or dared perhaps, to claim;
The dead child in her belly still unborn,
Might have passed, momentary as a shooting star,
Quenched like the misery of her personal life,
Had not the foremost surgeon of Italy,
Giulio Casserio of Padua,
Bought her for science, questioned her with his knife,
And drawn her for his great *Anatomy*;

Where still in the abundance of her grace,
She stands among the monuments of time
And with a feminine delicacy displays
His elegant dissection: the sublime
Shaft of her body opens like a flower
Whose petals, folded back expose the womb,
Cord and placenta and the sleeping child,
Like instruments of music in a room
Left when her grieving Orpheus left his tower
Forever, for the desert and the wild.

Naked she waits against a tideless shore,
A sibylline stance, a noble human frame
Such as those old anatomists loved to draw.
She turns her head as though in trouble or shame,
Yet with a dancer's gesture holds the fruit
Plucked, though not tasted, of the Fatal Tree.
Something of the first Eve is in this pose
And something of the second in the mute
Offering of her child in death to be
Love's victim and her flesh its mystic rose.

No figure with wings of fire and back-swept hair
Swoops with his: Blessed among Women!; no sword
Of the spirit cleaves or quickens her; yet there
She too was overshadowed by the Word,
Was chosen, and by her humble gift of death
The lowly and the poor in heart give tongue,
Wisdom puts down the mighty from their seat;
The vile rejoice and rising, hear beneath
Scalpel and forceps, tortured into song,
Her body utter their magnificat.

Four hundred years since first that cry rang out:
Four hundred years, the patient, probing knife
Cut towards its answer – yet we stand in doubt:
Living, we cannot tell the source of life.
Old science, old certainties that lit our way
Shrink to poor guesses, dwindle to a myth.
Today's truths teach us how we were beguiled;
Tomorrow's how blind our vision of today.
The universals we thought to conjure with
Pass: there remain the mother and the child.

Loadstone, loadstar, alike to each new age,
There at the crux of time they stand and scan,
Past every scrutiny of prophet or sage,
Still unguessed prospects in this venture of Man.
To generations, which we leave behind,
They taught a difficult, selfless skill: to show
The mask beyond the mask beyond the mask;
To ours another vista, where the mind
No longer asks for answers, but to know:
What questions are there which we fail to ask?

Who knows, but to the age to come they speak
Words that our own is still unapt to hear:
'These are the limits of all you sought and seek;
More our yet unborn nature cannot bear.

Learn now that all man's intellectual quest
Was but the stirrings of a foetal sleep;
The birth you cannot haste and cannot stay
Nears its appointed time; turn now and rest
Till that new nature ripens, till the deep
Dawns with that unimaginable day.'

JOHN THOMPSON

1907-68

A Latter-Day Polonius to His Sons

The inwardness of woman yields
To touches softer than a flower,
Holding, behind its shifting shields,
Funds of inviolable power.
Insistence and abrupt command
Will win you scant surrender here:
Be patient, with your metal hand:
Go softly, with your crystal spear.

*

Beware the deist's wrath and hate
Whom facile saints exonerate,
For while he drones of truth and love
His conscience works at one remove,
Answerable to his gods and then,
And only then, his fellow men.
Your disbeliever cannot dodge
Himself the witness and the judge;
His case is tried within the steel
Walls of a court of no appeal:
There, subject to his own decree,
He knows himself confined or free.

*

Each man, however he may live,
Hankers for an alternative;
Yet, if he lose his *status quo*,
He'll often lose his temper too,
Constant in little else but his
Compulsive inconsistencies.
Life's an ad lib. impromptu play,
Unsafe, unstable, where we strive

(Pushing or pushed) as best we may
From tragi-comic scene to scene,
Seldom fathoming what we know
And seldom knowing what we mean.
Your best resource, if you can split
Your tastes between the stage and pit,
Is both to act a role and sit
Where you may humorously view
Yourself, a skilful schizophrene.
The man of undivided mind
In this rich age is wholly blind.

*

Excess in moderation! Take
This principle for your health's sake,
Shunning the curst insipidness
Of moderation in excess.
Constraint's a thing to disregard
In pleasures personal or shared,
Unless, through liver, heart, or head,
Admonitory twinges spread.
Be, above all things, straight and kind,
But never stoop or shrink your mind
To wheedle prudes or flatter fools
Who stint their lust with others' rules
Till all life's golden glory's gone
Through being too long gazed upon.

*

Earth is a graveyard filled with dead
Where, when we stir, with every pace
We pack the soil more tightly down
Into some once-expressive face.
We too shall bed there. None the less,
Minds with the needful gladsomeness
May still pursue with peace and grace
The ways the wise have ever known.

Monsters or madmen still may rise
To rot the very seas and skies,
Yet, in this time of teeming life
Which you, my thinking sons, inherit,
The best adventures of the spirit
Are still to find. Go bravely, then,
And be, however rough the strife,
Fulfilled and philosophic men.

Attis

(Procul a mea tuus sit furor omnis, era, domo.
Alios age incitatos, alios age rabidos.)

Attis, ten years in service
To an abstraction, dedicated as though
To some inflexible goddess thronged around
With thick delirium and flowers of blood,
Having to her fierce usage pledged his powers
And, in his fierceness, having as often plunged
The blade of sacrifice in his own flesh
As in the flesh of others – this pious Attis
Suddenly faltered, suddenly fell sick.
Irrational angers, wanderings, fits of tears,
And impermissible melancholy exploded
From the one deadly stroke of understanding
By which, beyond resumption or repair,
He knew himself denatured and unmanned.
Unmanned – by his own willing!
'Now, now, now, I rue what I have done.'
He was not found in the iron congregation
Where for so long he had stood so hard, so hot,
So absolute for the rituals; was not heard
In the great hammering shoutings of the believers
Whom he had led so often; was not seen
In council, for he had crept off on his own;

And far away, near the disorderly turbulence
Of ordinary living where he dared not swim,
Crouched like a fugitive. His glaring eyes
Rolled wildly, and he shuddered as he sobbed:

'Dawn, with a rosy edge,
Peeled me an early apple. The morning star
My diadem, the frosty wind my wrap,
The birds my clocks, the bronco sea my horse,
Myself my warmth – thus to the waking world
My boyhood woke. The dayspring and the spring
Chimed with my cooeeings. All the ways of joy
(Why did I choose a blind way?) stretched and branched
Around me as I grew. Alas, my truth,
My youth, my strength, betrayed me: I renounced
My ease, my games, my plenteous liberty,
For that peremptory logic which engrossed
All my fresh passions: rapture winged me on
Beyond recanting, while the force of love
Hatched me the force of hatred. Who could stir,
As I could do, the sluggish hearts and wits
Of the drab mob? Who with a like devotion
Stood front-man for a doctrine and never probed
Its seed and premise? And who with purer frenzy
Lost himself – as I have lost myself –
In lies, lies, lies? I am sown through with lies,
Vilely invaded, monstrously usurped,
So much that I must be what now I am,
Corrupt with full self-knowledge, till I die.'

Attis fell down and swooned
And almost died forthwith, but could not. Waves
Of ordinary living lapped the shores
He sprawled upon, but did not reach or rouse
His dried and shrunken senses.
Meanwhile, those who had missed him set their spies
To prove his absence, and, this done, at once
Put dogs and trackers everywhere about,

Who, quickly fastening on his scent and spoor,
Trailed and surrounded him. They hauled him up,
They struck at him, they drove him at a run
Before them, till they cast him down beneath
The tight cold terrible faces of the implacable
Hierarchs he must yield to. He was judged
Already, as he knew: and his own voice
Expounded his defection, his own voice
Commanded his submission, his own voice
Doomed him to be degraded. From that time,
Banished and yet not banished, he was locked
In unequivocal serfdom. Never again
Did Attis dare to pine, to stray, to weep.
From that time (even to himself) he seemed
Less man than thing, apathetic and neuter,
Without fault but without virtue, a menial unit
Which limped from chore to chore as it was bid.

Goddess of cruelties, Mother of the creeds,
Queen of fanaticisms – diffuse your poisons
Anywhere rather than upon mine or me.

HARRY HOOTON

1908-61

Moonlight

Oh I've got to write a poem about the moonlight –
Oh dead world! Diana! Disc of silver!
Oh dripping beams through leaves a-quiver.
Oh tremulous adjectives and ings, pleasant participles.
Oh men and maids beneath you in infinite combinations –
    if only
This could be the last poem written about you thus for all
    time. . . .

But that's old time stuff, our modern poets are so much
    better;
They don't rhyme, and they start every line with a little
    letter.
And they've found so many deft, delicate nuances of hue
    and allusion,
Painfully elaborated, or just carelessly tossed off effusions,
Nice, precise, or deliciously vague constructions – poems
Containing exactly nothing. . . .

But the Freudians – now they are modern.
They have no truck with moonshine and flowers –
For them the depths of the psyche, desires and dreams,
    and scowers.
Do you know the symbol of phallus?
The pencil, the phoenix, the sword, the snake, the
    telegraph pole
(Anything longer than it is broad)
The cable, the cork, writing pad
(Everything is longer than it is broad)
Have you prescribed for fascism, communism, every other
    ism, wasm,
The furiously revolutionary ooze of a Reichian orgasm?

Have you glibly quoted your complexes, ids, libidos, other
    spasms,
Other things you can't eat, put in a test-tube, under a
    microscope, through a prism?
Well, you're ready – to pile bombs on the cities of these men
    whose manic-depressive half-conscious demonology has
    driven them to sublimated wish-fulfilment induced by
    paranoiac delusions in the crass conscience stricken
    mind of a sadistic masochist.

Have it your own way – ancient moon-worshippers, modern
    mind-mappers.
Analyse your fellows – dissect your witches with explosives,
    bayonets.
Turn from the moon you moderns – rightly its muse is
    blind.
Turn your eyes within to the superstition, mind.
Introspect, look at the looker who looks at the looker,
    psychoanalyse
Turn yourself inside out, strain your wizard eyes!
Drive the priests from the temple with virtuous intent –
And put politicians in their place, in houses of parliament,
Or submit your sick soul to the psychiatrist's infinitely viler
    lies.

Just look at this moon; What a clear night for planes!
These people are all suffering from psychopathological
    abnormalities of one kind or another, let's go
And drop our healing cargoes on the heads of the foe.

The Word is Too Much Withered

There was a time (when man was wide awake)
When this world seemed as fresh as day –
In a clear, sensible and logical light.
It is foul night now – the murkiness and squalor of a
    dream.

Frazer frigs us all to sleep, beneath golden boughs;
Freud lifts our clothing up to seek
The sub-man – counting sheep or Pharaoh's cows?
God no. His phallus in the phrenzy of wet dreams, his
    drab spouse
Reading tealeaves in a cup, his weak
Poets spewing the sewer of consciousness technique.
I'll say that glory's passed away from their words' worth –
But we'll still wipe our artsouls on the earth.

The world is soul enough for us; and it is ours!
There is nothing in this whore Nature which is hers.
Getting and spending, wasting – it occurs
To me that saving, conserving ends in constipation,
    scowers.
Let us not save, be saved, like all these modern
    Worthwords,
But get and spend – expend and let it fall excreted
    earthwards;
And expand to worlds above these clouds and flowers.

Let us lust steel, uranium – manless, manureless, deathless;
We have given these away in words that prate and drool
About the soul. Hell, I'd rather be a tool –
Rather than soulful be at least a holeful
To some soft whore –
That I might, sated, search for something other, more;
So might I as some noble 20th century savage raise another
    horn
And seduce, ravage, rape, reach orgasm with worlds as yet
    unborn.

RONALD McCUAIG

b. 1908

Au Tombeau de Mon Père

I went on Friday afternoons
Among the knives and forks and spoons
Where mounted grindstones flanked the floor
To my father's office door.

So serious a man was he,
The Buyer for the Cutlery. . . .
I found him sketching lamps from stock
In his big stock-records book,

And when he turned the page to me:
'Not bad for an old codger, eh?'
I thought this frivolous in him,
Preferring what he said to them:

They wanted reparations paid
In German gold and not in trade,
But he rebuked such attitudes:
'You'll have to take it out in goods.'

And what they did in time was just,
He said, what he had said they must:
If Time had any end in sight
It was, to prove my father right.

The evening came, and changed him coats,
Produced a rag and rubbed his boots,
And then a mirror and a brush
And smoothed his beard and his moustache;

A sign for blinds outside to fall
On shelves and showcases, and all
Their hammers, chisels, planes and spades,
And pocket-knives with seven blades.

Then, in the lift, the patted back:
'He's growing like you, Mr Mac!'
(The hearty voices thus implied
A reason for our mutual pride.)

And so the front-door roundabout
Gathered us in and swept us out
To sausage, tea in separate pots,
And jellies crowned with creamy clots.

And once he took me on to a
Recital, to hear Seidel play,
And Hutchens spanked the piano-bass,
Never looking where it was.

When I got home I practised this,
But somehow always seemed to miss,
And my cigar-box violin,
After Seidel's, sounded thin.

And once he took me to a bill
Of sporadic vaudeville.
A man and woman held the stage;
She sneered in simulated rage,

And when he made a shrewd reply
He'd lift his oval shirt-front high
And slap his bare and hairy chest
To celebrate his raucous jest.

Then, as the shout of joy ensued,
Uniting mime and multitude,
And mine rang out an octave higher,
A boy-soprano's in that choir,

My father's smile was half unease,
Half pleasure in his power to please:
'Try not to laugh so loudly, Ron;
Those women think you're catching on.'

But far more often it was to
The School of Arts we used to go;
Up the dusty stairway's gloom,
Through the musty reading-room

And out to a veranda-seat
Overlooking Hunter Street.
There in the dark my father sat,
Pipe in mouth, to meditate.

A cake-shop glowed across the way
With a rainbow-cake display;
I never saw its keeper there,
And never saw a customer,

And yet there was activity
High in the south-western sky:
A bottle flashing on a sign
Advertising someone's wine.

So, as my father thought and thought
(Considering lines of saws he'd bought,
Or, silence both his church and club,
Feeling close to Nature's hub,

Or maybe merely practising
Never saying anything,
Since he could go, when deeply stirred,
Months, at home, without a word,

Or pondering the indignity
Of having to put up with me),
I contemplated, half awake,
The flashing wine, the glowing cake:

The wine that no one can decant,
And the cake we didn't want:
As Mr Blake's Redeemer said,
'This the wine, and this the bread.'

ELIZABETH RIDDELL

b. 1909

After Lunik Two

It was like falling out of love, a wisp of grief
Identifiable pain, unease, regret
As for the end of summer when a brilliant feather
Lies on the grass and the bright bird flown on.

It was a sort of cruelty, a small torture,
A shudder in the skin, and yet
That night the pure moon floated like a leaf
Moist, pale, and patterned in her familiar way
Between her stars and clouds, the candid moon.

No mark of the insolent arrow on her cheek,
No crimson kiss or tear to show her wound
She passed on her dark acres to the deep
Green gulf of day, and so with her
My fears and sorrows into caves of sleep.

R. D. MURPHY

b. 1910

In the Train

Seven rows of severed heads,
Domed women's, dimmed men's,
Neatly posed and mounted, carefully numbered
On uniform malachite bases, life-size, live.

Shedding the flesh, they share a grace
Of faded innocence; endearing, helpless
Cherubs emeriti, a few seeking the nipple
Of nicotic comfort or the touch of a ghostly hand.

And tric-trac tricoteuses, the wheels
Tumbril these trophies on their way
To what convention of secular decollation,
Martyrology of less than More?

Anonymous, unanimous,
Delphic sign of contradiction,
They tease the hand to tighten all their stringed
Attentiveness and pluck its muted music.

Notation spelling form and sense
Or mere inconsequence, the more
The mind strains to read illegible silence
Under the pointless, metallic counterpoint?

WILLIAM HART-SMITH

b. 1911

The Inca Tupac Upanqui

The Inca Tupac Upanqui,
suffering from a surfeit of idleness,
amuses his scalp with a golden comb.

For the sun does not stand still, the Sun,
embracing nightly the fairheaded
daughters of the Sun, rises,

arms himself and goes forth.
But the Inca Tupac Upanqui, Son of the Sun,
is hidden. He dreams on his couch,

drowns in the sweat of his body, dreams
the rugs are pleated reeds,
his bed a raft of thong-bound balsa logs

groaning and complaining on the sea.
The curtain of his bed bends like a sail
marked with his regal emblem.

                            . . . All his wives,
a fleet of sails attending.

He has taken the look of the condor now
he has shaken off sleep, has bound
his hair in a loop of wire. His ears

enclose twin suns in their thin-stretched lobes.
He has taken a comb
of ships and set it lightly on the sea

to comb the sea for islands and for gold.
Four hundred ships,
each one in sight of two,

each two in sight of four . . .
drifting in a line across the main.
They look like shepherds moving on a plain.

Postage Stamp

If you should ever have to
part from someone dear, tear
yourself away, be sure

the tear is where
the perforations are. Please,
please do not ever

recklessly sever, sheer
yourself from some one other
so that their stamp is torn

and you have part of their
living, bleeding
flesh at your side worn.

Razor Fish

If you were
to draw
lightly
a straight line
right
down
the margin
of this
sheet of
paper
with your
pen

it wouldn't be
as thin
as a
Razor Fish
seen
edge
ways
on

If you were
to cut
the shape
of a
fish
out of transparent
cellophane
with a
tiny
tail fin
and a mouth
as long
and sharp
as
a
pin
and let it drift
tail up
head down
you wouldn't see –

the Razor Fish
See
what
I
mean?

IAN MUDIE

b. 1911

They'll Tell You About Me

Me, I'm the man that dug the Murray for Sturt to sail
    down,
I am the one that rode beside the man from Snowy River,
and I'm Ned Kelly's surviving brother (or did I marry his
    sister?
I forget which), and it was my thumbnail that wrote that
    Clancy
had gone a-droving, and when wood was scarce I set the
    grass on fire
and ran with it three miles to boil my billy, only to find
I'd left the tea and sugar back with my tucker-bag,
and it was me, and only me, that shot through with the
    padre's daughter,
shot through with her on the original Bondi tram.
But it's a lie that I died hanging from a parrot's nest
with my arm in the hollow limb when my horse moved
    from under me;
I never die, I'm like the Leichhardt survivor I discovered
fifty years after the party had disappeared; I never die,
I'm Lasseter and Leichhardt both; I joined the wires of
    the O.T. *overland telegraph*
so that Todd could send the first message from Adelaide
    to Darwin;
I settled everywhere long before the explorers arrived;
my tracks criss-cross the Simpson Desert like city streets,
and I've hung my hat on Poeppel's Peg a thousand times.
It was me who boiled my billy under the coolabah,
told the bloke in the flash car to open his own flamin'
    gates, *fancy house fancy car rich guy*
put the goldfields pipe-line through where the experts said
    nobody could, *1400 miles hundry inland*

224

wanted to know 'Who's robbing this coach, you or Ned
    Kelly?',
had the dog sit on my tucker-box outside of Gundagai,
yarned with Tom Collins while we fished for a cod
    someone'd caught years before,
and gave Henry Lawson the plots to make his stories from.
Me, I've found a hundred wrecked galleons on the
    Queensland coast,
dripping with doubloons, moidores and golden Inca
    swords,
and dug a dozen piles of guilders from a Westralian
    beach;
I was the one that invented the hollow wood-heap,
and I built the Transcontinental, despite heat, dust, death,
    thirst, and flies.
I led the ragged thirteen; I fought at Eureka and Gallipoli
    and Lae;
and I was a day too early (or was it too late?) to discover
    Coolgardie,
lost my original Broken Hill share in a hand of cribbage,
had the old man kangaroo pinch my coat and wallet,
threw fifty heads in a row in the big game at Kal,
took a paddle-steamer seventy miles out of the Darling on
    a heavy dew,
then tamed a Gippsland bunyip and sooled him on
to capture the Tantanoola Tiger and Fisher's Ghost
and become Billy Hughes's secretary for a couple of weeks.
Me, I outshore Jacky Howe, gave Buckley his chance,
and have had more lonely drinks than Jimmy Woods;
I jumped across Govett's Leap and wore an overcoat in
    Marble Bar,
seem to remember riding the white bull through the
    streets of Wagga,
sailed a cutter down the Kindur to the Inland Sea,
and never travelled until I went to Moonta.
Me, I was the first man ever to climb to the top of Ayers
    Rock,

pinched one of the Devil's Marbles for the kids to play
    with,
drained the mud from the Yarra, sold the Coathanger for
    a gold brick,
and asked for beer off the ice at Innamincka.

Me, yesterday I was rumour,
today I am legend,
tomorrow, history.
If you'd like to know more of me
inquire at the pub at Tennant Creek
or at any drover's camp
or shearing-shed,
or shout any bloke in any bar a drink,
or yarn to any bloke asleep on any beach;
they'll tell you about me,
they'll tell you more than I know myself.
After all, they were the ones that created me,
even though I'm bigger than any of them now
– in fact, I'm all of them rolled into one.
For anyone to kill me he'd have to kill
every single Australian,
every single one of them,
every single one.

In Sunny Days of Winter

Now that the sunny days of winter are with me
I feel myself down amidst the roots of the grasses,
down where all life has its beginning and ending;
I feel myself amidst the roots of the grasses,
feeding on humus and the warm black blanket of decay,
the diet of decomposed leaves, of last year's weeds,
of chemicals manufactured in those blind factories,
the bellies of tirelessly working worms.

This is the diet on which all living for ever feasts,
the fertility that is skin-deep upon the world

– rotted weeds, rocks fretted down to marl,
crumbled leaves, twigs fallen and perished,
earth transmuted by blind chemistry of worms –
the humus-rich nine inches that enwraps the earth,
and upon which feeds everything that lives,
all beasts and birds, man, and all green creatures.

Now that the sunny days of winter are with me
I am deep amidst the roots of the grasses,
where everything but steel and concrete and ledgers
have their beginning and ending,
and without which even they, even they,
would be less powerful and more meaningless
than the fractured ploughshare and the broken adze,
more blind and meek and vacant of conscious purpose
than the burrowing and all-powerful worm
that down in his dark and fertile universe
toils tirelessly among the roots of the grasses
where in these sunny days of winter I have hidden my
    thoughts
that they too may feed upon the diet that sustains the
    world.

The North-Bound Rider

Tombstone country –
so the pioneer described it.
'Patches of tombstone country,'
he wrote, 'exist in this area; indeed
at one place the north-bound rider
observes for more than ten miles
this horrible terrain.'
The north-bound rider. . . . Surely,
I thought, it must exist
for him who travels
west or east or south, besides
occurring for the eye
of him who merely northward rides.

At each of the stations round about, however,
it was always the same.
Blue would scratch his head.
'Tombstone country;
did you say tombstone country?
Never heard of it.'
And Mulga would ask:
'Who told you about it?'
And at my answer
they would give me sidelong looks.
'Books!' they would snort.
'Huh – books!'

Tombstone country. . . .
Ask and ask, as I did,
I never found it.
Only, a dozen times over,
the same reply to my question:
'Tombstone country, did you say?
Never heard of it.'
. . . Yet as years pass I grow more certain
I must return to those ranges once again
and somehow reach that dreaded region
that only in my dreams I now attain
(the north-bound rider nudging at my elbow)
– ten barren miles of horrible terrain.

HAL PORTER

b. 1911

Hobart Town, Van Diemen's Land (11th June, 1837)

Sir John Franklin, Governor of V.D.L., 1834-43, perished on
11th June 1847 in attempting the North-West Passage.

Mike Howe's head with frozen frown
Is on display in Hobart Town.

By Wapping Stairs the alley whale-oils blaze;
The tap-room skittle-grounds are stews of din
Where tripeman, shepherd, fence and whitesmith daze
Pock-pitted doxies with the Sky Blue gin.

Now, knuckle-bashers soak chapped fists in brine;
The cockpit curs lick bloody-feathered paws;
The chandler, sinking Bengal Rum like wine,
Brags at the Cornstalks and the Johnny Raws.

The gibbet chandeliers sag down –
Glass-frosted thieves of Hobart Town.

On night-tubs, water-butts and cobbled mud
Ice knits its mica-spiked and bitter wheels;
By the Jew's slop-shop pot-boy barks out blood;
The chill-struck tollgate-keeper dreams hot eels.

Through Russia tweed and kerseymere and smock
And red shell jackets and Valencia vests
Cold, like a watchman's cutlass, drives its shock;
The apple-woman shawls her stony breasts.

In Geneva-stinking gown
Venus paces Hobart Town.

By his last lucifer the forger's fooled,
His jackal stumbles cursing in the mire.
Governor Franklin shuts his *Birds* by Gould,
Says, 'Far too hot!' and leaves the cedar fire.

Return, and ring for extra logs, Sir John;
Refill the Monteith with a burning brew:
The final decade left ticks freezing on
And North-west icebergs inch upon your view.

Watchman Death – eternal clown –
Crows the hour through Hobart Town.

C. B. CHRISTESEN

b. 1912

The Desecrated Valley

'And he was preparing to cry out to show he wasn't dead.'

DIONYSIOS SOLOMOS

My stay-at-home dog has long held
To a Taoist ideal:
To live within sound of a bitch barking
In the next village but never bother to go there.
Now he has given the game away
And who can blame him?
Like Lord Chesterfield he keeps his lips
Firmly over his teeth and disdains modernity.

I confess to a certain empathy.
What with bulldozers and freeways
Chromium supermarkets and paved roads
Rotary-mowers and toothbrush hedges
Fenced-in garden plots trim and respectable
The valley is no longer a place of grace.

Even the bellbirds have all pissed off.

Yet I seem to recall a distant time
When I lived like Shelley in the Eugenian Hills
Far from the 'polluted multitude'.
On morning walks my dog and I
Were staggered by miracles;
And the verbal energy of birds
Made us pause in disbelief:
The lush diction of the gentle song-thrush
The fractured syntax of Indian myna
The juvenescence of blue wren and zebra finch.

He'd cock an eye as if to say,
What prolixity and purple rhetoric!
He is indiscreet by conviction.

And who am I to blame
When even the bellbirds have all pissed off?

In the stream below my ruined garden
The last platypus has been washed away
In an eroding flood of yellow mud.
Now all is quiet, save
For a lone crow who has one eye
And the whine of the new freeway.

I'd like to be civil to my old mate –
My stay-at-home Taoist dog –
But somehow, sitting here like Blake
Naked in his garden, the thought
Of this desecrated valley still rankles.

If only the bellbirds had not pissed off . . .

ROLAND ROBINSON

b. 1912

I Had No Human Speech

By stopping talking you will notice more.

I had no human speech. I heard
the quail-thrush cry out of the stones
and cry again its crystal word
out of the mountains' crumbling bones.

I had no human word, beyond
all words I knew the rush of ash-
grey wings that gloomed, with one respond,
storm-grey, to swerve with crimson flash.

The speech that silence shapes but keeps:
a ruin and the writhe of thin
ghost-gums against their rain-blue deeps
of night and ranges I drank in.

I lived where mountains moved and stood
round me; I saw their natures change,
deepen and fire from mood to mood,
and found the kingfisher-blue range,

and found, where huge dark heliotrope
shadows pied a range's power,
mauve-purple at the foothills' slope,
the parakelia, the desert flower.

even though I'm human

Yet, human, with unresting thought
tormented turned away from these
presences, from converse sought
with deserts, flowers, stones and trees.

Australian poetry about Austr. Patriotic poetry

233

Altjeringa

Nude, smooth, and giant-huge,
the torsos of the gums
hold up the vast dark cave
as the great moon comes.

Shock-headed black-boy stands,
with rigid, thrusting spear,
defiant and grotesque
against that glistening sphere.

In clenched, contorted birth
black banksias agonise;
out of the ferns and earth,
half-formed, beast-boulders rise;

because The Bush goes back,
back to a time unknown:
chaos that had not word
nor image carved on stone.

Passage of the Swans

How could I sleep? The moon rose at its full,
broadening the night. Through mauve-grey gum
and gum I heard, in distant swell and lull,
thunder and crash of ocean never dumb.
I lay and waited for the light, to hear
the first birds, wakening in the silent bush
and, rising through their chorus, loud and clear,
on and on, the day's harmonious-thrush.

Too late, too long I slept. It was a wind,
a rush of wings, a storm of blendless cries
that brought me, stumbling, in the daylight-thinned
darkness, to stand there, in a dazed surmise.
Far down the dawn those trumpet-throated ones
called, and I knew them . . . the swans, the swans.

The Seed Goes Home

Cave-man locked in her thighs.
Dancers pound the earth,
hurl their loudest shout,
trees beyond all height.

Clansmen rise from the gorse,
steel-chill the mountain's
sweep with skirl of their charge.
Grandstands burst in a crimson

football roar as the leather
spears in. Cave-man buries
his teeth in his kill. Her nails
rip deep. The seed goes home.

JOHN BLIGHT

b. 1913

Death of a Whale

When the mouse died, there was a sort of pity:
the tiny, delicate creature made for grief.
Yesterday, instead, the dead whale on the reef
drew an excited multitude to the jetty.
How must a whale die to wring a tear?
Lugubrious death of a whale: the big
feast for the gulls and sharks; the tug
of the tide simulating life still there,
until the air, polluted, swings this way
like a door ajar from a slaughterhouse.
Pooh! pooh! spare us, give us the death of a mouse
by its tiny hole; not this in our lovely bay.
– Sorry, we are, too, when a child dies;
but at the immolation of a race, who cries?

Mud

Fat, flabby as a woman's belly, jelly-like mud:
neither land nor water, but a black, crude
substitute lying primitive and rude
in squalor and poverty; a quadroon of the blood
that the sea and the land mixed with a skeleton of wood
belonging to neither, conceived in the flood,
the blind surge, and low urge of flats that intrude
under the white sea; the worm-infested, nude
land, deserted by the tide; flesh that's never had
the bones of ice to brace it, a skeleton of wood
rotting in its carcass; black, filthy mud
conceived in the mad swirl of torrent and flood;
green slime and grey ooze seeping through its blood:
yet, stone in embryo, firming into nationhood.

Helmet Shell

Something martial, some bestiality of Rome,
incongruous shellfish, bestirs your home.
Such a slow mucous brain filled that dome
that I cannot think other than that some
imperial artist shaped it – helmet, or tomb?
Surely a mind is buried that wears for Rome,
or Russia, or America, or any Caesar whom
the gods make mad, such head-gear.
And, now, on display in a city shop, 'mid fear
of the Bomb, helmet shell, you appear:
dead, dead, and polished like a skull. Wear
such apparel, Life, when Death is near.
This has the shape of a skull, and is a mere
skull in effect, that cannot keep out Fear.

Lamprey

To see, on film, the Great Lakes invaded
by the lamprey to the stage where, unaided,
the great northern salmon faces
certain extinction, places
a complex of guilt upon Man.
Because of his ingenuity,
his clever skipping of aeons of knowledge,
he has let in the lamprey;
and, now, that rare meal of fox and bear, the salmon,
in those great waters drifts to the edge
of extinction. True, man let them in, the lamprey,
the gruesome devourers of salmon. They
attach to the fish like Medusa's serpent locks.
Oh how first sight of them chills one. Man needs such
    shocks.

FLEXMORE HUDSON

b. 1913

Our World

The gas chambers of the concentration camp
looked forbidding but harmless enough
from the outside;
they could actually have been
what the murderers pretended them to be –
shower rooms for hygienic delousing.

But in the walls were glass peep-holes,
and through these the high German officials,
like depraved voyeurs at bedroom windows,
spied on the Jewish prisoners packed within –
men and women, naked, filthy, afraid, ashamed,
holding their silent children above their heads.

And when the hydrocyanic acid sprayed
from the nozzles in the ceiling,
the high officials watched their victims
choking, clawing, showering excrement,
springing convulsively into the air
like decapitated fowls. . . .

Even as hideous is the evil we discover
if we pry behind the fair exterior of our world.
Behind the masquerade of parliaments,
behind the wealthy culture and the high-sounding laws,
behold! cheating and lies, cruelty and disease,
lust for oil, lust for uranium, lust for steel –
volcanic lusts as perilous and ugly
as the subliminal pressures of the sickest mind;
and, like a skyscraper fractured in an earthquake
teetering above defenceless streets,
death overhanging us all.

REX INGAMELLS

Earth-Colours

Earth-colours, rich, primeval, blaze and smoulder
on claypan-flat and river-cliff and cuesta-boulder.
My heart should burn to praise yet fear gripes, cold and
    colder.

Blood blinds the world: in war-zones blood is running.
Where Ethiopian lizards scuttled, sunning,
all the air is filled with the smoke of gunning.

Death's keen minstrels
ping like rain
through the pleasant
land of Spain.

Death's engined angels
range the sky
where China's smouldering
temples lie.

I watch the streaks of sunset metafusing:
my heart should burn to praise but it rebels, refusing . . .
I see the wake-waves of dark carnage-squadrons cruising.

Dare you now behold the new day dawning?
There comes no radiant goddess to your fawning –
Smoke-clouded Mars, blood-hungry, cavernously yawning.

Black Mary

Mary, the lubra,
walks wonderfully.
She came along the dust-track,
swinging her body freely, stepping
lithely and with perfect measure.

The beautiful rhythm of her body
flooded my heart with joy as do leaf-calls
in a place of many birdsongs,
flooded my heart with joy
such as must be
to apprehend perfection.

Superbly swung her supple form
along the dust-track,
for she walks wonderfully.

But she saw Tommy, and
her resentment of yesterday
rose, instant,
to tear all harmony to harsh-edged coarseness.
Suddenly all rhythm died
and in its place
was jarring discord of a nagging voice,
disrupting all the
vision of her I had.
Tommy, her husband, fled like a bush-rat
from her ugly, angular gesticulations.

History

These are the images that make my dreams,
strong images but frail; dimmed-with-glow yet clear:

Pioneer ships lumbering in the sunset,
lumbering along our sombre eastern coastline,
swaying, awkward but beautiful, north to Port Jackson . . .

The stark hatred and reeking soul-fire of men's faces,
men pent in penitentiaries and chained in road-gangs,
herded as cattle, worked as cattle, fierce in their misery . . .

Stern-hearted freemen, felling tall trees, building
rough homesteads amid far, unfamiliar places,
hoping, cherishing their preconceived
visions of beauty and propriety . . .

Herds of cattle, lowing by the fertile banks
of eastern rivers; drowsing under redgums,
where the black-and-white magpie sits calling
      ecstatically . . .

Flocks of sheep bleating perpetually on green hillsides,
tired of fine feeding, joyous at life . . .

Deserted station-houses, quiet in drought.
Bones of cattle, camels, horses, men.
And the despised black who lives through it all,
finding himself water, native plums, yams,
and wild-honey from the honey-ants . . .

Cities growing up,
towering into the future;
and this land's destined
vast cities of imagination.

KENNETH MACKENZIE

1913-55

The Moonlit Doorway

The peacock-eye of the half-moon long since up;
the peacock-blue of the iridescent sky
moonlit to starless pallor; the scream of peacocks
across the bay from here mock night together
outside my windows – a wild, gritty scorn,
a jeer at memory, a blue-lit laughter
at man and me.
    Once, though, there was a doorway
set full of night and this same genial pallor
of moon-made sky-magic. Memory
does not give jeer for jeer. Memory's faithful
and so am I to memory – even tonight
when the imperial birds across the bay
scream out their scornful warning through the light
of blue darkness: 'She was white and golden
in that dark room the moonlight entered no more.
She was a pale woman lying there
whom you have never seen, whom you have known
well at night only – never well by day.'
And that mad scream through the doorway of my windows,
though less with distance, still cries out 'Beware.'
Beware of you, it says, your man's fallibility
in keeping faith. Beware of moons and midnights
lest the white body of the beloved suffer
a sad sky-change, and through that moonlit doorway
pass headlong into the hell of discontent,
the double hell of conscience and of scorn,
the final hell of hate. Beware, beware. . . .
    Of what, I say? Of my heart? Of my mind?
Of the dark entry of this blood and flesh
into that younger and more innocent
flesh and blood, when the night was not far worn?

And I say, this was my fortune and delight,
and my long dreamed yet long withheld desire –
but more yet: my momentary destiny
that dream should harden into softest flesh
which, melting to the tongue, almost returns
to dream. This was my fortune, that her breasts
should stand upright and for an hour or more
tell me this body warmed and tensed and turned
with love to mine. This was my fine reward
for nothing more than kisses and caresses –
that in some hour or two there should have been
utter forgetfulness of me and life
in the profundity of face-to-face
against a doorway full of the moonlit sky,
silence, solitude, and she and I
alone and together.
    Against the moonlit doorway is a tree,
flowered with a sparse but vigorous red by day
and black as a groping hand's lean skeleton
at night, when the moon's high. As I lay looking
I thought you had flown into it like a bird,
my child, my darling, silent and solitary
and watchful of the peacock treachery
of night, like a wary bird above the pool
of green lawn and new coming-together,
green knowledge and new understanding,
question, request, confession, answer, silence
as still as water. Then you were there again
with laughter in your mouth (I could not see
your clear eyes laughing in that silken darkness)
and in your hands a sudden secret cunning
as the desire and the will were mixed into
the slow and speechless deed itself. The tree
clawed kindly at the opal of the sky
with its red talons, and your own hands
are a mile away from you in space; and you
are a mile away from me, in space and time
and in intention. I, the servitor,

243

the bolder yet more humble of us two
who so astonishingly lie together,
am here no longer; I am in your body,
and, as the tree grown out of earth is earth,
so am I you, and you are my protection
against the tempests of the hated surface.
And into you I shall dissolve at last
with a great falling crash and sigh, contented.

   With your cool graveness of a painted angel,
what do you think of, child, bedded in darkness
with your feet towards the peacock-coloured panel
of the open door? Just that the game is over?
Just that the night is cold and I am warm?
(This is what we were made for.) Just that the doorway
is beautiful in its silky moonlit splendour
slashed once with the dagger-sounds of a dog's barking
and once again with the unholy cry
of the royal birds impassioned by the night?
Tell me now – so long afterwards but so soon –
what you think lazily about, stretched here at ease
across my arm and shoulder and my heart.
Or yet – these are your own words – why should you speak?
I speak enough for both. My tongue's uncaged,
the padlock opened by a key of passion,
the door sprung wide, the wooing moon of love
luring it out and on, across the lawns,
down through the trees of your own silences
into the valley of your quiet body,
into the shadow of your lidded eyes,
between the moonlike mountains of your bosom,
through the whole world that's you, until it falls
silent, and with a sigh we almost sleep.

Through the tall moonlit doorway night looks in,
and once again the peacocks cry at us.

KENNETH MACKENZIE

The Wagtail's Nest

Moulded in cobweb, horse-hair, cow-hair, grass and soft,
　　stray feathers
the nest is a cup shaped by the beak of desire and the
　　breast of love
accurately yet with a careless look set in the joint of a
　　slender
sloping branch of the dying pepper tree. The hen's touch
　　is tender,
she smoothes the lip of the cup with her black throat and
　　every amorous move
she makes is a pledge of the nest's strength against time
　　and all weathers.

The eggs in the bowl of the grey nest are the fruits of love
　　that flowered apart
in a petalled spreading of wings when the wind was cold
　　and the days came blue and bright
and the dying tree with a gallant desperate gesture plumed
　　its age with green
feathery pinnate leaves more perfectly curved than even
　　its youth's had been
so that when the increasing moon of the month shone
　　stronger late at night
fluttering shadows touched the sitting bird with dark and
　　delicate art.

The cock unsleeping sings all night in the besom crown of
　　the dead tree
stripped of its bark last year and sweeping still the floor of
　　the moonlit sky.
He says without fail *You sweet innocent creature* in clearly
　　whispering notes.

Derelict

God! what a lot of beauty to be dead on a Sunday:
so much fine fur, such delicate claws and eyes
dedicated to life; such sweet intention
ended in the inevitable 'here lies . . . here lies . . .'

Here, then, lies cat. Cat lies here that loved the moonlight,
loved fine fur, loved delicate eyes and claws
and went about her business like a woman,
watching the scraps and concerned about her paws.

The rain came down like death, like clubs of water
smashing this white and grey one open-eyed
(for what cat ever died with its eyes closed?) ;
and so she must have looked at the night, and died.

And died, I say; thinking that night was nothing,
nothing to this, the night that won't end ever,
swift to catch a cat that was limber and nimble,
cutting down quickly the caution, fervour, fever

of cat-at-large. Poor wild and dainty creature,
you could not dodge the last blow – not you
who walked proud as a ship, shining in darkness,
and found your port, and suddenly were signalled through.

An Old Inmate

Joe Green Joe Green O how are you doing today?
I'm well, he said, and the bones of his head looked noble.
That night they wheeled Joe Green on a whisper away
but his voice rang on in the ward: I'm a terrible trouble
to all you girls. I make you work for your pay.
If I 'ad my way I'd see that they paid you double.

Joe Green Joe Green for eighty-two years and more
you walked the earth of your grandad's farm down-river
where oranges bigger than suns grow back from the shore
in the dark straight groves. Your love for life was a fever
that polished your eye and glowed in your cheek the more
the more you aged and pulsed in your voice for ever.

Joe Green looked down on his worked-out hands with scorn
and tears of age and sickness and pride and wonder
lay on his yellow cheek where the grooves were worn
shallow and straight: but the scorn of his look was tender
like a lover's who hears reproaches meet to be borne
and his voice no more than echoed its outdoor thunder;

Gi' me the good old days and the old-time folk.
You don't find that sort now you clever young fellers.
Wireless motorbikes all this American talk
and the pitchers and atom-bombs. O' course it follers
soon you'll forget 'ow to read or think or walk –
and there won't be one o' you sleeps at night on your
        pillers!

Joe Green Joe Green let us hear what your grandad said
when you were a lad and the oranges not yet planted
on the deep soil where the dark wild children played
the land that Governor King himself had granted
fifteen decades ago that the Green men made
a mile-square Eden where nothing that lived there wanted.

Joe Green lay back and smiled at the western sun:
'Fear God and the women, boy,' was his only lesson,
'and love 'em – but on the 'ole just leave 'em alone,
the women specially.' Maybe I didn't listen
all of the time. A man ain't made of stone. . . .
But I done my share of praying and fearing and kissing.

No. I 'ad no dad nor mum of me own –
not to remember – but still I'd a good upbringing.

The gran'ma raised thirty-two of us all alone
child and grandchild. . . . Somewhere a bell goes ringing.
Steps and the shielded lanterns come and are gone.
The old voice rocks with laughter and tears and singing.

Gi' me the good old days. . . . Joe Green Joe Green
how are you doing tonight? Is it cold work dying?
Not 'alf so cold as some of the frosts I've seen
out Sackville way. . . . The voice holds fast defying
sleep and silence, the whisper and the trifold screen
and the futile difficult sounds of his old girl's crying.

DOUGLAS STEWART

b. 1913

Rock Carving

The lines grow slack in our hands at full high-water;
The midnight rears in the sky; and beneath the boat
Another midnight, dwarfing the flare of a match
Or flare of a mind, expands and deepens. We float
Abandoned as driftwood on a tide that drowns all speech,
Where movement of hand or keel can make no mark
That will stand in space or endure one moment in time.
Flashing in shallows or hiding in murderous dark,

The fish live out their lives in weeds and silence;
And, locked like them in some alien struggle or peace,
No business of ours, from the moon to the water's edge,
Looming above us, tower the gigantic trees.
Among those rocks where time has ravaged the ridge,
In all that pattern cold and inhuman as the tide's,
Where shall the mind make camp? How in that darkness
Shall the mind ride tranquil with light as the high moon
    rides?

Shine the torch on the rock: we are not the first
Alone and lost in this world of water and stone.
See, though the maker's life has vanished like a leaf's,
The carvings living a hard strange life of their own
Above the water, beneath the tormented cliffs.
They glow with immortal being, as though the stone fish
May flap and slither to the tide, and the kangaroo
Bound from the rock and crash away through the bush.

The moon lights a thousand candles upon the water,
But none for the carver of stone; and nobody comes
Of his own long-scattered tribe to remember him
With dance and song and firelight under the gums;

But he walks again for me at the water's rim
And works at his rock, and a light begins to glow
Clear for his sake among the dark of my mind
Where the branches reach and the silent waters flow.

I watch him working through a summer afternoon,
Patient as the stone itself while his tribesmen sleep;
The children jostle, the girls cry out in the sun,
And first the fish and then the great 'roo take shape.
The work is crude, and he knows it; but now it is done;
And whoever laughs is a little afraid in the end,
For here is a swimmer in stone, and a beast that leaps
Nowhere for ever, and both can be touched with the hand.

I could have sat down with that man and talked about
    fishing,
How the bream are fish of the night, and they take the bait
With a run before you are ready; of the fabulous catches
For which we always got there a week too late;
And of how a man in the lonely midnight watches
Becomes himself a part of night and the tide
And, lost in the blackness, has need of a wife or a dog
Or a blackfellow's ghost to sit in peace by his side.

Centuries dead perhaps. But night and the water,
And the work of your hands on the rock have brought us
    together,
Fishermen both, and carvers both, old man.
I know as you how the work goes naked to the weather,
How we cut our thought into stone as best we can,
Laugh at our pain, and leave it to take its chance.
Maybe it's all for nothing, for the sky to look at,
Or maybe for us the distant candles dance.

The boat tugs at the kellick as it feels the ebb.
Good-bye, old wraith, and good luck. You did what you
    could
To leave your mark on stone like a mark on time,

That the sky in the mind and the midnight sea in the blood
Should be less of a desolation for the men to come;
And who can do more than you? Gone, you are gone;
But, dark a moment in the moonlight, your hand hovers,
And moves like the shadow of a bird across the stone.

The Dosser in Springtime

That girl from the sun is bathing in the creek,
Says the white old dosser in the cave.
It's a sight worth seeing though your old frame's weak;
Her clothes are on the wattle and it's gold all over,
And if I was twenty I'd try to be her lover,
Says the white old dosser in the cave.

If I was twenty I'd chase her back to Bourke,
Says the white old dosser in the cave.
My swag on my shoulder and a haughty eye for work,
I'd chase her to the sunset where the desert burns and reels,
With an old blue dog full of fleas at my heels,
Says the white old dosser in the cave.

I'd chase her back to Bourke again, I'd chase her back to
    Alice,
Says the white old dosser in the cave.
And I'd drop upon her sleeping like a beauty in a palace
With the sunset wrapped around her and a black snake
    keeping watch –
She's lovely and she's naked but she's very hard to catch,
Says the white old dosser in the cave.

I've been cooling here for years with the gum-trees wet and
    weird,
Says the white old dosser in the cave.
My head grew lichens and moss was my beard,
The creek was in my brain and a bullfrog in my belly,
The she-oaks washed their hair in me all down the gloomy
    gully,
Says the white old dosser in the cave.

My eyes were full of water and my ears were stopped with
      bubbles,
Says the white old dosser in the cave.
Yabbies raised their claws in me or skulked behind the
      pebbles.
The water-beetle loved his wife, he chased her round and
      round –
I thought I'd never see a girl unless I found one drowned,
Says the white old dosser in the cave.

Many a time I laughed aloud to stop my heart from
      thumping,
Says the white old dosser in the cave.
I saw my laugh I saw my laugh I saw my laugh go
      jumping
Like a jaunty old goanna with his tail up stiff
Till he dived like a stone in the pool below the cliff,
Says the white old dosser in the cave.

There's a fine bed of bracken, the billy boils beside her,
Says the white old dosser in the cave.
But no one ever ate with me except the loathsome spider;
And no one ever lay with me beside the sandstone wall
Except the pallid moonlight and she's no good at all,
Says the white old dosser in the cave.

But now she's in the creek again, that woman made of
      flame,
Says the white old dosser in the cave.
By cripes, if I was twenty I'd stop her little game.
Her dress is on the wattle – I'd take it off and hide it;
And when she sought that golden dress, I'd lay her down
      beside it,
Says the white old dosser in the cave.

The Brown Snake

I walked to the green gum-tree
Because the day was hot;
A snake could be anywhere
But that time I forgot.

The Duckmaloi lazed through the valley
In amber pools like tea
From some old fossicker's billy,
And I walked under the tree.

Blue summer smoked on Bindo,
It lapped me warm in its waves,
And when that snake hissed up
Under the shower of leaves

Huge, high as my waist,
Rearing with lightning's tongue,
So brown with heat like the fallen
Dry sticks it hid among,

I thought the earth itself
Under the green gum-tree,
All in the sweet of summer
Reached out to strike at me.

One Yard of Earth

Darwin, that diffident wise patient man
Who proved that men were monkeys as they are,
When working out how apes and men began
Could well have whirled his thought from star to star
Chasing the far Creator and his plan,
But knew that for the origin of species
Or all of truth one yard of earth suffices –

DOUGLAS STEWART

One yard of earth where ant and bird have trod
Where time lies fossilized in sand or stone
Where spike of plant comes green from the dark sod
Where prowling beast has passed and sunlight shone
Where starlight has looked down and maybe God,
One yard of earth, ragged, obscure and humble,
Where truth hangs trembling as its wildflowers tremble;

So took one naked yard of English earth
And watched to see how many weeds it grew
And how the weeds got on; and lo came forth
Warmed by the sunlight, watered by rain and dew,
Three hundred and fifty-seven at a birth;
Yet only sixty-two survived of that vast total;
The rest (alas) were slain by slug or beetle.

And once above the forest in the heather
He took one yard of the high turfy earth
To find out why the fir-trees climbed no further,
And saw them there like fairies in the heath
Thirty-two tiny fir-trees all together,
But if one raised its head above the rough
Some browsing quadruped would bite it off.

Delighted thus to learn with such precision
How Nature multiplied then had the wit
To eat herself to check her own profusion,
He seized a yard of mud and studied it;
And instantly in his astonished vision
He flew, he flew, far high and wide he flew
With water-birds when all the world was new;

Vast glaciers crushed their weight across the plain
And hurled their icebergs into ancient seas;
The mountains sank, and then stood up again;
Great scaly lizards sang in the green trees
Then changed to duck and heron, swan and crane;
And flying like stars through all this whirling dance
Over the earth dispersed the seeds of plants;

254

For when he watched that simple yard of muck,
Three tablespoons he took, to be precise,
From some wet haunt of heron, goose and duck,
And kept it moist for six months under glass,
He found as he recorded in his book
In words of fire, it grew from hidden seeds   — *indices*
Five hundred and thirty-seven aquatic weeds —   *from*

And saw at once, what troubled him before,
How the same weeds could grow in stream or pond
From Europe to the world's most distant shore.
In Pitcairn, Patagonia and beyond,
Wherever winds could blow and waters lure,
The fertile seeds, all eager for release,
Flew on the muddy feet of ducks and geese.

So neither by some quite incredible fluke
Had the same forms evolved in every land,
Nor dealing all his thought a deadly stroke
Had God upraised them with a strange command,
But all was due to the most useful duck.
Darwin blessed ducks, and geese and swans and herons,
And almost felt the light that shone was Heaven's —

e would not have blessed plants

For though he had grave doubts of the Creator
Who had not done all he was said to do
There was no doubt each yard of earth or water
Let the most curious light come shining through
From what far source? He left all that for later;
But noted with some reason for men's good
We should do well to keep our eyes on mud.

B Flat

Sing softly, Muse, the Reverend Henry White
Who floats through time as lightly as a feather
Yet left one solitary gleam of light
Because he was the Selborne naturalist's brother

And told him once how on warm summer eves
When moonlight filled all Fyfield to the brim
And yearning owls were hooting to their loves
On church and barn and oak-tree's leafy limb

He took a common half-a-crown pitch-pipe
Such as the masters used for harpsichords
And through the village trod with silent step
Measuring the notes of those melodious birds

And found that each one sang, or rather hooted,
Precisely in the measure of B flat.
And that is all that history has noted;
We know no more of Henry White than that.

So, softly, Muse, in harmony and conformity
Pipe up for him and all such gentle souls
Thus in the world's enormousness, enormity,
So interested in music and in owls;

For though we cannot claim his crumb of knowledge
Was worth much more than virtually nil
Nor hail him for vast enterprise or courage,
Yet in my mind I see him walking still

With eager ear beneath his clerical hat
Through Fyfield village sleeping dark and blind,
Oh surely as he piped his soft B flat
The most harmless, the most innocent of mankind.

The Silkworms

All their lives in a box! What generations,
What centuries of masters, not meaning to be cruel
But needing their labour, taught these creatures such
    patience
That now though sunlight strikes on the eye's dark jewel
Or moonlight breathes on the wing they do not stir
But like the ghosts of moths crouch silent there.

Look it's a child's toy! There is no lid even,
They can climb, they can fly, and the whole world's their
    tree;
But hush, they say in themselves, we are in prison.
There is no word to tell them that they are free,
And they are not; ancestral voices bind them
In dream too deep for wind or word to find them.

Even in the young, each like a little dragon
Ramping and green upon his mulberry leaf,
So full of life, it seems, the voice has spoken:
They hide where there is food, where they are safe,
And the voice whispers, 'Spin the cocoon,
Sleep, sleep, you shall be wrapped in me soon.'

Now is their hour, when they wake from that long swoon;
Their pale curved wings are marked in a pattern of leaves,
Shadowy for trees, white for the dance of the moon;
And when on summer nights the buddleia gives
Its nectar like lilac wine for insects mating
They drink its fragrance and shiver, impatient with
    waiting,

They stir, they think they will go. Then they remember
It was forbidden, forbidden, ever to go out;
The Hands are on guard outside like claps of thunder,
The ancestral voice says Don't, and they do not.
Still the night calls them to unimaginable bliss
But there is terror around them, the vast, the abyss,

And here is the tribe that they know, in their known place,
They are gentle and kind together, they are safe for ever,
And all shall be answered at last when they embrace.
White moth moves closer to moth, lover to lover.
There is that pang of joy on the edge of dying –
Their soft wings whirr, they dream that they are flying.

Firewheel Tree

Round and round, those wheels of fire,
My hurt, my fear, delight, desire,
Hung whirling in that dark-green tree.
I could not tell, so fast they spun
Like scarlet star and crimson sun
In all the leaves' intricacy,
What incandescence clear or sombre
Might light one flower from another,
Delight or fear or agony;
But all in that same shape they blazed
Of flame whirled into symmetry.
And round they went – I stood amazed
In hurt, in fear, delight, desire,
To see my life in wheels of fire
Go round that dark and silent tree.

Fence

Fence must be looked at; fence is too much neglected;
Most ancient indeed is fence; but it is not merely
White ants' and weather's ravage must be inspected,
The broken paling where we can see too clearly
The neighbours at their affairs, that larger hole
Where Hogan's terrier ate it, or very nearly;
But fence most quintessential, fence in its soul.

For fence is *defensa*, Latin; fence is old Roman
And heaven knows what wild tribes, rude and unknown,
It sprang from first, when man took shelter with his woman;
Fence is no simple screen where Hogan may prune
His roses decently hidden by paling or lattice
Or sporting together some sunny afternoon
Be noticed with Mrs Hogan at nymphs and satyrs;

But fence is earthwork, *defensa*; connected no doubt
With *fossa*, a moat; straight from the verb to defend;
Therefore ward off, repel, stand guard on the moat;
None climbs this fence but cat or Hogan's friend.
Fence is of spears and brambles; fence is defiance
To sabre-toothed tigers, to all the world in the end,
And there behind it the Hogans stand like lions.

It is not wise to meet the Hogans in quarrel,
They have a lawyer and he will issue writs;
Thieves and trespassers enter at deadly peril,
The brave dog bites the postman where he sits.
Just as they turn the hose against the summer's
Glare on the garden, so in far fiercer jets
Here they unleash the Hogans against all comers.

True it is not very often the need arises
And they are peaceable people behind their barrier;
But something is here that must be saved in a crisis,
They know it well and so does the sharp-toothed terrier.
They bring him bones, he worships them deeply and
    dankly,
He thinks Mrs Hogan a queen and Hogan a warrior,
Most excellent people, and they agree with him, frankly.

The world, they feel, needs Hogans; they can contribute
To its dull pattern all their rich singularity;
And if, as is true, it pays them no proper tribute,
Hogans from Hogans at least shall not lack charity.

Shielded by fences are they not free to cherish
Each bud, each shoot, each fine particularity
Which in the Hogans burgeons and must not perish?

It is not just that their mighty motor mower
Roars loudest for miles and chops up the insolent grass,
Nor that the Iceland poppies are dancing in flower,
Nor the new car all shiny with chromium and glass,
Nor the fridge and T.V., nor that, the bloom of their
    totem,
Their freckled children always come first in the class
Or sometimes at least, and never are seen at the bottom;

It is all this and so much more beside
Of Hogans down the ages in their proud carriage
And Hogan young and Mrs Hogan a bride
And napkins washed and babies fumbling their porridge,
Things which no prying stranger can know or feel –
All locked in the strange intimacy of marriage,
Which by all means let decent fences conceal.

So let us to work, good neighbour, this Saturday morning,
Nail up the paling so Hogans are free to be Hogans
And Stewarts be Stewarts and no one shall watch us
    scorning
And no one break in with bullets and bombs and slogans
Or we will stand guard at the fence and fight as we can.
World is against us, but world has had its warning;
Deep out of time is fence and deep is man.

Professor Piccard

Some said it was a shooting star,
Some said it was a pheasant;
It was the most surprising thing
To villager and peasant.

To see it floating and shining there
Over the alps of snow –
Some said it was a bubble of air,
The others they said no;

It could not be just snow or cloud
Or any such phenomenon,
It could not be a water spout,
At least it was no common one

For they could see a shape inside
That stood too straight and tall
To be a weed or fish caught up –
If it was there at all.

Some said it was a man in a bottle,
But they had drunk too well;
Some said it was a shining spirit
Released from heaven or hell;

Some said it was a thing from Mars
And some the man in the moon;
And some said it was Professor Piccard
Ascending in his balloon.

His bright blue eyes were filled with heaven,
His hair like wisps of cloud,
And straight like an exclamation mark
In the high noon he stood.

And up and up to the stratosphere,
Always sublimely vertical,
Ten miles above the earth he rose
In his astounding vehicle.

What is the colour of outer space
Above the mountain snows?
Purple and violet, sombre, deep –
But look, down down he goes;

He will not sleep in the stars tonight
Or camp on Augsberg's peaks;
Seventeen hundred fathoms down
Another world he seeks,

And hardly pausing to change his craft
Or see that it is safe
Down to the Ponza Deep he dives
In his strange bathyscaphe.

The yellow light dies out in green,
The green dies out in purple
And all in utter blackness now
Swim round him the sea's people,

The shadowy fish with bulging eyes
The flying phosphorescence,
The mighty shapes that loom in the shades
That never have known man's presence.

But now they know for here he comes
As radiant and orbicular
The bathyscaphe sinks with Piccard inside
Proud, calm and perpendicular.

Oh like a bubble of living sunlight
Down to the bottom they plunge
Where the specks of jelly drift in the murk
And silently breathes the sponge.

From the top of the sky to the bottom of the sea –
How much I wish I were able
To set Professor Piccard now
In his appropriate fable:

How like some mythological hero
Down in that shuddering dark
He wrestled for life with an octopus
Or fought with a giant shark;

How some great lumbering whale or ray
Mistaking him for Jonah
Loomed from the shadowy fog and swallowed
The bathyscaphe and its owner;

Or how like some new Orpheus
Wandering through dim Hades
He saw the queen of the mermaids there
Surrounded by all her ladies

And up and up she followed him,
Divinely fishy and fair,
Out from the dark and the purple gloom
To the breaking wave and the air,

Until at last as the bathyscaphe
Rose bubbling out of the water
The professor yearned for his gleaming prize
And so looked back and lost her.

Or how when he rose up and flew
High to the sun like Icarus
Down from that light he fell, he fell
Through space as black as licorice.

Or like some modern saint, more happily,
Soaring in his uprightness
He felt in his strange globular car
A lift, a sudden lightness,

And saw bright angels wafting him,
Their feathers soft as pullets,
Impervious to cosmic rays
And meteorites like bullets,

To his celestial home. Alas,
He did not see one feather
But studied in the stratosphere
The cosmic rays and the weather;

And when he dived to the floor of the sea
All eager though he stood,
The bathyscaphe half-buried itself
And he saw nothing but mud.

Yet when I think how from that deep
Where life first moved and flickered
His craft rose up like some great egg
And hatched Professor Piccard,

When I reflect how his brave stance
Of perpendicularity
In posture and in motion both
Is man's whole singularity,

Who rose from that same depth and stood
And climbs on to infinity,
He seems more legendary now
Than any old divinity;

And up towards the stars of heaven
Or down to look at zero
I leave Professor Piccard now,
Our emblem and our hero.

HAROLD STEWART

b. 1916

Orpheus and the Trees

Lips only sing that cannot kiss:
Orpheus had suffered in his bliss
An arid metamorphosis.
But now Eurydice is dust,
The thirsty desert waste of lust

That drained, with drinking overlong,
Pierian sources dry of song,
A barren spell no longer brings.
His inspiration's secret springs
Gush forth again: the poet sings.

Now passion, broken in, has grown
Sublimated wings, and flown.
But where its hoof once struck, his scene
Of inner wilderness is green
With overflowing Hippocrene.

His fluency can move with ease
The oak of bones, the willow-trees
Of branching veins and arteries.
The ever-trembling poplar curves
To catch his air, that stirs the nerves.

Eradicated from their trance,
The vegetative trunks advance
And ivy-sinewed join the dance;
While Daphne her remembered limb
Sways to keep in time with him.

Their dance has ramified until
A glade of quiet crowns the hill:

For where he sat, a spell has bound
The audience of trees around
Melody bubbling from the ground.

The vocal fountain rises higher,
As though emotion would aspire
In slender exaltation where
The heights of contemplation bear
Aloft the dome of summer air.

The waters at their summit play,
Then part, and shower a sunlit spray
Of tones. Their cadence falls away.
The silver lyric soars and sighs:
No sooner born than music dies

JOHN COUPER

b. 1914

A Sydney Scot When the Boat Comes In

Snow and haggis and the bagpipes, half a cheer
for a terrible trio. Thank God you left Scotland for those.
Bare feet, cauld doup, kilt and sporran for clothes,
a de'il's brew of porridge and whisky, and Scotsmen are
    nothing but queer.

Leave the damn lot to the imaginary Hielandmen. Steer
well windward of Caledonian capers: which goes
for the Burns sprees, and the cabers, and thinking a thistle
    a rose,
and every raw-boned accent for gathering gear out here.

But I wasn't for saying to tramp on your gude Scots
    bonnet.
Fine do I ken o' my hame as well as you
and while there's breath in my body I'm minding on it.

Green braes and the whistle of the wind in the winter days;
man's hand by land and sea; lang syne standing new;
and the bonnie lift of the hills at the sky, man, that's
    beyond praise.

For You Angela
Horace, Odes, 1, 5

Surfers' Paradise

What cheerful bastard
reeking of sun-tan
goes for you, Angela,
flat on the sands?

Just the old boy-friend
writing to ask you
who cops the hair-do,
coolest of bitches?

My, but he's in for a
tough old time there,
tossing the seas of your
greedy libido.

Won't know it yet, though,
now he enjoys you,
always plain sailing,
so easy always.

Sucker, like the rest of us,
silly at the sight of
that dropping lee shore, your
sunsmitten bottom.

Here am I writing this
thankful tribute and
drying my wings like a
shag on a rock.

DOROTHY AUCHTERLONIE

b. 1915

Apopemptic Hymn

All was as it was when I went in:
The pictures right-side up, the chairs in place,
The flowers stood stiff upon the mantelpiece,
I knew the voice, I recognised the face.

Outside, the same sky held the same earth fast,
The green leaves shone, dogs barked, the children played;
But suddenly, inside, the air grew cold,
The evening ceased to sing, I was afraid.

The chairs began to dance, the pictures screamed,
The suppurating flowers smelt sickly-sweet,
The white walls clashed together, silence howled,
The floor collapsed in darkness at my feet.

The door slams shut, the wind is in my hair,
The sun has gone, and in its place there stands
The mighty stranger, blotting out the sky;
I turn and feel my way with cold, blind hands.

But where I turn, he stands before me still,
Annihilating time, bestriding space,
Chaos is come, my daughter is unborn,
And blank and featureless my own son's face.

No point of recognition but the grass –
Even the tree betrays me in the end –
Oh blind hands, feel the toughness of the blades
And the cold ground beneath them as your friend.

DAVID CAMPBELL

b. 1915

Men in Green

There were fifteen men in green,
Each with a tommy-gun,
Who leapt into my plane at dawn;
We rose to meet the sun.

We set our course towards the east
And climbed into the day
Till the ribbed jungle underneath
Like a giant fossil lay.

We climbed towards the distant range
Where two white paws of cloud
Clutched at the shoulders of the pass;
The green men laughed aloud.

They did not fear the ape-like cloud
That climbed the mountain crest
And hung from twisted ropes of air
With thunder in its breast.

They did not fear the summer's sun
In whose hot centre lie
A hundred hissing cannon shells
For the unwatchful eye.

And when on Dobadura's field
We landed, each man raised
His thumb towards the open sky;
But to their right I gazed.

For fifteen men in jungle green
Rose from the kunai grass
And came towards the plane. My men

In silence watched them pass;
It seemed they looked upon themselves
In Time's prophetic glass.

Oh, there were some leaned on a stick
And some on stretchers lay,
But few walked on their own two feet
In the early green of day.

They had not feared the ape-like cloud
That climbed the mountain crest;
They had not feared the summer's sun
With bullets for their breast.

Their eyes were bright, their looks were dull,
Their skin had turned to clay.
Nature had met them in the night
And stalked them in the day.

And I think still of men in green
On the Soputa track
With fifteen spitting tommy-guns
To keep a jungle back.

Windy Gap

As I was going through Windy Gap
A hawk and a cloud hung over the map.

The land lay bare and the wind blew loud
And the hawk cried out from the heart of the cloud

'Before I fold my wings in sleep
I'll pick the bones of your travelling sheep,

'For the leaves blow back and the wintry sun
Shows the tree's white skeleton.'

A magpie sat in the tree's high top
Singing a song on Windy Gap

That streamed far down to the plain below
Like a shaft of light from a high window.

From the bending tree he sang aloud,
And the sun shone out of the heart of the cloud

And it seemed to me as we travelled through
That my sheep were the notes that trumpet blew.

And so I sing this song of praise
For travelling sheep and blowing days.

Night Sowing

O gentle, gentle land
Where the green ear shall grow,
Now you are edged with light:
The moon has crisped the fallow,
The furrows run with night.

This is the season's hour:
While couples are in bed,
I sow the paddocks late,
Scatter like sparks the seed
And see the dark ignite.

O gentle land, I sow
The heart's living grain.
Stars draw their harrows over,
Dews send their melting rain:
I meet you as a lover.

Under Wattles

Now, here and there, against the cold,
The hillsides smoulder into gold
And the stockman riding by
Lifts to the trees a yellow eye.

It's here the couples from the farms
Play in one another's arms
At yes and no – you'd think the trees
Sprang from their felicities.

So may our children grow up strong,
Got while the thrush drew out his song,
And love like you and I when we
Lie beneath the wattle tree.

Droving

Down the red stock route, my tall son
Droves with his girl the white-faced steers
From the high country, as we would years
Ago beneath a daylight moon.
But now these two must bring them down
Between the snow-gums and the briars
Hung with their thousand golden tears,
To camp beside the creek at noon.
And finding them so sure and young,
The flower-fat mob their only care,
The days I thought beyond recall
Are ringed about with magpie song;
And it seems in spite of death and war
Time's not so desperate after all.

Windy Nights

Naked in snowdrifts, we've made love,
In city parks, at the front gate,
And thought no deeper truth to prove
Than this, that lovers cannot wait.
What if the whole world disapprove,
Though it should be a crowded street?
See how instinctive lovers move
To get their clothes off when they meet.
O what do lovers love the best,
Upstairs naked or downstairs dressed?
Windy nights and hot desire
Or an old book and a steady fire?
Ask your mistress. Should she pause,
She has a lover out of doors.

J. S. MANIFOLD

b. 1915

The Tomb of Lieut. John Learmonth, A.I.F.

At the end on Crete he took to the hills, and said he'd fight
it out with only a revolver. He was a great soldier . . .
One of his men in a letter

This is not sorrow, this is work: I build
A cairn of words over a silent man,
My friend John Learmonth whom the Germans killed.

There was no word of hero in his plan;
Verse should have been his love and peace his trade,
But history turned him to a partisan.

Far from the battle as his bones are laid
Crete will remember him. Remember well,
Mountains of Crete, the Second Field Brigade!

Say Crete, and there is little more to tell
Of muddle tall as treachery, despair
And black defeat resounding like a bell;

But bring the magnifying focus near
And in contempt of muddle and defeat
The old heroic virtues still appear.

Australian blood where hot and icy meet
(James Hogg and Lermontov were of his kin)
Lie still and fertilize the fields of Crete.

*

Schoolboy, I watched his ballading begin:
Billy and bullocky and billabong,
Our properties of childhood, all were in.

I heard the air though not the undersong,
The fierceness and resolve; but all the same
They're the tradition, and tradition's strong.

Swagman and bushranger die hard, die game,
Die fighting, like that wild colonial boy –
Jack Dowling, says the ballad, was his name.

He also spun his pistol like a toy,
Turned to the hills like wolf or kangaroo,
And faced destruction with a bitter joy.

His freedom gave him nothing else to do
But set his back against his family tree
And fight the better for the fact he knew

He was as good as dead. Because the sea
Was closed and the air dark and the land lost,
'They'll never capture me alive', said he.

*

That's courage chemically pure, uncrossed
With sacrifice or duty or career,
Which counts and pays in ready coin the cost

Of holding course. Armies are not its sphere
Where all's contrived to achieve its counterfeit;
It swears with discipline, it's volunteer.

I could as hardly make a moral fit
Around it as around a lightning flash.
There is no moral, that's the point of it,

No moral. But I'm glad of this panache
That sparkles, as from flint, from us and steel,
True to no crown nor presidential sash

Nor flag nor fame. Let others mourn and feel
He died for nothing: nothings have their place.
While thus the kind and civilized conceal

This spring of unsuspected inward grace
And look on death as equals, I am filled
With queer affection for the human race.

The Showmen

From the French of Leconte de Lisle

It's vile to live like you; to drag along
Senile, decrepit as the infertile earth,
Castrated by this murderous age, from birth,
Of every passion that is deep and strong.

Your heads secrete no plan, your hearts no song;
You pullulate, soiling the round world's girth
With mere corruption, so Disease and Dearth
May batten well and decimate the throng.

You have outlived your Gods – and what shall save
You, wallowing in gold in some dark cave,
When you have sucked the good soil bare and dry?

The day draws on when time and space shall press
Down with an awful weight of emptiness,
And you, stuffing your money-bags, shall die.

DAVID MARTIN

b. 1915

Gordon Childe

From this far, late-come country that still keeps
A primitive and ancient dream he drew
That which is name- and changeless. Here he grew
And, all his work accomplished, here he sleeps.

Scholar and man, his road lay straight through time.
With rational affection he restored
From shards the road by which the race explored
Its world and heaven, risen from the slime

Not on the wings of mystery but through shared
Dread and experience. Ranging free he saw
The gods, with Caesar one before the law
Of birth and death, decay, and God not spared.

Our pre-historic father who was sent
To his last journey with an axe of stone,
With this same axe cut through the dark unknown
The road on which Saul to Damascus went.

And so, come home, he closed the book and cast
Upon the fertile wind his unwrit page.
Dying, the hills stood round him, age on age.
Man makes himself. Each crest out-tops the last.

JUDITH WRIGHT

b. 1915

The Company of Lovers

We meet and part now over all the world.
We, the lost company,
take hands together in the night, forget
the night in our brief happiness, silently.
We who sought many things, throw all away
for this one thing, one only,
remembering that in the narrow grave
we shall be lonely.

Death marshals up his armies round us now.
Their footsteps crowd too near.
Lock your warm hand above the chilling heart
and for a time I live without my fear.
Grope in the night to find me and embrace,
for the dark preludes of the drums begin,
and round us, round the company of lovers,
Death draws his cordons in.

Bullocky

Beside his heavy-shouldered team,
thirsty with drought and chilled with rain,
he weathered all the striding years
till they ran widdershins in his brain:

Till the long solitary tracks
etched deeper with each lurching load
were populous before his eyes,
and fiends and angels used his road.

All the long straining journey grew
a mad apocalyptic dream,
and he old Moses, and the slaves
his suffering and stubborn team.

Then in his evening camp beneath
the half-light pillars of the trees
he filled the steepled cone of night
with shouted prayers and prophecies.

While past the campfire's crimson ring
the star-struck darkness cupped him round,
and centuries of cattlebells
rang with their sweet uneasy sound.

Grass is across the waggon-tracks,
and plough strikes bone beneath the grass,
and vineyards cover all the slopes
where the dead teams were used to pass.

O vine, grow close upon that bone
and hold it with your rooted hand.
The prophet Moses feeds the grape,
and fruitful is the Promised Land.

South of My Days

South of my day's circle, part of my blood's country,
rises that tableland, high delicate outline
of bony slopes wincing under the winter,
low trees blue-leaved and olive, outcropping granite –
clean, lean, hungry country. The creek's leaf-silenced,
willow-choked, the slope a tangle of medlar and crabapple
branching over and under, blotched with a green lichen;
and the old cottage lurches in for shelter.

O cold the black-frost night. The walls draw in to the
    warmth
and the old roof cracks its joints; the slung kettle

280

hisses a leak on the fire. Hardly to be believed that summer
will turn up again some day in a wave of rambler roses,
thrust its hot face in here to tell another yarn –
a story old Dan can spin into a blanket against the winter.
Seventy years of stories he clutches round his bones.
Seventy summers are hived in him like old honey.

Droving that year, Charleville to the Hunter,
nineteen-one it was, and the drought beginning;
sixty head left at the McIntyre, the mud round them
hardened like iron; and the yellow boy died
in the sulky ahead with the gear, but the horse went on,
stopped at the Sandy Camp and waited in the evening.
It was the flies we seen first, swarming like bees.
Came to the Hunter, three hundred head of a thousand –
cruel to keep them alive – and the river was dust.

Or mustering up in the Bogongs in the autumn
when the blizzards came early. Brought them down; we
    brought them
down, what aren't there yet. Or driving for Cobb's on the
    run
up from Tamworth – Thunderbolt at the top of Hungry
    Hill,
and I give him a wink. I wouldn't wait long, Fred,
not if I was you; the troopers are just behind,
coming for that job at the Hillgrove. He went like a luny,
him on his big black horse.

                Oh, they slide and they vanish
as he shuffles the years like a pack of conjuror's cards.
True or not, it's all the same; and the frost on the roof
cracks like a whip, and the back-log breaks into ash.
Wake, old man. This is winter, and the yarns are over.
No one is listening.
                South of my days' circle
I know it dark against the stars, the high lean country
full of old stories that still go walking in my sleep.

281

Woman To Man

The eyeless labourer in the night,
the selfless, shapeless seed I hold,
builds for its resurrection day –
silent and swift and deep from sight
foresees the unimagined light.

This is no child with a child's face;
this has no name to name it by:
yet you and I have known it well.
This is our hunter and our chase,
the third who lay in our embrace.

This is the strength that your arm knows,
the arc of flesh that is my breast,
the precise crystals of our eyes.
This is the blood's wild tree that grows
the intricate and folded rose.

This is the maker and the made;
this is the question and reply;
the blind head butting at the dark,
the blaze of light along the blade.
Oh hold me, for I am afraid.

The Cycads

Their smooth dark flames flicker at time's own root.
Round them the rising forests of the years
alter the climates of forgotten earth
and silt with leaves the strata of first birth.

Only the antique cycads sullenly
keep the old bargain life has long since broken;
and, cursed by age, through each chill century
they watch the shrunken moon, but never die,

for time forgets the promise he once made,
and change forgets that they are left alone.
Among the complicated birds and flowers
they seem a generation carved in stone.

Leaning together, down those gulfs they stare
over whose darkness dance the brilliant birds
that cry in air one moment, and are gone;
and with their countless suns the years spin on.

Take their cold seed and set it in the mind,
and its slow root will lengthen deep and deep
till, following, you cling on the last ledge
over the unthinkable, unfathomed edge
beyond which man remembers only sleep.

Our Love is so Natural

Our love is so natural,
the wild animals move
gentle and light on
the shores of our love.

My eyes rest upon you,
to me your eyes turn,
as bee goes to honey,
as fire to fire will burn.

Bird and beast are at home,
and star lives in tree
when we are together
as we should be.

But so silent my heart falls
when you are away,
I can hear the world breathing
where he hides from our day.

My heart crouches under,
silent and still,
and the avalanche gathers
above the green hill.

Our love is so natural –
I cannot but fear.
I would reach out and touch you.
Why are you not here?

Black-Shouldered Kite

Carved out of strength, the furious kite
shoulders off the wind's hate.
The black mark that bars his white
is the pride and hunger of Cain.
Perfect, precise, the angry calm
of his closed body, that snow-storm –
of his still eye that threatens harm.
Hunger and force his beauty made
and turned a bird to a knife-blade.

The Harp and the King

Old king without a throne,
the hollow of despair
behind his obstinate unyielding stare,
knows only, God is gone:
and, fingers clenching on his chair,
feels night and the soul's terror coming on.

Bring me that harp, that singer. Let him sing.
Let something fill the space inside the mind,
that's a dry stream-bed for the flood of fear.

Song's only sound; but it's a lovely sound,
a fountain through the drought. Bring David here,
said the old frightened king.

Sing something. Comfort me.
Make me believe the meaning in the rhyme.
The world's a traitor to the self-betrayed;
but once I thought there was a truth in time,
while now my terror is eternity.
So do not take me outside time.
Make me believe in my mortality,
since that is all I have, the old king said.

I sing the praise of time, the harp replied:
the time of aching drought when the black plain
cannot believe in roots or leaves or rain.
Then lips crack open in the stone-hard peaks;
and rock begins to suffer and to pray
when all that lives has died
and withered in the wind and blown away;
and earth has no more strength to bleed.

I sing the praise of time and of the rain –
the word creation speaks.
Four elements are locked in time;
the sign that makes them fertile is the seed,
and this outlasts all death and springs again,
the running water of the harp-notes cried.

But the old king sighed obstinately,
How can that comfort me?
Night and the terror of the soul come on,
and out of me both water and seed have gone.
What other generations shall I see?
But make me trust my failure and my fall,
said the sad king, since these are now my all.

I sing the praise of time, the harp replied.
In time we fail, alone with hours and tears,

ruin our followers and traduce our cause,
and give our love its last and fatal hurt.
In time we fail and fall.
In time the company even of God withdraws
and we are left with our own murderous heart.

Yet it is time that holds,
somewhere although not now,
the peal of trumpets for us; time that bears,
made fertile even by those tears,
even by this darkness, even by this loss,
incredible redemptions – hours that grow,
as trees grow fruit, in a blind holiness,
the truths unknown, the loves unloved by us.

But the old king turned his head sullenly.
How can that comfort me,
who see into the heart as deep as God can see?
Love's sown in us; perhaps it flowers; it dies.
I failed my God and I betrayed my love.
Make me believe in treason; that is all I have.

This is the praise of time, the harp cried out –
that we betray all truths that we possess.
Time strips the soul and leaves it comfortless
and sends it thirsty through a bone-white drought.
Time's subtler treacheries teach us to betray.
What else could drive us on our way?
Wounded we cross the desert's emptiness,
and must be false to what would make us whole.
For only change and distance shape for us
some new tremendous symbol for the soul.

Clock and Heart

The trap of time surprised my heart –
its hidden teeth of circumstance
that draw the child into the clock
upon the cogs of tick and tock.
No logic, artifice nor chance
could silence my protesting heart.

Then poetry's electing shade
enclosed me with its darkening ray,
left me no face to recognize,
no eyes to meet my searching eyes.
The solitude of poetry
locked me within its second shade.

To light that shade and set me free
no flame had power but human love.
Against my will I caught and burned,
but then the key of time was turned,
the dark ray blazed, and from above
it lit the hour that set me free.

Set free at last in human time –
that long-rejected tyranny –
I found in ordinary love
the solitudes of poetry.

Typists in the Phoenix Building

In tiled and fireproof corridors
the typists shelter in their sex;
perking beside the half-cock clerks
they set a curl on freckled necks.
The formal bird above the doors

is set in metal whorls of flame.
The train goes aching on its rails.

Its rising cry of steel and wheels
intolerably comes, and fails
on walls immaculate and dumb.

Comptometers and calculators
compute the frequency of fires,
adduce the risk, add up the years.
Drawn by late-afternoon desires
the poles of mind meet lust's equators.

Where will the inundation reach
whose cycle we can but await?
The city burns in summer's heat,
grass withers and the season's late;
the metal bird would scorch the touch;

and yet above some distant source,
some shrunken lake or spring gone dry,
perhaps the clouds involve the day
in night, and once again on high
the blazing sun forgets its course,

deep-hidden in that whirling smoke
from which the floods of Nile may fall.
But summer burns the city still.
The metal bird upon the wall
is silent; Shirley and her clerk

in tiled and fireproof corridors
touch and fall apart. No fires
consume the banked comptometers;
no flood has lipped the inlaid floors.

The Beanstalk, Meditated Later

What's fortune, that we pray it may be mild?
The beans I carried home that careless day
I thought were toys, and I a clever child –

but mother scolded, throwing them away:
'The subtlest traps have just such pretty bait.'
Well, she was right. That beanstalk reached a sky
where giants cheat us. We must skulk and wait
and steal our fortune back to mock them by.

Who was my father? See where that doubt leads –
the ladder grew so pat out of our garden
perhaps my mother recognized its seeds.
Giants have trampled earth and asked no pardon –
Well, nor did I. He took our family's gold.
I stole it back and saw the giant die.
(Four days to bury him.) Now I've grown old,
but still the giants trample in the sky.

Yes, still I hear them; and I meditate
(old, rich, respected, maudlin – says my son)
upon our generations and our fate.
Does each repeat the thing the last has done
though claiming he rejects it? Once I stood
beside my beanstalk – clever boy – and crowed
I'd killed the giant, Tom Thumb whose luck was good;
but now – what farmer saved the seed I sowed?

For somewhere still that dizzy ladder grows –
pathway for tit-for-tat from here to there –
and what's the traffic on it, no man knows.
Sometimes I hug my gold in pure despair
watching my son – my cocky enemy –
big, ugly, boastful. It's the giant strain
come out in him, I think. I watch, and he
watches me. The gold is in his brain.

I'll post a proclamation – advertise –
find that farmer, buy his whole year's crop,
burn the lot, and see the last seed dies.
But one seed – yes – I'll plant. That's for my son.
I'll send him up it, wait; and when he's crawled
far enough, I'll lay the axe-blows on
and send him sprawling where his grandpa sprawled.

NANCY CATO

b. 1917

Moon and Pear-Tree

Pale as the pear-tree blossom, the new moon floats
Like a fragile petal fallen into the sky.
The bees are busy among the white and green,
But ignore that flower, they could not climb so high.

Here in the blossoming orchard where the grass
Grows long and green, a thousand insects' flight
Against the sun becomes a cloud of fire,
Each one a fleck of golden, living light.

And the blossoms hang like clusters of white moons,
And the moon is soft as a petal; so senses mock,
Making of inky specks a dance of flame,
And a delicate flower of an old, scarred lump of rock.

JAMES McAULEY

b. 1917

Terra Australis

Voyage within you, on the fabled ocean,
And you will find that Southern Continent,
Quiros' vision – his hidalgo heart
And mythical Australia, where reside
All things in their imagined counterpart.

It is your land of similes: the wattle
Scatters its pollen on the doubting heart;
The flowers are wide-awake; the air gives ease.
There you come home; the magpies call you Jack
And whistle like larrikins at you from the trees.

There too the angophora preaches on the hillsides
With the gestures of Moses; and the white cockatoo,
Perched on his limbs, screams with demoniac pain;
And who shall say on what errand the insolent emu
Walks between morning and night on the edge of the plain?

But northward in valleys of the fiery Goat
Where the sun like a centaur vertically shoots
His raging arrows with unerring aim,
Stand the ecstatic solitary pyres
Of unknown lovers, featureless with flame.

The Incarnation of Sirius

In that age, the great anagram of God
Had bayed the planets from the rounds they trod,
And gathered the fixed stars in a shining nation
Like restless birds that flock before migration.

For the millennial instinct of new flight
Resolved the antinomy that fixed their light;
And, echoing in the troubled soul of Earth,
Quickened a virgin's womb, to bring to birth

What scarce was human: a rude avatar
That glistened with the enclosed wrath of a star.
The woman died in pangs, before she had kissed
The monstrous form of God's antagonist.

But at its showing forth, the poets cried
In a strange tongue; hot mouths prophesied
The coolness of the bloody vintage-drops:
'Let us be drunk at least, when the world stops!'

Anubis-headed, the heresiarch
Sprang to a height, fire-sinewed in the dark,
And his ten fingers, bracketed on high,
Were a blazing candelabra in the sky.

The desert lion antiphonally roared;
The tiger's sinews quivered like a chord;
Man smelt the blood beneath his brother's skin
And in a loving hate the sword went in.

And then the vision sank, bloody and aborted.
The stars that with rebellion had consorted
Fled back in silence to their former stations.
Over the giant face of dreaming nations

The centuries-thick coverlet was drawn.
Upon the huddled breast Aldebaran
Still glittered with its sad alternate fire:
Blue as of memory, red as of desire.

Tune for Swans

Black swan leaving
Your reedy nest
To sail on the waters
With quiet breast,
While you are far
The grey rat has come
Destroying, despoiling:
Turn again home.

Black swan dipping
Your neck to feed
In the half-lit pastures
Of wavering weed,
While you are far
The marauder has come:
Where is your treasure now?
Turn again home.

Celebration of Divine Love

The infant laughs beneath the cosmic tree,
Joyful to see it put forth leaf and flower
Under angelic husbandry.
He names the creatures in his father's bower,
Filled with the magic savour of the words.
Not time, it seems, nor wild beasts, can devour
The innocent delight that girds
His tender flesh. The leopard
Gambols, and the harmless bear
Licks honey from its paw; the drowsing shepherd
Lets his flock drift like clouds. Yet even here
Things turn and show an underside of fear;
Night-terrors come; the Eden colours fade;
The joy that seemed a supernatural power
Weakens and grows discouraged and afraid.

While time seems motionless the child must learn
The outer life of exile on the plain,
Where creaking carts, lurching beneath the grain,
Deepen the winding ruts as the slow wheels turn;
And chatter rises round the grinding quern;
And bees within their murmuring temples hive
Merit by which the race of Cain may thrive;
While Abel guards the herd in contemplation,
Or fends the yearling from the lion's claw.
Whether in dream or act, his heart acquires
An obscure guilt; he feels love's shattered law
Piercing his breast, and all creation
Grown tuneless and distraught, like his desires
Which drive him, marked with an inward flaw,
To wander in the earth without vocation.

Sad childhood world, long vanished in the flood!
Now in the sexual night the waters rave,
Drowned earth is mingled with a sky of mud,
And cresting the abyssal wave
Leviathan uprears a hundred heads
To bellow over the destructive tide.
Waters of judgment! Yet they might have been
Living waters, sanctified.
Pity the castaways of that vast storm,
Who, passing through the deathly element,
Survive unliving and are not reborn:
For them the frightful dreams do not relent;
They have no kin, and pass their days unknown,
And in the hour of their delight receive
A stranger to their bed, and wake alone.

Fled from his own disaster, he consults
The learned magi casting horoscopes
For the New Babylon. Plan by plan
They raise the scaffold of terrestrial hopes:
'For thus,' they say, 'when exiled man
Disowns Jerusalem which we destroy,

And learns to live, as the enlightened should,
The desecrated life, he will enjoy
The sweet fruition of all earthly good.'
Yet, ill at ease, his steps are led apart
Where the despised and hated remnant clings
To the old way with undivided will:
Out of the bowed darkness a voice sings,
'If I forget thee, O Jerusalem . . .'
He listens; and his heart stands still.

Faintly at first then clearer each day brings
Like an Annunciation a deep sense
Of natural order in the way of things,
In star and seed and in the works of love,
Whose violation brings sure recompense.
This meaning old mysterious symbols bear:
The Ark, the Rainbow, the returning Dove,
Requiting piety, rewarding care;
And secret patterns printed in our being,
The Wheel, the Pillar, and the abstract Rose,
Denying which we lose the power of seeing.
And soon with a submissive joy he knows
The benediction that an infant's birth
Can bring to those
Who share the old fidelities of earth.

Then in his sight the living Temple stands,
The sacred mother of terrestrial things;
Her head is crowned with stars, her feet are shod
With peace, and in her hands
She bears the Child, the Mystery of God,
Declared to angels and adored by kings.
Tributes of gold and frankincense and myrrh
Lie gleaming at her feet: her hands confer
Far other wealth than these; for in her courts
Music reflects angelic hierarchies,
And crafts that Wisdom has perfected shine;
There Holy Poverty with Joy resorts,

And Love that is most human grows divine.
Caught in her splendour other glories fade,
And earthly kingdoms turn to dust and shade.

The figure on Eternity's gold ground,
Behold Christ reigning on the cosmic tree,
His blood its sap, his breath its respiration,
In him are all things in perfection found.
He is the bond and stay of his creation,
Unmeasured measure of immensity;
The nails that pierce his hands and feet make fast
The axis of the world, his outstretched arms
Give falling nature its stability.
Now is the three hours' darkness of the soul,
The time of earthquake; now at last
The Word speaks, and the epileptic will
Convulsing vomits forth its demons. Then
Full-clothed, in his right mind, the man sits still,
Conversing with aeons in the speech of men.

You gentle souls who sit contemplative
In the walled garden where the fountain flows,
And faint with longing have desire to live
But the brief flowering of the single rose,
Knowing that all you give
Into the keeping of your tender Lord
Shall be enriched and thousandfold restored:
Before the herons return
Abide the sharp frosts and the time of pruning;
For he shall come at last for whom you yearn
And deep and silent shall be your communing;
And if his summer heat of love should burn
Its victim with a sacrificial fire,
Rejoice: who knows what wanderer may turn,
Responsive to that fragrant hidden pyre!

A Leaf of Sage

This is a tale from the Decameron;
Truant to good advice the poet returns
To the lost art, which he is told to shun,
Of narrative; hoping this time to have won
Some part of the perfections he discerns.

Let me be Love's cantor, and have power
To breathe the solemn neums of temple song
In pure unsweetened verse, neither harsh nor sour,
And may this five-leaved stanza come to flower
With graces that to youth and art belong.

A woolmonger's apprentice used to carry
Yarn to a poor household that was paid
To spin a weekly task of thread. And very
Often he would find excuse to tarry
For reasons not connected with his trade.

Pasquino lingered while Simona span;
And as he watched, her spindle seemed to draw
The fibre of his feelings till they ran
Twisting to coloured threads, which Love began
To weave into the pattern he foresaw.

Those fierce uncertain ardours of first love,
Who can quite recall them? Later, it's true,
Love may be jubilant in its summer grove,
Golden as noonday, pungent as the clove,
But gone is that trembling light like morning dew.

Clumsy, vehement, tongue-tied and aflame,
Pasquino's wishes yet found means to advance.
Each blurred encounter through the mesh of shame
And shyness was rewarded with the same
Confused surrender in Simona's glance.

Walking to her house he would devise
Conversations full of love's intent,

Supplying in his fancy her replies;
And if he ventured on these colloquies
She would return almost the words he'd lent.

They touched; they kissed; and passed incontinently
To the next stage of love (is it not so?)
Deceit of elders. Longing to be free,
She of her parents, of his master he,
They plotted what to say and where to go.

And thus one Sunday, with another pair,
They found a garden; each couple sat remote;
The sky laughed; a curling baroque air
Ruffled the colours of the bright parterre;
A bird sat by with soft recording note.

Spring had resumed its liturgy of light.
The sun's gladness like a festal garment
Fell on Simona's body and flowed bright
About her. Suppliant in her presence, sight
And touch and other senses sought preferment.

She seemed the virgin of Love's calendar.
Her mood of stillness, flushing with desire,
Resembled as Pasquino worshipped her
The delicate alternation of a star
Whose cold blue radiance has a pulse of fire.

A sage plant in this garden of their bliss
Like a small tree of knowledge grew at hand.
Laughing she plucked a leaf and said, 'Rub this
Against your teeth and it will give your kiss
Its aromatic virtue.' Her command

Pleased him, and he quoted the old saw,
'Eat sage in May if you would live for aye.'
He crushed the grey-green leaf as if to draw
Immortal joy from it under Love's law;
And then the thumb of Darkness bruised the day.

For not long after, as if plague-stricken, he
Grinced and sweated; livid spots appeared
Upon his face and hands; quite suddenly
His body swelled; he ceased to hear or see;
And while Simona, fixed in horror, stared,

The strange distemper with rough spasms tore
His life out by the cringing roots, and left
A swollen corpse. Beside the unseen door
The hidden bird sang sweetly as before.
And then the girl shrieked, utterly bereft.

O high untraceable permissive Will!
I stare into the whirlpool of your eye
Where our intentions, whether good or ill,
Sink to destruction swift and terrible:
These are your counsels, Lord, which terrify.

The other couple ran up at the sound,
And saw the spotted flesh, deformed and grim;
Then strangers too began to gather round,
And since no cause could readily be found
Suspicion grew that she had poisoned him.

The appetite for random accusation
Woke in a dozen mouths, which flowed with blame
And the sweet slaver of anticipation:
Our virtue loves the sauce of indignation
With which to eat another's life and name.

Hurried weeping to the magistrate,
She is too speechless to deny the crime.
He, unconvinced by what the accusers state,
Comes to the spot and bids the girl relate
Minutely all that happened at the time.

Then somewhat mastering her shock and grief,
Fearful of her accusers' lowering rage,

She tells the story, though her words are brief.
The tale seems hardly worthy of belief,
For why should death come from a harmless sage?

And now in her confusion and despair,
To show exactly how Pasquino died
She rubs the suspect herb against her bare
White teeth, commends her soul to Mercy's care,
And pitifully shows she has not lied.

In silence they cut down the shrub; beneath,
They find a foul toad squatting at the root,
The Satan of that bower, whose noisome breath
Proclaims it the dark minister of death;
For toads were venomous then by long repute.

I fear this business of the toad may seem
Unsatisfactory to those inclined
To live within a scientific scheme;
Why spend one's art upon a tale whose theme
Turns on a fable? But – ah well, never mind.

And then the keeper of the garden came
And with piled timber burned both bush and toad,
Cleansing the garden with a timely flame.
So may the lovers, purified from blame,
Ascend from fire to win a clear abode.

Rest now, my youth, under this hieroglyph,
This figured seal of silence; do not start
Up once more in agony and grief.
Sing, hidden bird, sing mercy and relief
To wanderers in the darkness of the heart.

Aubade

It was the hour of spells and charms.
Right at the crowing of the cock
She turned herself into my arms
And whispered tenderly: 'Unlock
In me the paradise of pleasure;
Now is the hour, and this the key.
Make haste, sweet, to possess each treasure
That searching shall create in me.

'Taste on my lids the tears that float
On the dark iris of my eyes.
Drink deeply from my murmuring throat
The yielded body's inmost cries.
O quickly, before dawn shall break
And day renew its thousand things,
Enter my paradise, touch and take
Your pleasure while the robin sings.'

Our loves were mingled in that hour,
Pure as the robin's piping call,
Scented with mystery like the flower
Of dusk-blue iris by the wall.
Thereafter day, from us renewing
Its eastern fires, drew from their rest
All things that move, their loves pursuing,
While our love slumbered on the breast.

Pietà

A year ago you came
Early into the light.
You lived a day and night,
Then died; no-one to blame.

Once only, with one hand,
Your mother in farewell
Touched you. I cannot tell,
I cannot understand

A thing so dark and deep,
So physical a loss:
One touch, and that was all

She had of you to keep.
Clean wounds, but terrible,
Are those made with the Cross.

St John's Park, New Town

Often I walk alone
Where bronze-green oaks embower
John Lee Archer's tower
Of solid Georgian stone.

Tradition is held there,
Such as a land can own
That hasn't much of one.
I care – but do I care?

Not if it means to turn
Regretful from the raw
Instant and its vow.

The past is not my law:
Queer, comical, or stern,
Our privilege is now.

Because

My father and my mother never quarrelled.
They were united in a kind of love
As daily as the *Sydney Morning Herald*,
Rather than like the eagle or the dove.

I never saw them casually touch,
Or show a moment's joy in one another.
Why should this matter to me now so much?
I think it bore more hardly on my mother,

Who had more generous feelings to express.
My father had dammed up his Irish blood
Against all drinking praying fecklessness,
And stiffened into stone and creaking wood.

His lips would make a switching sound, as though
Spontaneous impulse must be kept at bay.
That it was mainly weakness I see now,
But then my feelings curled back in dismay.

Small things can pit the memory like a cyst:
Having seen other fathers greet their sons,
I put my childish face up to be kissed
After an absence. The rebuff still stuns

My blood. The poor man's curt embarrassment
At such a delicate proffer of affection
Cut like a saw. But home the lesson went:
My tenderness thenceforth escaped detection.

My mother sang *Because*, and *Annie Laurie*,
White Wings, and other songs; her voice was sweet.
I never gave enough, and I am sorry;
But we were all closed in the same defeat.

People do what they can; they were good people,
They cared for us and loved us. Once they stood
Tall in my childhood as the school, the steeple.
How can I judge without ingratitude?

Judgment is simply trying to reject
A part of what we are because it hurts.
The living cannot call the dead collect:
They won't accept the charge, and it reverts.

It's my own judgment day that I draw near,
Descending in the past, without a clue,
Down to that central deadness: the despair
Older than any hope I ever knew.

The Cloak

With fifty years not lived but gone, we find
Death the Magician, his dark cloak crimson-lined,
    Performing to the crowd we've known.
    No volunteer? But the cloak is thrown

Over this or that one, and they disappear,
Leaving in us an astonished void, a fear,
    A decent numbness, or raw grief,
    And sometimes that obscene relief

We feel when one we've wronged, or who knew
    our shame,
Is not there to cast a shadow of blame –
    He may have forgotten, or forgiven:
    We wish him very well in heaven.

The cloak's lining, is that red for pain,
Or promise? Death doesn't comment or explain.
    Caped in darkness, do they fly
    Into the land of symmetry,

To the jade mountain veined with crystal streams,
Or whatever else they saw in dreams?
    We don't know. The house is packed;
    He doesn't need to change the act.

W. S. FAIRBRIDGE
1918-50

Consecration of the House

House, you are done . . .
                    And now before
The high contracting parties take
Final possession, let us stand
Silent for this occasion at the door,
Who here a lifelong compact make:
That you were not for trading planned,
Since barter wears the object poor,
But are henceforth our living stake
– And hereunto we set our hand.
    Be over us, be strong, be sure.

You may not keep from world alarms,
But from the daily wind and rain
Of guessed, or real, or of imagined wrong
Shadow us between your arms;
Be our sincere affection, and maintain
A corner here for art and song;
Yet no mere image of benumbing calms,
But a bold premiss, where the mind may gain
Purchase for adventurous journeys long.
    Be round us, and protect from harms.

A roof well timbered, hollow walls
Where the damp creep never comes,
Kiln-hardened joists no worm can bore;
Low sills where early daylight falls
Beneath wide eaves against the summer suns;
Huge cupboards, where a child might store
Surfeit of treasures; and no cramping halls,
But spacious and proportioned rooms;
A single, poured foundation, perfect to the core.
    Be our security against all calls.

305

Six orange trees, a lemon, and a passion vine.
All the lush living that endears
A home be yours: some asters for a show,
And roses by the wall to climb,
Hydrangeas fat as cauliflowers.
We who (how arduously!) have watched you grow,
We feel you in the very soil; and time
Shall tie your flesh with ours, your piers
And pipes intestinal, that anchor you below.
   Be through us, and prevent our fears.

Your windows face the north: the sun
At four o'clock leaps in;
By breakfast-time has swung so high
We lose him; till upon his downward run,
Swollen and yellow as a mandarin,
We catch his amber from the western sky.
Then when the night's dark web is spun,
Let your glass like a stationary comet gleam,
And lantern to our light supply.
   Be our sure welcome, and a wakeful beam.

Though we designed and built you, we
Will not outlive what we have done.
And if our children here succeed,
Our gain is now, and yours. Let this mortar be
Consecrate to death – a place where one
Gladly might wither to his glowing seed.
We serve you then in all humility
Who serve us, and by our sweat were won
When we had most need.
   Give us the obligations that make free.

House, you are done. . . . And nevermore
So painted, new, so arrogantly clean;
The tang of lime, the horrid clang
Of footsteps on the naked floor
Will fade to a serene

Patina of sounds and smells that hang
Like the reverberations of a shore
Of history: a hive where love has been,
And whence the future sprang.
    Be powerful above us all. Be sure.

ROSEMARY DOBSON

b. 1920

The Mirror

Jan Vermeer Speaks

Time that is always gone stays still
A moment in this quiet room.
Nothing exists but what we know,
The mirror gathers in the world,
Time and the world. And I shall hold
All summers in a stroke of gold.

Twilight, and one last fall of sun
That slants across the window-sill,
And, mirrored darkly in the glass
(Can paint attempt that unlit void?)
All night, oblivion, is stayed
Within the curtain's folded shade.

Upon the table bread and wine.
The earthen pitcher's perfect curve
Once spun upon the potter's wheel
Is pivot of the turning world,
Still centre where my peace abides,
Round moon that draws all restless tides.

There, it is done. The vision fades
And Time moves on. Oh you who praise
This tangled, broken web of paint,
I paint reflections in a glass:
Who look on Truth with mortal sight
Are blinded in its blaze of light.

Cock Crow

Wanting to be myself, alone,
Between the lit house and the town
I took the road, and at the bridge
Turned back and walked the way I'd come.

Three times I took that lonely stretch,
Three times the dark trees closed me round,
The night absolved me of my bonds
Only my footsteps held the ground.

My mother and my daughter slept,
One life behind and one before,
And I that stood between denied
Their needs in shutting-to the door.

And walking up and down the road
Knew myself, separate and alone,
Cut off from human cries, from pain,
And love that grows about the bone.

Too brief illusion! Thrice for me
I heard the cock crow on the hill,
And turned the handle of the door
Thinking I knew his meaning well.

Jack

My mortal husk is shelled at death
And shut inside a narrow box;
But he is coffined up in life:
Oh, what a bitter paradox!

He crouches low and supplicant,
His elbows knocking on the wood,
And with a cry too thin to hear
Implores the gods that somehow Good

Will bring him to a just release.
He waits the tapping at the locks,
He hears the children calling 'Jack!'
They think he sleeps inside his box.

They think he sleeps, but how he weeps,
His small tears falling with no sound
Like ghostly leaves that seem to fall
And fade upon a haunted ground!

We touched the lock and up he sprang,
Delight upon his simple face
As though he knew himself at last
The poet-prophet of his race –

All lowly Jacks shut up in boxes,
Composed of odds and ends of wood,
Who have such brief, amended chances
To see the world and find it good.

The children laughed and stretched their hands
And called again for Jack, for Jack,
But with a sudden brutal thrust
I caught his head and pushed him back,

Thinking, it does not do to muse
And give to toys of stick and straw
Emotions that belong to life
Lest the conclusions that we draw

Might yet be turned upon ourselves
To show each in his narrow piece
Of flesh and blood, like Jacks of straw
Shut down, and crying for release.

GWEN HARWOOD

b. 1920

The Wound

The tenth day, and they give
my mirror back. Who knows
how to drink pain, and live?
I look, and the glass shows
the truth, fine as a hair,
of the scalpel's wounding care.

A round reproach to all
that's warped, uncertain, clouded,
the sun climbs. On the wall,
by the racked body shrouded
in pain, is a shadow thrown;
simple, unchanged, my own.

Body, on whom the claims
of spirit fall to inspire
and terrify, there flames
at your least breath a fire
of anguish, not for this pain,
but that scars will remain.

You will be loved no less.
Spirit can build, make shift
with what there is, and press
pain to its mould; will lift
from your crucible of night
a form dripping with light.

Felix culpa. The sun
lights in my flesh the great
wound of the world. What's done
is done. In man's estate
let my flawed wholeness prove
the art and scope of love.

Triste, Triste

In the space between love and sleep
when heart mourns in its prison
eyes against shoulder keep
their blood-black curtains tight.
Body rolls back like a stone, and risen
spirit walks to Easter light;

away from its tomb of bone,
away from the guardian tents
of eyesight, walking alone
to unbearable light with angelic
gestures. The fallen instruments
of its passion lie in the relic

darkness of sleep and love.
And heart from its prison cries
to the spirit walking above:
'I was with you in agony.
Remember your promise of paradise,'
and hammers and hammers, 'Remember me.'

So the loved other is held
for mortal comfort, and taken,
and the spirit's light dispelled
as it falls from its dream to the deep
to harrow heart's prison so heart may waken
to peace in the paradise of sleep.

The Glass Jar
To Vivian Smith

A child one summer's evening soaked
a glass jar in the reeling sun
hoping to keep, when day was done
and all the sun's disciples cloaked
in dream and darkness from his passion fled,
this host, this pulse of light beside his bed.

Wrapped in a scarf his monstrance stood
ready to bless, to exorcize
monsters that whispering would rise
nightly from the intricate wood
that ringed his bed, to light with total power
the holy commonplace of field and flower.

He slept. His sidelong violence summoned
fiends whose mosaic vision saw
his heart entire. Pincer and claw,
trident and vampire fang, envenomed
with his most secret hate, reached and came near
to pierce him in the thicket of his fear.

He woke, recalled his jar of light,
and trembling reached one hand to grope
the mantling scarf away. Then hope
fell headlong from its eagle height.
Through the dark house he ran, sobbing his loss,
to the last clearing that he dared not cross:

the bedroom where his comforter
lay in his rival's fast embrace
and faithless would not turn her face
from the gross violence done to her.
Love's proud executants played from a score
no child could read or realize. Once more

to bed, and to worse dreams he went.
A ring of skeletons compelled
his steps with theirs. His father held
fiddle and bow, and scraped assent
to the malignant ballet. The child dreamed
this dance perpetual, and waking screamed

fresh morning to his window-sill.
As ravening birds began their song
the resurrected sun, whose long
triumph through flower-brushed fields would fill
night's gulfs and hungers, came to wink and laugh
in a glass jar beside a crumpled scarf.

Estuary
To Rex Hobcroft

Wind crosshatches shallow water.
Paddocks rest in the sea's arm.
Swamphens race through spiky grass.
A wire fence leans, a crazy stave
with sticks for barlines, wind for song.
Over us, interweaving light
with air and substance, ride the gulls.

Words in our undemanding speech
hover and blend with things observed.
Syllables flow in the tide's pulse.
My earliest memory turns in air:
Eclipse. Cocks crow, as if at sunset;
Grandmother, holding a smoked glass,
says to me, '*Look. Remember this.*'

Over the goldbrown sand my children
run in the wind. The sky's immense
with spring's new radiance. Far from here,
lying close to the final darkness,
a great-grandmother lives and suffers,
still praising life: another morning
on earth, cockcrow and changing light.

Over the skeleton of thought
mind builds a skin of human texture.
The eye's part of another eye
that guides it through the maze of light.
A line becomes a firm horizon.
All's as it was in the beginning.
Obscuring symbols melt away.

'*Remember this.*' I will remember
this quiet in which the questioning mind
allows reality to enter

its gateway as a friend, unchallenged,
to rest as a friend may, without speaking;
light falling like a benediction
on moments that renew the world.

Cocktails at Seven

Rhetorical trifles buzz and settle.
A bluestocking made bold by gin
leaves on a vulnerable face
some words like fingerprints of metal.
A tutor, who forgets his place,
laughs and does his promotion in.

All's covered up with frenzied sweetness.
Fudgy evasions circulate.
While A and B discuss the fitness
of fiddling with the failure rate
in X's subject, X is squeezing
the arm of B's young wife, and, seizing

a chance that seldom comes his way,
coaxes her to the balcony;
a group there, to his consternation,
is chopping up a book of verse.
B's wife, with brittle animation,
joins them. He goes inside to curse

colleagues and cocktail party women,
and gets an earful, with his wine,
of many-valued logics. Tired,
he looks around for someone human.
A leprous picture's being admired.
He yawns, and thinks of Wittgenstein.

If the question can be put at all
then we can answer it. How shall
the mind fly to its mark tonight?

The wine is eloquent, answering:
straight as an arrow means the thing
itself, the shaft, and not its flight.

X drinks, and grins. His wit is ready,
straight as an arrow, to be fired.
There's loathsome A, and B whose frown
is fixed on him; his aim's unsteady.
Those elegant harpies know he's tired.
Some other night he'll shoot them down.

COLIN THIELE

b. 1920

Up-Country Pubs

Each four-square limestone monument
Of praise to man's heroic thirsts
Heaves elementally and bursts
With gusty, shirt-sleeved merriment.

And though verandahs loll and sprawl
Or windows arch their lidless eyes,
And leaning posts apostrophize
The unsafe step and sagging wall

Yet Spring in street and paddock hurls
Its sap till every corner brims,
And morning jumps along the limbs
Of singing trees and ready girls.

With breasts and buttocks firm as trees
The barmaid-waitress blooms and sways;
And drinking timber-men appraise
How thighs grow upwards from the knees;

All day they dream and climb astride
Such satin-smooth and supple forks,
And cling and linger in their talks
Of stems so straight and scarfs so wide;

And tractor-drivers' glances state
That doors they know of have no locks
And love wears deftly zippered frocks
When sudden Spring and moonlight mate.

And shearers ask for leg and tart:
No matter what the table lacks
These come to them as midnight snacks,
Kept hot and served with lusty art.

And in the bar and Men's redoubt
Gargantuan drinkers handle beer
With massive feet apart, and steer
It grandly in or grandly out.

Australia Fair pursues its way,
And in its myth of malt and mirth
The nation's salt still goes to earth
On each up-country Saturday.

KATH WALKER

b. 1920

We Are Going

For Grannie Coolwell

They came in to the little town
A semi-naked band subdued and silent,
All that remained of their tribe.
They came here to the place of their old bora ground
Where now the many white men hurry about like ants.
Notice of estate agent reads: 'Rubbish May Be Tipped
    Here'.
Now it half covers the traces of the old bora ring.
They sit and are confused, they cannot say their thoughts:
'We are as strangers here now, but the white tribe are the
    strangers.
We belong here, we are of the old ways.
We are the corroboree and the bora ground,
We are the old sacred ceremonies, the laws of the elders.
We are the wonder tales of Dream Time, the tribal legends
    told.
We are the past, the hunts and the laughing games, the
    wandering camp fires.
We are the lightning-bolt over Gaphembah Hill
Quick and terrible,
And the Thunderer after him, that loud fellow.
We are the quiet daybreak paling the dark lagoon.
We are the shadow-ghosts creeping back as the camp fires
    burn low.
We are nature and the past, all the old ways
Gone now and scattered.
The scrubs are gone, the hunting and the laughter.
The eagle is gone, the emu and the kangaroo are gone
    from this place.
The bora ring is gone.
The corroboree is gone.
And we are going.'

KATH WALKER

Municipal Gum

Gumtree in the city street,
Hard bitumen around your feet,
Rather you should be
In the cool world of leafy forest halls
And wild bird calls.
Here you seem to me
Like that poor cart-horse
Castrated, broken, a thing wronged,
Strapped and buckled, its hell prolonged,
Whose hung head and listless mien express
Its hopelessness.
Municipal gum, it is dolorous
To see you thus
Set in your black grass of bitumen –
O fellow citizen,
What have they done to us?

MAX HARRIS

b. 1921

A Window at Night

And thus, intent, as if intention
Were a kind of looking into night
Through glass all stained with bright
Reflection of thought, returned unasked,

You mirror me unfleshed and glimmering,
As if I were but an image in your mind
That does me little credit, draws a blind
Gesture between intention and your heart.

You are intent, I judge, because you sense
The weather of me blows outside,
Yet you can discern only, wide
And smooth, your own discerning

Of an intention that I do not intend.
There are cold winds in the brain,
Leaves may whip and whirl, rain-
Drops roll down the outer unknown surface,

But neither this nor that, if love is real,
Is real, weather unseen or image thrown
By the light we light to make known
The thing outside us that moves our love.

Be easy, then, to love without intent,
To shelter from the darkness on a heath
In some calm innocence or deed of faith.
In which I'll join, to mirror your content.

MAX HARRIS

The Death of Bert Sassenowsky

A legend concerning the volcanic hole at Allendale,
in the Mount Gambier district of South Australia.

Let me set the elegiac tempo of this poem.
It is the slow, slightly anxious squeaking of a wagon
And the rolling eyewhites of its slavering oxen,
While a sky pitched low and flapping like a tent
Sheers up its winds from Cape Northumberland.

Above the faint steam of manure and leather
Bert Sassenowsky sits and rocks, spitting
Between his teeth at the ambling rumps below:
Shafts of late light impale his pale eyes:
In protest he stirs and threatens to come alive.

From under the shallow shadow of Mount Schanck
The pub at Bellum-Bellum slides into sight.
The plain of cows and lucerne, now in focus,
Has hidden its secret of aboriginal blood
That stained the soil black thirty years ago.

'Bellum-Bellum – aboriginal word for War'
In a thought more Greek than Latin, Sassenowsky
Scans the passing gums for scars of spears,
Imagines the snaking spines in the silent rushes,
The sudden shouts, the expert whistling nullahs

Of that great tribal war. Explosively
He leaps and slumps. 'They've got me!'
He weeps to the great round grinning bums
And lolls there dead until he smells the pub.

Morning rhythms past Bellum-Bellum are bleaker,
Full of echo. The winding track is etched
On a thin volcanic crust of porous rock.
In the great honeycomb of caves beneath
The dead sheep rattle to the thumping hooves.

Holes like sightless sockets beside the track
Bring Bert's hand to the whip. He yells
For company, and his beasts go delicate
As goats, picking their way in terror
To the wet and singing safety of the sea

Nine miles away. 'A bloody failure!
A carrier of dung! A servant of the servants
Of the soil!' Bert thought of Bert,
Of farms, of earth, of mangel-wurzels, mortgages,
Of the one true union his blind mind

Had wanted from the itching of his scythe
And the passionate bending, aching of his back.
'I love you not!' The caves give way
To the soft and lichenous bogs of Allendale,
His shout dissolves in a murmuring of springs.

His hate grows silent while the oxen strain.
Other than defeat, there is only irony
In return for the ardours of being human.
Only irony gives answer to the private prayer,
Dying is the common course of living.
'To hell with the district!' roars Bert in despair.

The wet soil on its wafer of rock collapses!
The first ox sits, and slides, a startled grotesque,
A stiffened corpse on a slippery dip,
And the next. A watery hole appears
Slimed with the rot of a million years.

Receives the mud, Bert, oxen, and the wheels,
The green scum spins, bobbles, settles,
Hisses, falls still, and listens, listens . . .
Through the hours and days the bodies sink
In quiet and blackness to the hot rivers

That rush and wind through the airless veins
Of the burning rocks miles down.

Envoi: the great stone wall built round this hole;
The road that bifurcates to either side;
The arum lilies that dream above the slime.

T. H. JONES

1921-65

My Grandfather Goes Blind

When the cataracts came down, he remembered
Verses, grew grumpier, but did not cry or break.
His bulk sagged, shrunk a little; he would have liked
The comforting presence of Mari, even as she was
Those last years, tiny woman in a big chair,
Talking mostly to her small boy sons, though
Sometimes she came back to this world for a moment.
When the cataracts came down, he remembered.
Was sometimes peevish, liked to talk in Welsh,
Was for the most part content with his old dog,
Blind, deaf, rheumatic, and pretty daft,
His firm stick, strong pipe, his memories – and me:
His grandson who could not speak his language,
Lacked his mountain skills, but in whom
He had a thorny faith not to be beaten
Down by any wind or language.
When the cataracts came down, creeping
Curtains over his shepherd eyes,
He talked to me.
            The old names still resound
For me of farms, men, ponies, dogs,
The old names that are all that I possess
Of my own language, proud then
And prouder now to call myself only
Young Crogau, old Crogau's grandson.

I remember when the cataracts came down.

NAN McDONALD

b. 1921

The Bus-Ride Home

'A bus will be provided for the mourners' –
That's common form at funerals down our way
But we would think it odd if someone said,
'A bus will be provided for the dead.'   *– provides a night*
And yet I almost thought the other day . . . *marxist trip*
No, it was just a normal bus-ride home
Or so it seemed at first. I always say
It's soothing to sit there, the day's work done,
Although you bump and rattle in your seat,
And watch blue dusk roll inland from the sea,
The darkening range loom up beyond the town,
The yellow lamps thin out along the street,
While scraps of talk float round you on a haze
Of smoke and beer. So, listening drowsily
I heard a voice: 'And how's old Jack these days?'
And the answer came: 'Old Jack? He's down six feet.'

Grinding our gears, we lurched and swung to take
The mountain road. '. . . buried last Tuesday week'
Was the next I heard, and then the first man said,
'Ah well, he was brought up to it.' And that,
It seemed, was that. They spoke of other things.
But I sat still, while through my empty head
The question echoed, startling me awake,   *We are all brought*
Brought up to it? Brought up to being dead? —   *up to die*

I remembered then, of course, these were old miners,   *poem is*
The words that fell with such a tolling sound   *full of ominous*
No doubt were ancient stuff to them, half joke,   *double meanings*
Half pride of trade. What's six feet to a miner?
Let others shrink from being laid underground.
Old Jack would fear no more the fall of the rock,

The water flooding in, the living tomb *[methane gas in air]*
Past help, the loaded air that waits the spark,
The creeping after-damp – those shapes of doom
Known all his years could never break his sleep
Or rise to haunt him, only six feet deep.

Yet my first thought would not be brushed away.
If that were true of him, true of us all?
The girl beside me held a bunch of jonquils, *[ride is metaphor for our passage through life to death]*
I had to turn my head, their scent had grown
So sickly sweet, so heavy. My hand lay
Across my bag, I saw how white the bone
Shone through the skin; and round us the weak light
Gave way before a stealthy tide of darkness
That scoured the hollows out in face and throat
And filled the sockets of the eyes with shade.
A cold breath drifted inward from the night
And someone shut the glass, as if in fear
Our flesh would crumble at its touch to dust.
The lamps had dropped behind us now and gone,
The trees like black plumes dipped above the road,
I thought of crying, 'Stop! I'll get off here –'
Too late, I knew. So the bus laboured on
Up the dark mountain with its mortal load
Brought up to death, in training for the grave . . .

That was the strangest ride I've had this year.

carpe Seim – make the best of it
This style of poem has been written for centuries – no positive suggestions of how we should live our life.

GEOFFREY DUTTON

b. 1922

Abandoned Airstrip, Northern Territory

At half past two on the moonlit taxiway,
Amongst the dispersal bays where only moonlight
Is dispersed, in trees around the silent runway
Where only the moon is airborne on the bright
Flash of an uncontrolling tower, sleep
Gliding crashed. Six warm, wakened people
Listening wider than daylight now. Terrible,
That cry, mixture of howl and bellow, deep
In the pale, tall Territory grass, fluid
As the building corridors the multitude
Of mountainous, solitary anthills hide.
Some lone creature silently pacing, quiet
As drought amongst hard nights of hated stars.
There! Again. A mad bull? No. The whites
Of woken eyes follow the whispers. The wounds in those
        cries
Are human, the pain and fury, they make the night
Air rub like a madman's cheek against a rifle.
Remember the drunk half-castes and a worse white
At that slatternly pub, murder would be a trifle
To as much rum as that. Again the height
Goes higher, and the roar climbs nearer to a howl.

There is always a man who makes a joke to prove
To himself that he is brave. He generally is.
'A bloody dingo, I tell you. Shove a towel
In it. Tell him I'm not going to move.
Bulls and half-castes! Yoo-raow-uh! Jesus!'

And so it is. The true, high, breaking note
Moving fast now, round the dispersal bays
Towards the take-off point of the empty strip.

328

One last word from a sleeping-bag. 'The ghost
Of some poor bastard who must have had his chips
Here, landing or taking off, plenty of ways
To go in.' A murmur from the bag beyond:
'More likely a Yank still wailing for a blonde.'

Dingo, lone howler on the strips of death,
No matter whether ghost or still drawing breath,
Outcast and individual you remain
And all we offer is the bait of pain.
This night, that also you have offered me,
To remember the reward of being free.

A few: Frank, Sandy, Sam, Paul, Geoff and Leigh.
Some shot or burnt in air, some hit by sea
As hard as land. What's left is left to me.
And when our friends go solo, we sing with all our might,
'Per Ardua ad Astra, up you, Jack, I'm all right.'

The parts of war were parts of a machine,
But all the machines were individual.
Spitfire, most elegant but not too lean,
Sensitive to the stroke of finger tips,
Easy mistress of the loop and roll.
Kittyhawk, broad back and solid hips,
Vertical Vengeance, dropping like a stone,
Brutish Buffalo of the big belly,
Mustang and Lightning, and the one home-grown,
Humble Wirraway, and humbler fellow,
The Tiger Moth that had all things done to it
And suffered all within its fabric suit.
Each landing, stalling, turning differently,
Not even one Tiger exactly like the next,
Yet all scrapped now, and like lost aircrew, dead.

Already the proof of being unperplexed
Sounds on the taxiway from each warm bed
In most untragic snores, and presently

329

The dingo too is quiet. There are men,
Odd, even, who value comradeship much more
Than singularity, and never again
Will comradeship be close as in a war.

One from the same battery at Alamein
Drove to Alice Springs to shake their hands,
At Port Augusta they were on the road again
In Syria, at Tennant Creek one spoke from the sands
Of Sidi Barrani. ('Who the hell was he?')
Good blokes all, or at least they used to be.

Moonlit airstrip, silent now, what high-octane
Illusions of freedom roared airborne from you!
In an age of dead kings we pilots were
Emperors of the empty sky. As plain
A target for holes to be shot through.
Our ermine was the clouds, a royal fur
For falling out of and revealing less
Of individual than of nakedness.
Yet when we landed, a beer mug in the mess
Frothed over all of that spare happiness.

It is perhaps the worst evil of war
To give that sense of belonging and of love,
And all for death, which peace cannot restore.
Freedom means loneliness, a place to move
About in, round which no one sets a border,
Names the time and target, gives the order.

Lacking lions and wars, our country bred
In us a fear of loneliness instead,
And when the two wars came it was no loss
To mates of the Birdsville Track or of The Cross.
Each man was free as a drunk A.W.L.,
And even if he wakened in a cell
At least it had a door that he knew well.

GEOFFREY DUTTON

Frank, Sam, and all the rest, I hear the oath
With which you'd greet the holy comradeship
Of Anzac Day. Greater bad luck you both
Would call it, leave the love. You'd rather slip
Out after the dingo than be yarded,
However highly cattle are regarded.

Dingo, lucky brute, no stranger calls you mate,
You are nobody's good bloke, you share no plate.
In a world where millions hanker to belong
You have the courage of a lonely song.
(Nice irony, that abos breed the dingoes up
To earn the Government bounty on each pup!)
But you at least may truly claim to be
Genuine vermin, the badge of being free.

An anthill shaped like a mother and a child
Is watching me. My friends and those I love
Are sleeping, while I alone still watch the moon.
Those cries that scarred the silence are all healed,
Fire-deaths have long burnt out, and where tyres spun
Little anthills are heaving through the tar.
Love can be shared, death not. However brave,
Years of freedom walk by on their own
And loneliness will never have a child.
Love takes its sharing moment, that we have,
High above ant and airstrip as the moon,
With friend or lover, mother, wife or child,
In bed or cloud or desert, none the same.
The sharing and the loneliness of love
We have. Where all are equal none are wild.

January

In summer when the hills are blond
O dark-haired girl with wave-wet ankles
Bare your skin to the sun and to me.
All summer go brown, go salt by the sea.

331

O dark-haired girl stay close to me
As grass that shivers on the hill's hot flank
Or your spine that trembles under my hand;
The pale grass is dead, but not so the sea.

Across the paddocks stooks and bales
In separate civilizations stand
Like tribesmen's tents and townsmen's cities,
While a dark girl swims in distant seas.

The sun's blond fire turns red and black,
A horrible army runs through hay
By flank of hill through hair of tree
And the ashes fall upon the sea.

Stook-tents, bale-cities all fall down
And fences keep the dead stock back.
O dark-haired girl, stay close to me,
All summer go brown, go salt by the sea.

Ky in Australia: A Postscript

Sometimes, to fool the people, most of the people,
It is enough to be cool, modest and sincere, so sincere.
You peel off your black jacket, take the guns from your
    hips,
And in a silk suit show no fear, no fear
Of being assassinated by a placard shrieking 'Murderer.'
Of course you have a beautiful wife, who also is sincere.
And the crass black word 'Fascist' on a banner,
Stale as the 1930's, is an old man being sincere.
It appears that in the background, the Uncles, Sam and
    Ho,
Are also being sincere, behind the same white beards,
Though it is very confusing to know that the North and the
    South
And the Vietcong would all join together to fight the
    Chinese,

(Who are appallingly sincere), when we thought all along,
    told
By our Harold, who is so sincere he cannot stop smiling,
That the faceless monster, communism, had Chinese eyes.
The helicopter, with the cool silk couple, chops over the
    city
Where the teacher lifts his head from the examination
    papers,
'Wordsworth was a great poet because he was so sincere,'
While the children in the puppet theatre do not hear for
    laughing
At the little man on strings whose fear is so sincere.

Our Crypto-Wowsers

No wowsers they, who drink and smoke
With decent wives who do not mind;
They know the latest dirty joke,
Progress never leaves them behind.
In fact, they are the ones who lead it,
Through Apex and the J.C.C. –
Public spirit for those who need it,
The ideals and smiles of Rotary,
Mateship worn on the lapel
Where every Joseph is a Joe,
And nothing is too dear to sell
And no one is too proud to know.
At night behind the sand-blasted doors
The sexes take their guided tour,
After the little woman pours
Crème de menthe and parfait amour
In stem-ware amongst soft furnishings;
A birch-tree keeps the wrought-iron cool
And a wagtail by the Holden sings
To a concrete flamingo in the pool.
The house is vacuumed every day
Which goes to prove that cleanliness,

GEOFFREY DUTTON

For living the most boring way,
Is certainly next to godliness.
The good men leave no lawn untrimmed;
There is no plot but they have fenced it;
And like the wowsers they have hymned:
'There ought to be a law against it.'
Fat boys whom middle age makes lean,
They aim to keep their children chaste,
Forgetting how, by seventeen,
Their hand had slipped below the waist
And many a month was filled with fear.
Those of their contemporaries
Who have not 'settled down' are queer,
Not queer like homosexual fairies
But even worse, the queer that means
'Most peculiar', 'odd', hell-bent
Like kids on motor-bikes in jeans,
Fit for corporal punishment.
They pray their children may emerge
Not brilliant, but ordinary,
Not grow a beard, or get an urge
To study biochemistry.
They may meet New Australians, but
Never ask an Italian home;
Our broken bottles never cut,
Not like the knives they use in Rome.
Support by all means leagues and clubs
And flock to lecturers who give
Our egos little pats and rubs
And praise the way of life we live.
With luck within a hundred years
Australia will have abolished crime
And surnames, dirty books and queers,
Dry wine, old buildings, art and rhyme
(Except for commercials on TV,)
And all across the great outback,
Made safe for kiddies, there will be
A barbecue for every shack;

On greens where now the desert sprawls
Golfers will knock their little balls,
While God, in the Safety Council's Chair,
Smiles down upon Australia Fair.

ALEXANDER CRAIG

b. 1923

Sea at Portsea

Blue, viridescent, with a cold edge
    against the biscuit
  hue, the yellow and brown
  of this nude, populated

rim, its light shifts with the light
    of sun moon stars,
  shafts stabbing from a beacon
  night-beams of flounder-spears.

We dared to slither from it once,
    now revisit
  no longer than we need to.
  Daylong its sunlit spray

is barely glimpsed, the sheerest drape
    drawn over
  the sand, across the shallows
  where the sharp-toothed prototype

of streamlined grace is driven in
    by hunger. Why
  do I seem baptized beneath
  my beach-umbrella, landlocked

in that evangelistic tent
    (its congregation
  the cold-eyed gulls, the sermon
  unspoken)? It's a dream

like others: it will pass. I watch
    with a kind of awe
  the vestals in bikinis
  tending the sacred fire.

DOROTHY HEWETT

b. 1923

Go Down Red Roses

'Go down all my blood-red roses' is the chorus of an old English
sea chanty

O when shall we two meet again
In thunder and in lightning and in rain,
By what strange waters and by what dry docks,
By what mean streets alive with summer frocks,
And girls, and men with grease across their lips,
Who fire the boilers on what lonely ships?

By the waters of the Yarra I sat down and wept
For you, timber-cutter, cane-cutter, black-faced stoker on
    the *Ellaroo*,
Melbourne to Newcastle, Sydney to Rockhampton . . .
Shipped out of port, anywhere, anything new,
And the Yarra waters are muddy with a thousand tears
Of shop girl, typist, process-worker and whore,
By the pitiless street light, the park and the empty door,
And the train in the cutting whispering nevermore . . .
When the footsteps die at the end of the empty street,
When the faces die in the neon sign and the pub closes,
The door shuts, the ship pulls out of the dock, this is the
    end –
And go down all my red roses.
I weep for you, my love, who will not be loved,
You wandering men with a swag of dust on your shoulders,
Carting a holey blanket to the world's end,
The Southern Cross over your right eye and your left
Turned inwards, fist in your pocket, punchy and warm,
A hole in your heart and a star where the blanket's torn,
Walking, ah! God knows where, the Yarra streets under
    your footsteps.

337

Look out for the bodgies! They swing a hard bottle at
    night,
And the Southern Cross has a wan and a wandering light,
And the neon sign's blood-red, blood-red as a rose.
Oh! tears and mud and regret where the Yarra flows,
And the seagull screams on the ship and the wild wind
    blows. Go down red roses . . .
'Dining in town tonight, a warm welcome awaits you.'
Arms and kisses and Melbourne draught at the London
    pub.
The bed is warm, the woman is warm and willing,
A breast to fondle, an early start to curse,
And promise is easy, conclusion is something worse.
Running before the tide out of Sydney to Rockhampton,
Do you carry my letter in your pocket like a promise of
    love?
Continents swing between us, desert and sand and scrub,
The plane dips, the Bight arcs in a sunlit dazzle of surf,
Two thousand miles measure two thousand years,
And you are gone . . . over the rim of the Tasman Sea,
And the Yarra mud has swallowed up all my tears.
I sleep alone with a kiss-print on my lips,
The thud of my heart beats in the engine-room,
Ah! the ship is hollow and hollow thuds my heart,
Ah! hollow, hollow, the cormorant flaps and crows.
On the Yarra bank the red rose blooms and blows.
The flowers of Spring sink in the muddied river,
And go down, go down all my red roses.

O when shall we two meet again
In thunder and in lightning and in rain,
By what strange waters and by what dry docks,
By what mean streets alive with summer frocks
And girls, and men with grease across their lips,
Who fire the boilers on what lonely ships?

Timber-cutter, cane-cutter, black-faced stoker on the
    Ellaroo,

Melbourne to Newcastle, Sydney to Rockhampton,
Shipped out of port, letters are following, anything new!
Nowhere to go, it's late and the last pub closes.
The pillow lies like a stone under your head,
The prostitute's shoes grow cold under your bed.
The bed's still warm in the last port where you slept.
By the waters of the Yarra I sat down and wept
Go down, go down all my blood-red roses.

NANCY KEESING

b. 1923

The Goat with the Golden Eyes

They are grooming a brindled goat for the judging ring.
His stubbed horns shine with wax, his delicate hooves
Twinkle blacking; his sparse beard combed to a fringe,
Coat crimped and brushed: a most elegant petty King
Whose wives, one lean-ribbed with kid, one heavy with milk,
Nuzzle at hay, awaiting their Lord. They are led
In single-file to the grey-dust-coated judge
Who garlands the Attic trio with ribbons of silk;
And the male goat shakes his whiskery head, he sees
An appraising crowd, pricks twitching ears at the noise
Of a bagpipe band – for who invented the Pipes?
Who led the wreathéd tribute on Marduk's frieze?
His blank, slot-pupilled, cold and golden eyes
Curtain an ancient frenzy – burnished hooves
That scuff in dust and papers once stripped flesh
And kicked hot blood from Maenads' streaming thighs.

ERIC ROLLS

b. 1923

Sheaf Tosser

The lone crow caws from the tall dead gum:
Caw. Caw. Caw-diddle-daw.
And judges the stack with one bleared eye
Then turns the other to fix its lie:
Caw. Caw. Caw-diddle-daw.
There are four tiers of sheaves on the waggon yet
And one more loaded is standing by;
My arms are aching and I'm dripping sweat
But the sun is three axe-handles in the sky
And I must toss sheaves till dark.

It is fourteen feet from the ground to the eaves:
Caw. Caw. Caw-diddle-daw.
And two feet six to the third roof row;
Six feet high stands the load below:
Caw. Caw. Caw-diddle-daw.
Ten feet six now must I pitch,
Into the centre of the stack I throw
To the turner and the short-handled fork with which
He thrusts sheaves to the builder in endless flow,
Butts out and long-side down.

There are twenty-five crows on the old dry gum:
Caw. Caw. Caw-diddle-daw.
Thirteen on one branch and twelve on the other
And each one calls as loud as his brother:
Caw. Caw. Caw-diddle-daw.
My hands are blistered, my sore lips crack
And I wonder whether the turner would smother
If a hard throw knocked him off the stack
In a slide of hay; but there'd come another
And I'd still toss sheaves.

341

There are thousands of crows on the gaunt white gum:
Caw. Caw. Caw-diddle-daw.
The reds are pale in the western sky
And the stack is more than sixty feet high:
Caw. Caw. Caw-diddle-daw.
My fork grows heavy as the light grows dim.
There are five sheaves left but I've fear of a whim
That one of the crows has an evil eye
And the five sheaves left will be there when I die
For each bird's forgotten how to fly
Till he drives out my soul with the force of his cry:
Caw. Caw. Caw. Caw.
Caw. Caw. Caw. Caw.

The Knife

There is the knife. See the blade curved
And ground as thin as a new moon;
And the handle: look at the wood carved
To fit the palm as trim as pain.
Though it is there, though I can reach it,
I do not dare to touch it.
Why from a calm chair should I trouble
To seize an angry blade laid on a table?
It is safer not to test oneself.
The fact is often less than the belief
And sometimes more. The silent steel
May gall the madness latent in the skull.
A knife is not a pretty thing to be fondled.
It must be taken and intently handled.

The knife is there. I look upwards away
And see on the ceiling shimmer a reflected ray;
Or out the window to tangle my thoughts in grass.
There are seven knives recurrent in the heavy glass.

My palm is hollow and the handle rounded.
Fingers cannot hold on shapeless air.
The knife. The knife. All other thought is blinded.
My sudden stretching oversets the chair.

DAVID ROWBOTHAM

b. 1924

The Candle is Going Out

Dear Lawson, – The candle is going out. Truth
Is the wick-flame. Once, in a Picton room, in the south
Cold alpine island, you wrote the story down
By night that I remember, now, alone
In another night, a northern room, beside
My page the going candle like a guide,
Like the candle that ended the guttering word it lit
When you, wick-blind, acknowledged the truth of it.

I should explain for truth my metaphor
Is neither forced nor fancied. Storm, an hour
Ago or longer, guttered and blew out
The blaze of my time's candle-power, more bright
Than any that you, lodger last century, knew,
And less inclined, keeping the page in view,
To give so closely to writers in the night
The sense time passes and word depends on sight.

This, then, is why I think of you there,
Of your tale of the young improvident traveller
Pencilled with provident living wit, and how
Your hand was stopped by the wick-flame falling low
To the dim Picton table. Even if the scene
Was not as you told or not as I take it to mean,
Not wholly, and the candle going out was tall
Really, your craft still saw the truth for all.

Writers by night today, as roomed, are yet
Shadowed the same as you and cannot forget,
Along with all men feeling as concerned,
That life, the candle, never can be burned

344

To match the work or worthiness in mind.
We aspire, and fatally invite the wind,
The wind of darkness that wears the great god-send
Of senses down and snuffs at the vigour we spend.

My candle here becomes the barometer
For time and storm, the destined dark and near
Visible invisible, outside and within,
That blows away the light and blinds the pen
I wield for providence unproved. Where you
Preceded me in this and the task I do,
Though borne under you yet bring comfort through,
The gain in the act of embarking to pursue.

Something, indeed much, was done. Though brief
The candle you lit, that burned, burning life,
Believing the journey suffered or enjoyed
From land to island and shade must so be said,
You in the distant Picton night are part
Of history's province of aspiring art,
Present, in your act of faith, your light of words.
The candle is going out. My kind regards.

First Man Lost in Space

I took in death
With your goodbye.
Then what have I
To fear of death?

I live with death
As with a star.
It is not far
To go with death

When death, the fear
That floats the earth,
Stars empty forth.
The earth dies here,

345

The seas, not I.
I mourn the earth.
And I mourn death
Its birth goodbye.

You buried me
With one red roar.
Do not grieve more
The given. See,

As I see now,
The atom's urn,
In which you turn
The seaborne prow

And craft of earth
About, for fear,
In seas of death,
So empty here. . . .

What is it bears
My craft to birth,
My ark of earth
Away from yours?

The thing I seem,
The time I have,
The light you gave,
The launch of dream.

And a great star
Is standing by.
I have gone through
The kingdom's eye.

I go before,
Before gods grew,
To where none knew
Creation, nor,

Trailing the plume
Of ice and fire,
The rose desire.
Another bloom

Shall summon me,
Shall save us all,
And the past be
Perpetual. . . .

VINCENT BUCKLEY

b. 1925

Late Tutorial

The afternoon dark increases with the clock
And shadows greening on the cabinet.
Teacher of youth, and more than half a fool,
How should you catch those shadows in your net?

Outside, the world's late colour calls us home:
Not to the refuge of familiar art
Nor house of settling wood, but to the first
Home, to the savage entry of the heart.

There, where the dry lips are cooled with words
And every hand worships the love it serves,
Perhaps we'll find some comfort: the deep spring
Rising, and soft renewal of the nerves

In poetry with its constant singing mouth.
Open the door, then; numbed with winter air,
They smile, and move inside; the colours fade
Ringing my head; they seat themselves, and stare.

So I must learn that these, the learners, come
To teach me something of my destiny;
That love's not pity, words are not mine alone,
And all are twined on the great central tree.

How shall I answer them, give ultimate name
To the nerves at war, the mind in dishabille?
Better to pace with the slow clock, and teach them
Quibbles with which to meet adversity.

Their thoughts come, slow, from a cold bed. Their needs
Are close to me as the smell of my own flesh.
Their timid guesses grow, soft-fallen seeds,
To grace my mind with pain. And should I say

'O man is sick, and suffering from the world,
And I must go to him, my poetry
Lighting his image as a ring of fire,
The terrible and only means I have;

And, yet, I give too much in rhetoric
What should be moulded with a lifetime's care,
What peace alone should strike, and hear vibrate
To the secret slow contraction of the air,'

The talk would die in loud embarrassment,
The books be rustled, and the noses blown
In frenzy of amazement at this short
Still youthful puppet in academic gown.

I cannot, but speak measured foolish words:
Shelley was fitful, Keats a dozing fire.
Pass with the light, poor comrades. You and I
Follow but feebly where our words aspire.

Colloquy and Resolution

All beasts are beasts of prey. We spend
Our nameless anger in the bruit
Against each other's loins, and end
Partners in our hot pursuit.

Or so we've heard, and heard. The case
Is argued nightly, while the moon
Runs on her level climbing course
And the trees loosen their weight for noon,

For a great sun striking leaf and breast.
Those thousand beds of argument!
But we will clasp, and feed, and rest
Still, as of old, impenitent.

The young moon heals her drowsy sky.
Ah, could I breathe my urgent breath
Into your nostrils, so decry
Those plaguing words, we'd ravish death

And bring all walls to bud, and make
Our senses prefaces of light,
A glitter of strands no cry might break,
Midsummer fibres of delight.

And what of what we've heard, that love
Is the scaly palm, the sweating bed?
Now in the twining arms' remove
Envision the uprising head:

When, out of the pit, from the hurt womb
That is our half-world of desire,
The child shall rise and, unconsumed,
Light with his hands the healing fire.

Places

For J. Golden, S.J.

I

Walking at ease where the great houses
Shelter the assorted trees that someone
Planted, once, to shelter them, I do
My voluntary patrol. The wind moves
Houses and trees together, till they breathe
As though I breathed with them, systole, diastole
Of the built and the growing.
Fair enough. We used to picture
Paradise both as a garden and a city.
Here it's a green hardihood, a tender
Rallying beyond concupiscence.
So I patrol. There's not a soul in sight.
It was an older, foreign voice that cried
'The swarm of bees enfolds the ancient hive'.

II

But love is a harsh and pure honey.
The world is brought alive with us
So many times. One night I learned the resurrection
In still water. Sea-mist moves
On a land that in its steeped
Peach-dark fruits,
Resin,
Pods,
Is warm as blood.
I lean on the bridge, looking down.
Under the utter moon all things reach
Their height in water; there the thin
Unbreathing tree touches the depth of cloud
Downward; there light vibrates in the sky.
In this voluptuous arrest of colour
I still feel the day's heat on my eyelids.
At noon the summer webbed us in; but now
I almost smell the next year's seed.

III

Bound from Mass, my blood fresh as the sea.
In the city light there are pools, deep-groined,
Where the gilled bodies leap down and glide;
And the sea-smell, drifting like the sounds of sleep,
Gives air a distance, not a shape,
And light itself is recreated, made
Native to all bodies. I think how once,
Hardly thinking, in a strange church,
A man, forgetting the common rubric, prayed
'O God, make me worthy of the world',
And felt his own silence sting his tongue.

Burning the Effects

By the chill winds to home. O cherry tree,
Cold flesh, cold stone, cold branch, and dripping leaves,
Stand near the house that could not fathom me
Or hold him, the earth your damp earth retrieves.

Mostly, I light a backyard fire to burn
The poor hoardings; a whole lumber-room,
Heaved out of doors, struggles to return
Some showing for a life's delirium;

Flakes whirl like gusts of breath or late desire
Upward; I learn in the new heat of air
How much seeks out its element in fire,
How much, too, mocks its own weakness there.

A mouse or lone rat scuttles in the wall
Where once, as indestructible, the bees
Swarmed with a sound like burning. Still and all,
Things get cleared away, and a cold breeze

Winnows the sparks enough to make a shine
Of the black air against the cherry tree.
Nothing of it is absolutely mine,
And he who hoarded it owned nothing. Free.

Fellow Traveller

Give him this day his bread of indignation,
For he is Inspector of our Consciences;
Give him his daily signature
To a joint letter; hear him explain,
Oh no it's not the case itself so much,
It's the principle;
And listen, with half an ear, to hear
Behind the almost-empty pipe,
The almost-empty eyes,
The high blast of a revolver shot.

Youth Leader

In the wedge head the eyes are
Too glibly moved, under hair combed forward
In the Roman fashion.
A programme in a hair style.
His torso holds the promise of a paunch.
He is big with history
And the streets go crazy at his lifted hand.
How many dead will bloat the gutters
When he learns to lower it?

LAURENCE COLLINSON

b. 1925

Hand in Hand

The unbearable elegance of young lovers
pardoning the pavement with their velvet steps;
the city receding, the ticking neon,
the hills and churches pleasurably tumbling,
the startled girders stiffening with pride.

The sky gapes with questions,
the night somersaults,
the day stutters morning,
the dawn still hurts after twenty-four hours.

Their own smile of the young lovers,
the detachable sadness of the young lovers
uncertain of knowledge of sadness,
transmutes all objects to chattels:
objects, men, women,
boxes and trees and persian kittens,
all bow at the waist and say please.

And I bow also
as the unbearably elegant young lovers drift by me,
and I sing in a joy without language;
and turn aside, in terror of the noon.

JILL HELLYER

b. 1925

The Way to the Headland

When the stranger asked how far I did not know.
The first time it had seemed so short a way
Straight from the humpback scrubland while the day
Closed like a bud around us.
                                I remembered the glow
Of dusk on yellow earth and how the sea
Seemed strangely near as it curled about the reef
And how solemn had been that moment of belief
That we were sharing this affinity.

Yet the way had been so long the second time,
Stumbling alone, and breathless: I remembered
The barren sky, the headland sparsely timbered
And facing the bleak harbour after the climb,
How I had leaned to watch the waves torment
The crumbling rocks and how the cliffs plunged down
And down to soundless currents where to drown
May or may not have been an accident.

Not so on known tracks where the image stuns,
Not in neat gardens spilling Latin names
Where stark japonicas emerge as flames
And wattles droop their melting yellow suns.
How far from one transience of understanding
To another shared on the wind-frozen edge
Of life? We had touched, out on that sandstone ledge,
The pulse beat of the infinite, demanding
Nothing of one another.
                                Yet, despite that,
Or because of it, on separate paths we left:
You, as a man, strong; I, as a woman, bereft,
With the long night stretched before me, dark and flat.

355

I could not tell how long it took to reach
The headland, if it could be reached again
Or was a fantasy that might remain
As so many bones for truth to strip and bleach.
I was as much a stranger there as he
And only knew the near familiar things,
Japonicas that open petalled wings
And the melting suns upon the wattle tree.
Sharp, rich and vivid things, the grass fresh-mown,
White apple blossoming and the summer-scent,
But all of it one dark imprisonment
As every place where I must walk alone.

If you should come to me, if we went back
And found the measure of each other's minds
I'd tell the stranger then how far it winds
And with new courage turn to face the track.

J. R. ROWLAND

b. 1925

Canberra in April

Vast mild melancholy splendid
Day succeeds day, in august chairmanship
Presiding over autumn. Poplars in valleys
Unwavering candleflames, balance over candid
Rough-linen fields, against a screen of hills

Sending invisible smokes from far below
To those majestic nostrils. A Tuscan landscape
On a larger scale; for olives eucalypts
In drifts and dots on hillheads, magpie and crow
For field-birds, light less intimate, long slopes stripped

Bare of vine or village, the human imprint
Scarcely apparent; distances immense
And glowing at the rim, as if the land
Were floating, like the round leaf of a water-plant
In a bright meniscus. Opposite, near at hand,

Outcrops of redbrick houses, northern trees
In costume, office-buildings
Like quartz-blocks flashing many-crystalled windows
Across the air. Oblivious, on their knees,
Of time and setting, admirals pick tomatoes

In their back gardens, hearty
Bankers exchange golf-scores, civil servants
Their after-office beers; the colony
Of diplomats prepares its cocktail parties
And politicians their escape to Melbourne.

This clean suburbia, house-proud but servantless
Is host to a multitude of children
Nightly conceived, born daily, riding bikes,

Requiring play-centres, schools and Progress
Associations: in cardigans and slacks

Their mothers polish kitchens, or in silk
White gloves and tight hats pour each other tea
In their best china, canvassing the merits
Of rival plumbers, grocers, Bega milk
And the cost of oil-fired heating or briquettes.

To every man his car, his wife's on Thursday
Plus one half-day she drops him at the office
(Air murmurous with typewriters) at eight-forty
To pick him up for lunch at home; one-thirty
Sees the streets gorged with his return to duty

And so the year revolves; files swell, are closed
And stored in basements, Parliaments adjourn
And reassemble, speeches are made and hooted.
Within the circle of the enfranchised
These invite those and are themselves invited,

At formal dinners, misprints of the *Times*
Compete with anecdotes of Rome or Paris
For after all, the capital is here.
The general populace sprays its roses, limes
Its vegetable patch and drinks its beer:

Golf at the weekend, gardening after five,
Indoor bowling, TV day and night
Lunchtime softball, shopping late on Friday –
As under glass the pattern of the hive
Swarms in its channels, purposeful and tidy,

Tempting romantics to dismay and spite,
Planners to satisfaction, both to heresy.
For everywhere, beyond the decent lawn
A visionary landscape wings the sight
And every child is rebel and unknown.

So long as daylight moon, night laced with stars
And luminous distance feed imagination
There's hope of strangeness to transcend, redeem
Purblind provincial comfort: summer fires
Under prodigious smokes, imperious storms,

A sense of the pale curving continent
That, though a cliché, may still work unseen
And, with its script of white-limbed trees, impart
A cure for habit, some beneficent
Simplicity or steadiness of heart.

Dawn Stepping Down

Dawn stepping down into the garden
Stepping down
Lightly about the roofs, sets in bare trees
Heavy lumps of birds, woodpigeons; places
Ladder against wall, uncovers
The houses' naked sleeping faces
And closed eyes

Sends overhead a film of cloud
Shallow blue
Spellbound vapour: stepping down
Across the printless lawn, invisible
Palpable being, whose presence all the choir
Of sparrow and pigeon now makes audible
In celebration

Till I, holding a feeding baby
Notice his eyes
Turn to the window, and following
Almost see the unhurried passing angel
Whose cool gauze brushes the crocus
Darts clustered under trees, the fleeting angle
Of a bent wing.

FRANCIS WEBB

b. 1925

On First Hearing a Cuckoo

It was never more than the two unchanging words
Heard first in the coming green of daybreak,
The sleepier green than sleep, with a sheer white
Between this yawning advancing green and the colour
Of all lights out. Not consciousness, the awakening early
    green:
For that was the steep curtain, immediate
Structure of pain and learning, familiar ratlings.

With this taut white wariness two words
Involved themselves, formed and changeless, cool and
    haunting.
Because they were of distance
I had tended to link them with the young tremulous
Begging green now scrambling in a tree,
Moon-eyed at the window, wanting to be let in
(Yes! now the breeze of green rejected distance
Pulled cleverly at the curtain, exposed a laundrymark,
Disordering the image while reaching not the self's
Hand-scoring rigs). But they were quite apart,
So freely entering, so at home,
Not softening, not disturbing, but making distant.
Old-story-devious green, all shapes and sizes
Of illusion, turned right out of doors:
Two words, always the same words, freely entering.

Heard next whilst playing cricket at eleven
In the robust green, long strider and talker
Of vital distances, while the Downs kept on and on –
Voyaging green – and chaffed the skyline's thin
Stalkage of personal mood along their sides;
Tree bulged, battening on a sleek green's
Passionate act and story, plump with spring.

And here among the withstood gross distances –
Green loggerheads – two level and small words
Never at odds with self, never with green.

And last at dinner, when the dissolute green
Summoned to bedside each image, unelectric
Against lights out: – gay sufferer with the syrinx,
Become this tree, enigmatic as a covered statue:
Green shoulders of the Downs, converge
To the humble, drooping lekythos,
The dead's soul unstirring at the folded forelock:
Shadows, freeze –
Sad elongated faces, fine hands extended
Downward, pouring the winds, shivering in the queasy
Grey trickle of nightfall and mixing airs.
Dissolving distances. Then the changeless words
Unelectric among the going green and the advancing
Colour of lights out and the nagging strands
Of an anger. And cool before the cavernous
Green of sleep which alone could lose them.

What in themselves? Twelve hours shaken away,
Not the abandoned green remained, not self,
Not spring, not Surrey, no, nor merely
A dead word-haunted man. Two words remained –
The language foreign, childish perhaps, or pitiable –
Heedless of enmity, again and again coming
To a taut candour, to a loose warbling green.

The Yellowhammer

Working, tumbling, doddering face of war,
Fog overruns without thunder a taut shire.
Deft and cynical mercenary winds
Inform the slewing grey, the errant wheels
Into intrigue upon browbeaten hills.
Age trickles from the docile lines of lands.

Colours grovel, the soused logos of the sun
Lisps a last word from sallow wash and glimmer.
Cloud-structures of reason crumble without sound.
It is the song, the footfall of the yellowhammer
Will not give ground
To earth, sky, day, and night crouching as one.

To know the ancient ritual brotherhood
Of light dispersed and sucked up piecemeal, dumb,
This is the grey rat nibbling at the soul:
For all that urgent blood,
Communiqué of the hammer-heart of God,
Flooding the wizened limb
Would leap past time, go spangling into truce
With snowfall, small hour, toss the ultimate news
To frontal dawn from tiny corpuscle.
Plasma in chains, here no veins intersect.
– It is the heel of summer,
It is the song, the footfall of the yellowhammer,
Leaps of a sudden past the intellect.

Fog-satellite, the street-lamp can but tell
Petty parables of the heretical will
Of power as conqueror: every yard's a swarm
Of furious atoms, bloodless, directionless,
At one another's throats in helpless harm.
We have known sober clouds run mad as this,
But sometimes the steep groan, steel-blue claws of search
And agony hither and thither scratched at earth,
Frantic to clutch the centre and the form –
Such fossicking could only end in death.
Outline of fog has no objective, clamour.
It is the song, the footfall of the yellowhammer
Continues on the march.

Wraiths of derelict cattle in a row
Moon round this muffled loiterer of a tree,
We never saw him so forlorn as now,
Arms asprawl to hostile nothing, creak and stammer

Pandering windward, off the living map.
It is the song, the footfall of the yellowhammer
Suggests trim elderly green, flagon of sap;
Yes, it is true
Even of such a ransacked fogey tree:
Worlds back, life cooked his supper zealously
And breasted him for certain hours with blue.

Pneumo-Encephalograph

Tight scrimmage of blankets in the dark;
Nerve-fluxions, flints coupling for the spark;
Today's guilt and tomorrow's blent:
Passion and peace trussed together, impotent;
Dilute potage of light
Dripping through glass to the desk where you sit and write;
Hour stalking lame hour . . .
May my every bone and vessel confess the power
To loathe suffering in you
As in myself, that arcane simmering brew.

Only come to this cabin of art:
Crack hardy, take off clothes, and play your part.
Contraband enters your brain;
Puckered guerilla faces patrol the vein;
The spore of oxygen passes
Skidding over old inclines and crevasses,
Hunting an ancient sore,
Foxhole of impulse in a minute cosmic war.
Concordat of nature and desire
Was revoked in you; but fire clashes with fire.

Let me ask, while you are still,
What in you marshalled this improbable will:
Instruments supple as the flute,
Vigilant eyes, mouths that are almost mute,

X-rays scintillant as a flower,
Tossed in a corner the plumes of falsehood, power?
Only your suffering.
Of pain's amalgam with gold let some man sing
While, pale and fluent and rare
As the Holy Spirit, travels the bubble of air.

Harry

It's the day for writing that letter, if one is able,
And so the striped institutional shirt is wedged
Between this holy holy chair and table.
He has purloined paper, he has begged and cadged
The bent institutional pen,
The ink. And our droll old men
Are darting constantly where he weaves his sacrament.

Sacrifice? Propitiation? All are blent
In the moron's painstaking fingers – so painstaking.
His vestments our giddy yarns of the firmament,
Women, gods, electric trains, and our remaking
Of all known worlds – but not yet
Has our giddy alphabet
Perplexed his priestcraft and spilled the cruet of innocence.

We have been plucked from the world of commonsense,
Fondling between our hands some shining loot,
Wife, mother, beach, fisticuffs, eloquence,
As the lank tree cherishes every distorted shoot.
What queer shards we could steal
Shaped him, realer than the Real:
But it is no goddess of ours guiding the fingers and the
        thumb.

She cries: *Ab aeterno ordinata sum.*
He writes to the woman, this lad who will never marry.
One vowel and the thousand laborious serifs will come
To this pudgy Christ, and the old shape of Mary.

Before seasonal pelts and the thin
Soft tactile underskin
Of air were stretched across earth, they have sported and
    are one.

Was it then at this altar-stone the mind was begun?
The image besieges our Troy. Consider the sick
Convulsions of movement, and the featureless baldy sun
Insensible – sparing that compulsive nervous tic.
Before life, the fantastic succession,
An imbecile makes his confession,
Is filled with the Word unwritten, has almost genuflected.

Because the wise world has for ever and ever rejected
Him and because your children would scream at the sight
Of his mongol mouth stained with food, he has resurrected
The spontaneous thought retarded and infantile Light.
Transfigured with him we stand
Among walls of the no-man's-land
While he licks the soiled envelope with lover's caress

Directing it to the House of no known address.

Wild Honey

Saboteur autumn has riddled the pampered folds
Of the sun; gum and willow whisper seditious things;
Servile leaves now kick and toss in revolution,
Wave bunting, die in operatic reds and golds;
And we, the drones, fated for the hundred stings,
Grope among chilly combs of self-contemplation
While the sun, on sufferance, from his palanquin
Offers creation one niggling lukewarm grin.

But today is Sports Day, not a shadow of doubt:
Scampering at the actual frosty feet
Of winter, under shavings of the pensioned blue,
We are the Spring. True, rain is about:
You mark old diggings along the arterial street

Of the temples, the stuttering eyeball, the residue
Of days spent nursing some drugged comatose pain,
Summer, autumn, winter the single sheet of rain.

And the sun is carted off; and a sudden shower:
Lines of lightning patrol the temples of the skies;
Drum, thunder, silence sing as one this day;
Our faces return to the one face of the flower
Sodden and harried by diehard disconsolate flies.
All seasons are crammed into pockets of the grey.
Joy, pain, desire, a moment ago set free,
Sag in pavilions of the grey finality.

Under rain, in atrophy, dare I watch this girl
Combing her hair before the grey broken mirror,
The golden sweetness trickling? Her eyes show
Awareness of my grey stare beyond the swirl
Of golden fronds: it is her due. And terror,
Rainlike, is all involved in the golden glow,
Playing diminuendo its dwarfish rôle
Between self-conscious fingers of the naked soul.

Down with the mind a moment, and let Eden
Be fullness without the prompted unnatural hunger,
Without the doomed shapely ersatz thought: see faith
As all such essential gestures, unforbidden,
Persisting through Fall and landslip; and see, stranger,
The overcoated concierge of death
As a toy for her gesture. See her hands like bees
Store golden combs amonng certified hollow trees.

Have the gates of death scrape open. Shall we meet
(Beyond the platoons of rainfall) a loftier hill
Hung with such delicate husbandries? Shall ascent
Be a travelling homeward, past the blue frosty feet
Of winter, past childhood, past the grey snake, the will?
Are gestures stars in sacred dishevelment,
The tiny, the pitiable, meaningless and rare
As a girl beleaguered by rain, and her yellow hair?

NOEL MACAINSH

b. 1926

A Small Dirge for the Trade

(exceptis excipiendis)

We are the sick men
   Wilted and blue
The words we scribble
   Never get through
We are the workmen
   No one employs
Foils for old women
   Masters for boys.

We were the chanters
   Loved at the fire
Quick to the people
   Deft at the lyre
Now all our poems
   End in themselves
Our prudent volumes
   Clutter the shelves.

True to our era
   We feel half dead
None of our visions
   Show paths ahead
Our stand in common –
   To stand alone
Dally with Jesus
   Or simply moan.

We are the sick men
   Aloof and kind
Prowling in bookshops
   Steeped in the mind

Spurning the rabble
   We spurn their case
In their tomorrow
   We have no place.

We are the sick men
   Lonely and true
The shrillest whistles
   That never blew
Our eyes are open
   The world is blind
Soon we are dated
   And left behind.

WILMA HEDLEY

b. 1927

Isaac

The way he acts,
the way he walks,
the way he looks,
the way he talks,
he is everything they say
at this somewhat privileged school,
(comprised of the usual scholar and fool)
that they do not wish to be.
'Dirty Jew' they call him, 'Stooge' and 'Fink',
and accompany the flick of their words
with a wink.
'Bastards!' Isaac mutters under his breath,
musing that after birth each day
one faces a little death.
But the Hebrew is a character
who's measured the Australian hide,
and knows that he'll survive.

Isaac assumes an ominous air
and the boys, anticipating the show,
hear him declare:
'God is alive and hiding in Argentina.
Regarding the Vietnam war he's awaiting a subpoena.'
He continues:
'I'm anti every revisionist freak
and every hawk who hates my beak.
I applaud Jim Cairns, Lord Russell and paisley ties,
and Enid Blyton, I have on good authority,
tells no lies.'

The boys gather round delighted,
and offer their reward –
a clip behind the ear.

Then one says: 'Listen Isaac, you no-good liar,
more than likely you'll end up an aristocrat
in a socialist state somewhere,
and be keel-hauled for rape after beer.'

Isaac grimaces . . . a passionate leer,
while his mind stands on tip-toe:
'Of course you know my ultimate fate, the real sequel,
I'm bloody well damned in a capitalist land
to become an equal.'

A screech assaults the air like the cry of cockatoos.
As the sixth formers bunch helpless with laughter –
Isaac strolls off, sardonic, well-satisfied, to his friends.
They discuss the questions on which Life depends.

GRACE PERRY

b. 1927

Red Scarf

Next, please.
Will you come in?
Cracked shoes squeak across the vinyl floor,
and shining blue-grey squares reflect the dust,
loose-hanging trousers, and the long-tongued belt,
limp shirt and bold flamboyant scarf.
What can I say?
You do not feel so well today?
You will be better soon. Sometime, but not now.
Remove your shirt and let me see.
Open your mouth and breathe for me.
Your scarf discarded on my chair,
laughs in the antiseptic air;
laughs at the sterile ritual, the sad futility
of this naked acolyte who must seek
eternal life in me.
Skin hangs in folds upon your frame,
and languor slows
the rhythm of living that remains
like pale twilight rain dripping unseen
through forests shadowed where the sun has been.
Upon your forehead, sweat gleams faint and cold;
your flushed cheeks seem unreal.
I stand behind you, so I do not see
the depthless eyes, the wordless loud appeal
shrieking in black pools of pain
I am powerless to heal.
Rapid and shallow, stale air moves
through your frosted mouth,
hungry no more for news of summer
sprawling in the leaping grass.
I listen.

And soon a wind disturbs the sea,
and undulating, deadly weed
is rustling to me.
Can you not feel the sprouting death,
the blaze of splitting buds,
frenzied foam and strangled breath,
insistent penetration of the bone?
Listen carefully.
Within your darkness, I can hear the sound,
crumbling and falling in slow decay,
milk-white honeycomb eaten away.
How is the cough?
Blood again, bright as a tartan scarf
crumbled on my empty chair in a crimson laugh.
It will be better soon. Sometime, but not now.
I cannot restore the squandered years;
I offer only a limit of long days
of drowsy poppy magic
trailing moist fingers on your throbbing eyes,
softly untwining tentacles of pain
and sinuously inundating the convolutions of your brain.
I give euphoria in deep injection,
yohimbine and male hormone
so that your flaccid flesh may rise again,
a fullbodied root of fire,
blood and pain forgotten in the white flood of desire.
And yet, I cannot tell you these mysterious things,
for when I listen to your lungs,
it is your death who sings.
You will be better soon. Sometime, but not now.
You dress and go out,
and I hear your feet disturb the sunlight in the street.
Your scarf, forgotten on my chair,
flames in the antiseptic air.

Time of Turtles

One time
Columbus said this island and the seas
were full of tortoises
living rocks swimming in troughs of sun.
Always after recognition – annihilation –
the turtles have been gone two centuries.

For us it is not difficult
to imagine wind among almond trees
soft eggs buried in moonwhite sand
flotillas of greenbacks slicing faceless water
long days of old men grazing on sea grass
evening homecoming rituals within the reef
and those less fortunate
skimming up the dusk
striking the widemeshed flags
that change direction with each lurch of tide.
All night the struggle the chest tightening
and in the silver daylight not yet death
hauled up armoured in amber and gold
to hang like some condemned god by the arms
hot metal entering the hands the feet.
Out of their element
they were not offered the alternative
to suffocate facedown by their own weight.

We keep our mouths shut breathing infrequently
and unobserved squeeze tears from hopeless eyes.
Wedged like turtles we submit
upon our backs our heads on pillows.
Slowly we lose our seabright colours
and wait to die.

ALAN RIDDELL

b. 1927

Goldfish at an Angle

Fish in the bowl have no depth at all
to my eye at this angle.

And even head-on
curiously they flatten

themselves against glass against eyes against
– the world. Fenced

round they are, yet not
round but flat

they are
there.

At the Hammersmith Palais ...

the woman is using a handkerchief
to wipe the sweat from under her armpits.
She has just finished dancing a medley
of Latin-American numbers, and is as well known
in the home
for her
intolerance towards children
as
on the floor
for
the sustained violence of her terpsichorean expertise.

BRUCE BEAVER

b. 1928

Exit

Behaviour is more human than we know.
All very well to quote the Book of Rules;
The catch is, if you stay, then I must go.

Some favour intermittence, some a flow;
The student keeps in touch with all the schools.
Behaviour is more human than we know.

Most fellow travellers vary fast with slow;
Adherence to a time-table soon cools.
The catch is, if you stay, then I must go.

The statistician hasn't got a show;
Mere expertise in figures is for fools.
Behaviour is more human than we know.

The small rains fall, the little winds do blow.
A myriad tadpoles pullulate in pools.
The catch is, if you stay, then I must go.

Mergers may fail, though sense of oneness grow;
Psychology can leave behind its tools.
Behaviour is more human than we know.
The catch is, if you stay, then I must go.

Holiday

For J. N.

I wanted facts.
                    'You see, it was like this . . .'
(Order book balanced on one knee, he drew
On the cardboard cover curves with a pencil)
'Here's the peninsula. They came down here

In dinghys from the ships, no ducks in those days,
No mechanised landing barges, only oars;
And that's what some of them believe to be
The cause of it all, currents taking them out
Of their course about here and pulling them around
And away to hell – And there's where they landed:
Right smack dead centre of the enemy's
Shore installations.

                    Now, if they'd only
Landed down here, say, and snuck up behind 'em
As planned – Well, no holiday today.
They'd have done a thorough job with noise enough
And loss of life but no repercussions
At G.H.Q. . . .

                There's another school of thought
Reckons that somebody ballsed the orders up
And sent 'em all to the wrong beach to start with,
But they never got around to blaming anyone;
Maybe they knew it could be used – There's a word for it –
Utilised at some future date with the rest of 'em,
You know, the ones they made the films about,
Bataan and Dunkirk –'

                  (Flanders, Rorke's Drift,
Balaclava, Yorktown – Why stop short
Of a few? The history books are full of them;
Names, embarrassing place names threaded with shame
And loss; so many shrouds to be embroidered
With convenient and apocryphal miracles
By a gelded clergy brooding on old powers;
To be memorised or sniffed over by pedants
Doing their best to mislead each generation
Back up the garden path to the lost lead soldiers;
So many sores for political leeches to suck at
And spew into fresh and public wounds
Now raw with new and private fears
The seething dark bacilli of old hates)
'And were they defeated?'

                    'All but annihilated –

Yet the enemy said later had there been more,
Say two hundred more, they wouldn't have stood a chance
Against 'em – And that's a tribute from a Turk.'

These were my facts in the language of the Fifties.
You know the fancies: Centuries of seedy
Poplars sown through the land; in capital cities
Cenotaphs; thousands given and taken
To house a portion of an unknown impersonal Death
While the living fret and procreate in boxes,
Kenneled like strays till home's a hollow laugh;
Mausoleums raised to harbour hate of the killer,
To hold the slain in effigy like small Christs
Upon a cross of turning time impaled
By an ignorant nation's pride.
                    The best we can offer
These ghosts and their sons' ghosts is a new ruin
For their sons' sons' haunting. – For the women
A dozen stagnant duckponds to reconnoitre
In the empty dusk and contemplate the honking
Of blatant birds ferrying in their young.

Sittings by Appointment Only

Some days I feel like a not-so-big
Nest of chairs.
People take me apart just to sit
On top of me
The easier to listen and look at others
Or rest themselves.
Then when the recital's over
I'm left fragmented
For something like a janitor to stack
Me back in my place,
One structure of many pieces.
One day I swear
I'll lock myself together or learn

The knack of collecting
My self in mid-performance and sandwich them:
Captives of the tower,
Cuckoo-guests of my nest of chairs.

Letters to Live Poets, 1

God knows what was done to you.
I may never find out fully.
The truth reaches us slowly here,
is delayed in the mail continually
or censored in the tabloids. The war
now into its third year
remains undeclared.
The number of infants, among others, blistered
and skinned alive by napalm
has been exaggerated
by both sides we are told,
and the gas does not seriously harm;
does not kill but is merely
unbearably nauseating.
Apparently none of this
is happening to us.

I meant to write to you more than a year
ago. Then there was as much to hear,
as much to tell.
There was the black plastic monster
prefiguring hell
displayed on the roof
of the shark aquarium at the wharf.
At Surfers' Paradise were Meter Maids
glabrous in gold bikinis.
It was before your country's
president came among us like a formidable
virus. Even afterwards –
after I heard (unbelievingly)

you had been run down on a beach
by a machine
apparently while sunning yourself;
that things were terminal again –
even then I might have written.

But enough of that. I could tell by the tone
of your verses there were times
when you had ranged around you,
looking for a lift from the gift horse,
your kingdom for a Pegasus.
But to be trampled by the machine
beyond protest . . .

I don't have to praise you; at least
I can say I had ears for your voice
but none of that really matters now.
Crushed though. Crushed on the littered sands.
given the *coup de grâce* of an empty beer can,
out of sight of the 'lordly and isolate satyrs'.
Could it have happened anywhere else
than in your country, keyed to obsolescence?

I make these words perform for you
knowing though you are dead, that you 'historically
belong to the enormous bliss of American death',
that your talkative poems remain
among the living things
of the sad, embattled beach-head.

Say that I am, as ever, the young-
old fictor of communications.
It's not that I wish to avoid
talking to myself or singing
the one-sided song.
It's simply that I've come to be
more conscious of the community
world-wide, of live, mortal poets.
Moving about the circumference

379

I pause each day
and speak to you and you.
I haven't many answers, few
enough; fewer questions left.
Even when I'm challenged 'Who
goes there?' I give ambiguous
replies as though the self linking
heart and mind had become a gap.

You see, we have that much in common
already. It's only when I stop
thinking of you living I remember
nearby our home there's an aquarium
that people pay admission to,
watching sharks at feeding time:
the white, jagged rictus in the grey
sliding anonymity,
faint blur of red through green,
the continually spreading stain.

I have to live near this, if not quite with it.
I realize there's an equivalent
in every town and city in the world.
Writing to you keeps the local, intent
shark-watchers at bay
(who if they thought at all
would think *me* some kind of ghoul);
rings a bell for the gilded coin-slots
at the Gold Coast;
sends the president parliament's head on a platter;
writes Vietnam like a huge four-letter
word in blood and faeces on the walls
of government; reminds me when
the intricate machine stalls
there's a poet still living at this address.

PETER PORTER

b. 1929

Your Attention Please

The Polar DEW has just warned that
A nuclear rocket strike of
At least one thousand megatons
Has been launched by the enemy
Directly at our major cities.
This announcement will take
Two and a quarter minutes to make,
You therefore have a further
Eight and a quarter minutes
To comply with the shelter
Requirements published in the Civil
Defence Code – section Atomic Attack.
A specially shortened Mass
Will be broadcast at the end
Of this announcement –
Protestant and Jewish services
Will begin simultaneously –
Select your wavelength immediately
According to instructions
In the Defence Code. Do not
Take well-loved pets (including birds)
Into your shelter – they will consume
Fresh air. Leave the old and bed-
ridden, you can do nothing for them.
Remember to press the sealing
Switch when everyone is in
The shelter. Set the radiation
Aerial, turn on the geiger barometer.
Turn off your Television now.
Turn off your radio immediately
The Services end. At the same time
Secure explosion plugs in the ears

Of each member of your family. Take
Down your plasma flasks. Give your children
The pills marked one and two
In the C.D. green container, then put
Them to bed. Do not break
The inside airlock seals until
The radiation All Clear shows
(Watch for the cuckoo in your
Perspex panel), or your District
Touring Doctor rings your bell.
If before this, your air becomes
Exhausted or if any of your family
Is critically injured, administer
The capsules marked 'Valley Forge'
(Red pocket in No. 1 Survival Kit)
For painless death. (Catholics
Will have been instructed by their priests
What to do in this eventuality.)
This announcement is ending. Our President
Has already given orders for
Massive retaliation – it will be
Decisive. Some of us may die.
Remember, statistically
It is not likely to be you.
All flags are flying fully dressed
On Government buildings – the sun is shining.
We are all in the hands of God,
Whatever happens happens by His Will.
Now go quickly to your shelters.

Competition Is Healthy
Es wartet alles auf dich

Everything. Yes. Some men holy enough
To have seen the Buddha may try to keep
His commandments – to clothe the ragged in lightweight
Dacron, to feed the hungry with milk bread
Or curious corn, to press salve of the sacred
Laboratories of America into sores
Too big to form scabs. Yet the underprivileged
Rich pray for a Goldwater victory
Within an ant's tremor of God's instep.
Your heavenly Father knoweth that
Ye have need of all these things.
He gives bells that walk the fields
When the unsteady rice is shooting,
He gives Sebastian Bach to the citizens
Of Leipzig. Out of reach of the philharmonic
That old man is planting his garden.
He nestles each seedling in the soil,
Contrives a cotton grid to keep the sparrows off,
Sweats in conscience of his easy goal.
Unknown to him his son has scattered
Radish seed in the bed and the red clumsy
Tubers shall inherit the earth.
Take no thought saying 'What shall we eat?
What shall we drink? or Wherewithal shall we be clothed?'
We shall eat the people we love,
We shall drink their fluids unslaked,
We shall dress in the flannel of their blood,
But we shall not go hungry or thirsty
Or cold. The old man writes with a post office nib
To his son. 'The Government has cut the quotas,
Here the bougainvillea is out,
The imported rose is sinking in the heat.

Moaning in Midstream

You can see the Master's latch-key
at the University of Anaconda,
plus a note from a girl who wanted
to write poetry ('I feel vowels like peaches'),
the picture he bought at the Salon –
'Sardanapalus Prepares for Death' –
and several letters to a Normandy vet
about boarding out his dog.
I looked in one hot day in June
before rehearsing my Organa
for Thirteen Orchestras. Lucky Master,
I thought, living at the doomed end
of a serious century, and went off
to hear Knipper's Concerto for Farts.
But there in the library gloom go
the dark geniuses, dapper and intense
in their fin de siècle silences,
caught by the camera ridiculously
at Seine boating parties, or heavy-glanded
watching balloons go up: arrogant,
incurable, hell in the home –
No point in regretting them or lauding
their relics: still, how nice just
not to be here at the fifth concert
of the series, trying hard to be fair, trying
harder still to like something, feeling
only breath won too easily on closed faces.

R. A. SIMPSON
b. 1929

Student

Talked at often;
Looked at often;
Given pamphlets telling of riots
And wars, she dreams of apples
She must not bite, that offer troubles.

She lets her hair fall down
While listening to lecturers
Who frown
And talk of deadly futures
She knows won't happen.

Her boy friend has ideas
And clumsily explores,
Finding sudden ice, doors
Shut tightly
Against him – rightly

So! she tells herself
While thinking of the shelf
Girls are sometimes left upon.
She must allow
For love somehow,

And yet a pit could open
To leave her there alone
Hating men
And, even more, herself – alone
Not daring to be alone.

R. A. SIMPSON

Carboni in the Chimney

'The shots whizzed by my tent. I jumped out of the
stretcher and rushed to my chimney facing the stockade.'
— from *The Eureka Stockade* by
Carboni Raffaello

Do all men live
In chimneys? Though some appear to give
Expansively,

Love mostly fuels the self.
Some men, hating pelf,
Conflagrate

And go to God,
While others end as soot. My blood
Has rumours of fire in it;

My soul is smoke
That wants to wake,
But I stay here

Being neither fire
Nor ash. Desire
Turns to a monotone

As I regard
Dying friends — the hard
Collapse of their intentions:

Some were inept,
And some could not accept
Whatever confines that they chose.

BRUCE DAWE

b. 1930

How To Go On Not Looking

How to go on not looking
despite every inducement to the contrary,

How to train the dumb elephant, patience,
to balance by command on its circus stool
without betraying its inward teetering,

How to subdue the snarling circle of ifs
by whip-crack, chair-twirl, seeming to look each steadily
in the eye while declining to unwrap
the deadly golden bon-bons of their hate,

How to forget also the silence
tenting itself over the old once wildly-applauded acts,
over Beppo and Toni, the Heavenly Twins,
not to mention Bucephalus, the Wonder Horse,

How to cry 'Ladies and Gentlemen!' to an empty marquee
where only the canvas flaps in the night wind,
how to people the vacant benches without bitterness,

And how to go on not looking and not looking
until the good years, the good pitches
return and the crowds gasp again
at the recurrent miracle of the balancing elephant,
the dutiful big cats, the Heavenly Twins
making it all look too easy, the ring-master
merely an accessory after the fact.

The Not-So-Good Earth

For a while there we had 25-inch Chinese peasant families
famishing in comfort on the 25-inch screen
and even Uncle Billy whose eyesight's going fast
by hunching up real close to the convex glass
could just about make them out – the riot scene
in the capital city for example
he saw that better than anything, using the contrast knob
to bring them up dark – all those screaming faces
and bodies going under the horses' hooves – he did a terrific
    job
on that bit, not so successful though
on the quieter parts where they're just starving away
digging for roots in the not-so-good earth
cooking up a mess of old clay
and coming out with all those Confucian analects
to everybody's considerable satisfaction
(if I remember rightly Grandmother dies
with naturally a suspenseful break in the action
for a full symphony orchestra plug for Craven A
neat as a whistle probably damn glad
to be quit of the whole gang with their marvellous
    patience.)
We never did find out how it finished up . . . Dad
at this stage tripped over the main lead in the dark
hauling the whole set down smack on its inscrutable face,
wiping out in a blue flash and curlicue of smoke
600 million Chinese without a trace . . .

BRUCE DAWE

Life-Cycle

For Big Jim Phelan

When children are born in Victoria
they are wrapped in the club-colours, laid in beribboned
    cots,
having already begun a lifetime's barracking.

Carn, they cry, Carn . . . feebly at first
while parents playfully tussle with them
for possession of a rusk: Ah, he's a little Tiger! (And they
    are . . .)

Hoisted shoulder-high at their first League game
they are like innocent monsters who have been years
    swimming
towards the daylight's roaring empyrean

Until, now, hearts shrapnelled with rapture,
they break surface and are forever lost,
their minds rippling out like streamers

In the pure flood of sound, they are scarfed with light, a
    voice
like the voice of God booms from the stands
Ooohh you bludger and the covenant is sealed.

Hot pies and potato-crisps they will eat,
they will forswear the Demons, cling to the Saints
and behold their team going up the ladder into Heaven,

And the tides of life will be the tides of the home-team's
    fortunes
– the reckless proposal after the one-point win,
the wedding and honeymoon after the grand-final . . .

They will not grow old as those from more northern States
    grow old,
for them it will always be three-quarter-time
with the scores level and the wind advantage in the final
    term,

That passion persisting, like a race-memory, through the
    welter of seasons,
enabling old-timers by boundary fences to dream of
    resurgent lions
and centaur-figures from the past to replenish continually
    the present,

So that mythology may be perpetually renewed
and Chicken Smallhorn return like the maize-god
in a thousand shapes, the dancers changing

But the dance forever the same – the elderly still
loyally crying Carn . . . Carn . . . (if feebly) unto the very
    end,
having seen in the six-foot recruit from Eaglehawk their
    hope of salvation.

A Victorian Hangman Tells His Love

[handwritten margin note: Maybe be read as political propaganda. About state of Victoria]

Dear one, forgive my appearing before you like this,
in a two-piece track-suit, welder's goggles
and a green cloth cap like some gross bee – this is the
    State's idea . . .
I would have come

[handwritten margin note: Hangman describes preparation for hanging as marriage and love. absurd discourse]

arrayed like a bridegroom for the nuptials
knowing how often you have dreamed about this
moment of consummation in your cell.
If I must bind your arms now to your sides
with a leather strap and ask you if you have anything to say
– these too are formalities I would dispense with:
I know your heart is too full at this moment
to say much and that the tranquilliser which I trust
you did not reject out of a stubborn pride
should by this have eased your ache for speech, breath
and the other incidentals which distract us from our end.

Canadian Version of poem is???

morbid — anything we'd rather not hear about

Let us now walk a step. This noose
with which we're wed is something of an heirloom, the last three
members of our holy family were wed with it, the softwood beam
it hangs from like a lovers' tree notched with their weight.
See now I slip it over your neck, the knot
under the left jaw, with a slip ring
to hold the knot in place . . . There. Perfect.
Allow me to adjust the canvas hood
which will enable you to anticipate the officially prescribed darkness
by some seconds.

Langman says lies, + evasion being hanged is not a gentle 'sinking'

The journalists are ready with the flash-bulbs of their eyes
raised to the simple altar, the doctor twitches like a stethoscope
– you have been given a clean bill of health, like any
modern bride.   With this spring of mine

parody of while s death

from the trap, hitting the door lever, you will go forth
into a new life which I, alas, am not yet fit to share.
Be assured, you will sink into the generous pool of public feeling

This is to discuss us

as gently as a leaf – accept your role, feel chosen.
You are this evening's headlines. Come, my love.

Victim not heard, he is inconsequential, he is of no concern

Home-Coming

All day, day after day, they're bringing them home,
they're picking them up, those they can find, and bringing them home,
they're bringing them in, piled on the hulls of Grants, in
trucks, in convoys,
they're zipping them up in green plastic bags,
they're tagging them now in Saigon, in the mortuary coolness

they're giving them names, they're rolling them out of
the deep-freeze lockers – on the tarmac at Tan Son Nhut
the noble jets are whining like hounds,
they are bringing them home
– curly-heads, kinky-hairs, crew-cuts, balding non-coms
– they're high, now, high and higher, over the land, the
    steaming *chow mein*,
their shadows are tracing the blue curve of the Pacific
with sorrowful quick fingers, heading south, heading east,
home, home, home – and the coasts swing upward, the old
    ridiculous curvatures
of earth, the knuckled hills, the mangrove swamps, the
    desert emptiness . . .
in their sterile housing they tilt towards these like skiers
– taxiing in, on the long runways, the howl of their home-
    coming rises
surrounding them like their last moments (the mash, the
    splendour)
then fading at length as they move
on to small towns where dogs in the frozen sunset
raise muzzle in mute salute,
and on to cities in whose wide web of suburbs
telegrams tremble like leaves from a wintering tree
and the spider grief swings in his bitter geometry
– they're bringing them home, now, too late, too early.

CHARLES HIGHAM

b. 1931

Still Lives

A fish, a tangled net, a pear;
A half-cut loaf upon the board.
Your mind, or someone's, lighting there,
Might think their quiet hutched a lair,
Might try to probe it with a word.

He, the mongrel painter, purged
The darkness from the fishing-net
And all the common things he'd urged
Out of the dark where something surged
Calcined them all of his regret.

Salvaged them from the October hour
Despite the critical clock that strove
With passionless hands to slow the dour
Noon in the basement where his power
Grew out and outward like a grove.

And she, his usual subject, lay
Contemptuously near at hand,
Loathing the shabby hands at play,
With brush and brush till end of day,
The canvas naked on its stand.

The cat inked out the azure rug,
The window rattled in the breeze,
Outside, a bench where they could hug
When he was loosened from the tug,
Melpomene's disastrous fees.

Outside, a birch-tree young and white.
Inside, the four consuming walls.

And she agaze at all his might
Slipping away within her sight,
The sexless passion which appals.

She almost rose to dash it down –
The easel where he stood and limned,
But changed her mind and slept alone,
Dreaming she tore him to the bone
While the evening candle dimmed.

Might try to probe it with a word?
Might think their quiet hutched a lair?
Your mind, or someone's, lighting there,
Saw just one loaf upon the board,
One fish, one tangled net, one pear.

Dusk at Waterfall

Night's down now: the cold voice
Of a bird, trapped
In the elbow of a fleshless arm,
Shivers through the bone-white trees.

Mauve velvet sweeps the ground,
The sea falls in the ear,
The tent tilts to clouds,
Great ages gather,

And the heart is emptied.
Lonely, watch
Through the night, the far
Lights of the city

Like a friendly fire
Where no fire is,
Where the cold hands
Of the trees smother

The hope, the dream,
Of all who long
For a storm of voices,
And a haven of limbs,

For children and falling
Fruit, for seasons.
Here we are unwanted;
Unknown. The trees watch.

Harbourscape

All, here, is molten. The gold down from the bridge
Sinking in prodigal fountains,
Over and over, from the transcendent lights strung
Like fished-up pearls in dripping nets;
And the wash of blue over the dreaming sea
By some prodigal sea-god flung
Far from the wavy mountains
Into the trapped mirror of the shining harbour,
Reflected always in a frozen symmetry.

A thousand sails! And the tossing, shining of them
In a fabulous argosy!
And amid, in curving, steady sweeps, the ferries
Illume a rust-brown course, a streak of age
In the newness, the eternal newness of the deeps,
Scrap-heaps of mysteries
And that great heresy
Called love: for love burns like a banner here
In a surrounding flame that never sleeps.

Celebrate them now. The torpid green of trees,
The resplendent folly
Of villas, the thin veneer of the city's edges,
Yet know that only one thing

Is divine here; sacred, though known by a flock of ships –
The blue, whose ages
Can never fully
Be fathomed; whose great heart beats in the narrow ribs
Of the land; whose sheen the revengeful sky outstrips.

It is aloof, though; lonely, like the land it decks,
South, far south, and sometimes by evening
An Antarctic gleam blights it; the impersonal smile
Of the bright waters freezes to a deathly grin.
But in high summer see it – tossed, warm as honey,
That dreamed-of image
In blue Australia,
Blue as the smoky bush in the low, ripe mountains,
Blue as the dusk-striped plains of its inland; the funnel-web
    evening sky.

The War Museum at Nagasaki

Here are two helmets, stamped
With the marks of burning death,
A twisted toy in a case,
Its glass smoked by the breath
Of a passer-by;
Dim in the photograph
A dying patient's face
Smiling patiently;
Where the moment tramped
He holds a bitter staff.

A woman pauses now,
Fixing her face in the glass,
Squinting to read the words
That summon up the crass
Immoment, silly facts:
The dates of birth and dying,

396

Name, height, the broken sherds
Of long-dead artefacts;
Broken is that bough;
The rest is useless lying.

Our pity, *their* regret
Are lost before the face
Of truth, the hollow bowl,
The twisted, worthless trace
Of broken wedding-rings.
Nothing, nothing can work,
Not love nor sorrow, yet,
One registers those things,
Throwing the dead a net
Across that foundering dark.

The Creature

For James Dickey

I am looking out of my bones' cage
And the oval box of my skull, stern
Into the eyes of a leopard. Fuelled

With red hate, life blazes from her throat,
And her laugh is an old accusation.
Fat with her kicking litter she is,

Wallowing in a green sloughing, leaves
Shed by cabbage-palms under a cool
Moon, the exact colour of lanterns

In that decisively encroaching
Garden. Her muscles shine like the ribs
Of polished trunks. On her paws the spots

That mark where she pounded through puffballs
And slow fungus fat as lechery.
Her claws are bare as thorns, her crying

Resounds with the precise tone of my
Brain, harsh, austere and repetitive,
Measured out in drams of anguish. Eyes

Catching mine, are as uncertainly
Focused on the real world; on nettles
And briars, the small sloughs that absorb

Our dreaming, the springs set by each path.
I have life on her authority,
And death as well, for she holds both: in

Her mouth she bears suddenly a numb
Blood-black bird, an egret with pen legs
And stupid stare she caught in the bush,

Each bone splintering like balsawood,
Its heart the size of a severed thumb-
Top, thick and still after a meagre

Fluttering, a dense no. In her blood
Her brood, spidery cubs in hot env-
Elopes, pulsing and kicking her

Belly, waiting for release to white
Days, to crackling twigs and buzzing sand,
To the erotic stench of prey. Hard

They beat, the bird falls from her mouth. She
Screams and hisses. To the noonday. I
Leash her tight, lead her to the blue house,

Trying to capture all she means: look there,
There she is, tame as a cat, purring
On the library carpet, pelted

And proud under golden lamps. You can come
Pat her now. But under her lids she
Dreams of your dying, for energy.

Must consume. Strip our skins, we are pale
Parchment. Shades, drab hangings for cold rooms.
But animal hides blaze still. They seem

To breathe and glow. Here in the evening
Kill her, stretch her furs high, her spots stare
Back at you, walls of eyes, walls of eyes.

EVAN JONES

b. 1931

Noah's Song

The animals are silent in the hold,
Only the lion coughing in the dark
As in my ageing arms once more I fold
My mistress and the mistress of the Ark.

That, the rain, and the lapping of the sea:
Too many years have brought me to this boat
Where days swim by with such monotony,
Days of the fox, the lion and the goat.

Her breathing and the slow beat of the clock
Accentuate the stillness of the room,
Whose walls and floor and ceiling seem to lock
Into a space as single as the tomb.

A single room set up against the night,
The hold of animals, and nothing more:
For any further world is out of sight –
There are no people, and there is no shore.

True, the time passes in unbroken peace:
To some, no doubt, this Ark would seem a haven.
But all that I can hope for is release.
Tomorrow I'll send out the dove and raven.

Boxing On

When the bell rings you come out feeling wary,
Knowing yourself you lack that brilliant snap.
Things change: you've lost your old need to be lairy,
And when the opening comes you see a trap.

You're mad with craft: even your slightest move
Has years of it, each step, each feinting lead
As smooth as when there's weight behind the glove;
You box with shadows just to keep up speed.

It hurts much more now when you're really hit,
But years of training never let it show:
Shocked in your stance, you give no sign of it
But moving in to clinch and hitting low.

You smile for cameramen who call you Kid
(Seen from the right, you're hardly marked at all)
And make with jokes, large gestures where you hid
The years of clipping marking every fall.

At thirty you're already getting old –
Time to hang up the gloves? That's time to kill,
Say twenty years: I'd rather take it cold,
And when I have to then I guess I will.

JOHN CROYSTON

b. 1933

Reconciliation

Paused at his apogee like the hawk
He saw the sharp descending stair;
He needed now for her to talk,
Else fall into the evening air.

His feet had had their own momentum
Motored by his angry word,
And now the terrible interregnum,
Would the homing call be heard?

Was that a movement? Does she mean
To start a hare from out the cover?
Does he fly, or does he lean
Against the angry air, and hover,

Until, the moment full in sight,
He falters, falling down the hill
Of air, to where he loses in her night
The urgency to claim a kill?

The image on his eye was still.
At his feet the sharp descent.
The hawk could only hang until
The heated plume of air was spent.

But she had seen his hesitation,
His half-halting at the height,
And his ebbing irritation
In the angled evening light,

So she let him hover there
With cloud confusion in his head,
But when his feet felt for the stair,
She plunged, 'Don't go,' she softly said.

VIVIAN SMITH

b. 1933

Dialogue

And so you see your life before you
not like mountains seen through trees,
but like a book of shapeless poems:
glittering felicities

but botched and not a verse that works,
the brilliant image and the random phrase,
but where's the poem? It's not here before you
in days divided into different ways.

And so you say perfection's not for man,
and that is true: but laziness you mean.
Division has its comforts like despair:
the odd convenience of the in-between.

But look, these words are wrong, a verbal play:
despair is voiceless or is not at all.
Distraction and evasion aren't implied
as man's whole nature since his primal fall.

Let's face the facts: this is a botched-up job;
these days, these verses don't belong to art.
You must begin again and turn and trust
the deep resistant silence of the heart.

Late April: Hobart

Turning from the mirror full of leaves
that draws the autumn garden through the room
I note that brown's the colour of decay,
but in the garden how it just achieves
a sense of balance between rot and bloom
where old chrysanthemums lean all one way

as if an angle meant avoiding change.
Thick with its burden of excess and loss
this time of year depresses and elates:
all points of stillness hover out of range;
wind strips the season to its sticks and dross
and days to a blue scratched out of southern slates.

This autumn garden is decay of gold,
a waste of mildew, fading reds that glow
as in bare boughs the brown and gold respond.
Each day the corners lengthen shades of cold
and silver rain gives way to mountain snow
and black and sour grows the lily pond.

Gone are the statements of the summer dawn
when love grew more abundant with excess;
sustained by filth, fertility survives.
Fulfilment needs its time to be withdrawn
in its own silence, much like holiness.
In time each shifting harmony arrives.

And now it's this dark brevity of gold
with so much withering as colours glow
as if the frugal with the fecund mates.
The sunlight dazzles with its April cold
and through the red the brown begins to show.
Beneath it all such final bareness waits.

Balmoral, Summer

All day the weight of summer and the shrill
spaced flight of jet planes climbing north.
The news at half past twelve brought further crimes.
Insane dictators threaten new disasters.

The light of summer with its bone white glare
and pink hibiscus in the yacht club garden.
The beach is strewn with bodies of all sizes.

How the sight of human nudity surprises –
cleft buttock, shaved arm-pit, nipple hair.

The heat haze hovers over Grotto Point
and skiers skim the violent flat water.
Incredible the feats that art demands.

Submarines surface to refuel
around this headland in a small bay's stillness.
History encroaches like an illness.
And children chase the gulls across the sand.

DAVID MALOUF

b. 1934

At a School Athletics Day

Strollers of April green: white tent-poles hold
the sky; the crowd's breath caught
on the heel of a javelin-thrower,
a boy as thick as two short planks, who never
will learn to distinguish
between perfect past and past conditional.

I walk between hurdles fallen,
on a cinder-track where sprinters kneel, with two
friends – my former students, freed
from blue serge to the daring
of corduroy and sideburns,
the faded blue-sky blue of washed-out jeans.

They argue: was Prince Hamlet hesitant
of murder lest the act
define him with its blood (he being, for his taste,
too narrowly defined
already by the too too sullied flesh)
or was he

(long shaft steady now)
caught, rat's-foot and star,
in the metaphysical mousetrap O so subtly
baited with death,
that his timid soul, nose twitching in the darkness,
sniffed and nibbled at?

Questions indeed for a clear spring day! – sun breeding
desire like daffodils,
the dead in green troughs nudging
our heels . . . And was he

twenty? – They mean like *them* –
or balding, short of breath, a cautious reader between the
    lines

of documents and faces,
well-meaning, impassioned, vague – an eternal student
    pushing thirty
like *me*? So time breaks
on the skull's bleak promontory. So idle fellows
exit underground. And April raises
questions – or daffodils – out of their end . . .

On the far side of the field, the crowd's breath lifts
over our head, steel
flies to nail its shadow in the grass.
Falling – not out of sight but where
two schoolboys in sneakers
run up, snow-footed, with a measuring-tape.

ANN TREGENZA

b. 1934

The Priestess of the Temple

I hesitated at the propylaeum,
Held like the hawk in the blue.
You picked me up
And galloped me round the frieze
Urging me to enter.
Outside,
Here in the sun and rain
Were clear shapes of mountains against sky,
Grey donkeys against white walls,
Smells of goat manure,
Garlic and home-made wine,
Crooked streets with people I knew,
Fish nets and undisturbed sleep,
Waves grasping a familiar shore –
But you were waiting –
And you a prince.

I passed through the propylaeum
The hawk dived.
Inside,
I searched for you among satin cushions
While lyras played love-songs.
I searched for you among blurred shapes
Of ships' captains, merchants, kings and princes;
I searched through sandalwood and musk-rose incense
I was lost on strange shores
Where waves of strong wines
Shipwrecked the senses.
And you were lost in too many disguises.
I asked the goddess.

'Go out into the sun, child, and see,' she said.
I saw you galloping round the frieze,
Another sharing your horse.
The hawk hung in the blue.
The sun was too bright.
I went inside for ever.

CHRIS WALLACE-CRABBE

b. 1934

Melbourne

Not on the ocean, on a muted bay
Where the broad rays drift slowly over mud
And flathead loll on sand, a city bloats
Between the plains of water and of loam.
If surf beats, it is faint and far away;
If slogans blow around, we stay at home.

And, like the bay, our blood flows easily,
Not warm, not cold (in all things moderate),
Following our familiar tides. Elsewhere
Victims are bleeding, sun is beating down
On patriot, guerrilla, refugee.
We see the newsreels when we dine in town.

Ideas are grown in other gardens while
This chocolate soil throws up its harvest of
Imported and deciduous platitudes,
None of them flowering boldly or for long;
And we, the gardeners, securely smile
Humming a bar or two of rusty song.

Old tunes are good enough if sing we must;
Old images, re-vamped *ad nauseam*,
Will sate the burgher's eye and keep him quiet
As the great wheels run on. And should he seek
Variety, there's wind, there's heat, there's frost
To feed his conversation all the week.

Highway by highway, the remorseless cars
Strangle the city, put it out of pain,
Its limbs still kicking feebly on the hills.
Nobody cares. The artists sail at dawn
For brisker ports, or rot in public bars.
Though much has died here, nothing has been born.

A Wintry Manifesto

It was the death of Satan first of all,
The knowledge that earth holds though kingdoms fall,
    Inured us to a stoic resignation,
    To making the most of a shrunken neighbourhood;

And what we drew on was not gold or fire,
No cross, not cloven hoof about the pyre,
    But painful, plain, contracted observations:
    The gesture of a hand, dip of a bough

Or seven stubborn words drawn close together
As a hewn charm against the shifting weather.
    Our singing was intolerably sober
    Mistrusting every trill of artifice.

Whatever danced on needle-points, we knew
That we had forged the world we stumbled through
    And, if a stripped wind howled through sighing alleys,
    Built our own refuge in a flush of pride

Knowing that all our gifts were for construction –
Timber to timber groined in every section –
    And knowing, too, purged of the sense of evil,
    These were the walls our folly would destroy.

We dreamed, woke, doubted, wept for fading stars
And then projected brave new avatars,
    Triumphs of reason. Yet a whole dimension
    Had vanished from the chambers of the mind,

And paramount among the victims fled,
Shrunken and pale, the grim king of the dead;
    Withdrawn to caverns safely beyond our sounding
    He waits as a Pretender for his call,

Which those who crave him can no longer give.
Men are the arbiters of how they live,
  And, stooped by millstones of authority,
  They welcome tyrants in with open arms.

Now in the shadows of unfriendly trees
We number leaves, discern faint similes
  And learn to praise whatever is imperfect
  As the true breeding-ground for honesty,

Finding our heroism in rejection
Of bland Utopias and of thieves' affection:
  Our greatest joy to mark an outline truly
  And know the piece of earth on which we stand.

The Secular

However you look at it,
The abundant secular,
How splendid it all appears
Shifting and coruscating
All over and everywhere,
All at once, repeatedly,
In little waves of motion
And stubbornly tangible.

Look, I grant all that you say:
Whoever the creator
He brutally botched the job,
But how tough his furniture
Really is made, piece by piece!
I jump on his solid stones
Or dance on these rustling fields
And hear the sap leap in trees
Already marked out for death.

Nature, Language, the Sea: an Essay

But what of the artist? Has he either knowledge
or correct belief? – *The Republic*

With such worn currency of models as
  Rivers and steps and roads, the mind
Does much of its diurnal labour;

Analogies its glory and its task,
  Into the shambling mess we call
Creation it plunges, asking 'Why?'

For the world is wonder, is profusion,
  A boundless brilliant orchard of
Sun-licked, thunder-shaken strangeness,

But nobody can claim it makes good sense
  Or testifies to clarity:
O, the mistakes of a creator!

Nature, language, sea: our great examples
  Of what must always be rebuked
By the modest radiance of art.

Where the thick ridges of a mountain range,
  Ruffled with unbroken forest
And innocent of bridge or roadway,

Roll like a stiff surf out from under you
  In one great Burkean rhythm
To shout, Sublime, Sublime, O Sublime,

And the gullies brim with a steely blue mist,
  Is there, as your heart takes pause,
Anything heard but a hymn of chaos?

There are no sermons in the Great Divide;
  The boundless overflows and
Its tide is no river of symbols;

Yet symbols must rise glittering from some
    Quick river or sullen current,
Dying as soon as their surface dries,

And sound roots must aspire from common soil
    Earning a sudden right to bear
The fire-featured apples of the sun.

Nature, language, the sea; and opposite
    These fluent fields of energy
Man feels that he is bound to chisel

The small hard statues of his poetry
    Which bear, like a sheen on marble,
All the assurance of being right,

All the assurance that we come to know
    Under the name of Form, and know
In the strong humming of completeness

Wherein the formal is at last the good.
    Both passionate and moral is
Music which has passed into a shape,

A river which has found its dimpling course
    Through the golden fields of Chronos,
Sounding not of loss but clarity.

Rustum

    Last week the Partisans
    Outflanked the Democrats,
    Sent a platoon out
    Five miles around
    A hair raising razorback,
    Came on them at the stream
    And shot them to pieces.

Yesterday the Democrats
Carried their justice
Into the market town
After a brisk siege;
The Mayor and six Partisans,
Marched to the river bank,
Were shot quick and neat.

Whose machine-gun fire
Pocks the escarpment?
Who was it that sustained –
Threatened, retreating –
Vital supply lines?
Who holds which bank of that
Neutral brown river?

Partisans, Democrats,
Black souls and white souls
Blindly confronting,
While at the river's edge
I am drawn through harsh light
To meet my only son
In mortal combat.

RODNEY HALL

b. 1935

The Hunter

Neighbourly day was over, a hunter ventured out
to await with prickling skin the mute attack,
for chilly night to waterfall
and wash along his back.

The hills ahead, grotesque and hung with misty beards,
like hope or understanding, shyly withdrew
from man's approach. The hunter crawled
in winter's residue.

He waited (eardrums throbbing, hands like metal, frosted
hair, and eyes as crisp as the moon at midnight)
to catch some hint of an angry tread:
the pigs of his own spite.

.

The Two Staircases of Consummation

He began to climb the staircase;
that had seemed the main thing.
Each step so tremendous
grew to dominate him.
Nothing else existed,
not heat of afternoon,
nor fragrance from an ocean
which lay as yet unseen.

There was nothing more to life
than the stairs below and stairs
ahead. The sun, bereft
of priesthood and factotum,
fought him for itself;

beat upon his crown
jabbed between his eyes
scorched his tender skin.

Though each weary bone
hung chiming in the light,
some grateful sense was shown
how several thousand years
had proved their force an ally
(who could help but marvel!)
had ground the stone, if slightly,
closer to his level.

With pain his every step
transfixed his crawling eyes.
Off-guard, he reached the top.
Then suddenly the columns
clustered round and cooled him
in the fountains of their shade,
refreshed the appetite
for securing his reward.

He crossed the temple floor.
From this great height he looked
upon the sea – that sphere
revolving in its socket,
a twitching retina
some fathoms deep in salt;
its iris burnt to death
where the seven winds exult.

Waves aligned gold edges
geometrical as stairs.
Gods, on the living ridges
leapt to possess their shrine.
He, a mortal, spat
at his bitter enterprise:
the hill of stones it took
before he dared to rise.

Heaven, in a Way

From my new world I'm waving.
See how far I've come?
Here it's perfectly alright
to turn however many somersaults you like
on all the roofs of town.
If anyone should care to live
in Gothic or in Romanesque cathedrals
that's alright too: you spread
your palliasse upon the altar or in the nave
and wake to find the morning sun
shattered to a flower of jewelled glass –
to find the ghost of a multicoloured
saint or two in bed beside you.

From my new world I'm waving.
See how far I've come?
It's no use being envious;
nothing but a life of heartbreak
can win you entry to this place.
Here the fish are naturally disguised
with scales that read as Hebrew letters.
The smells of every intimate ren_embrance
play your mind on their hook and line, until you do
achieve a state of re-experience.
And the colours here lie warm against the eye.
film upon film of unforgotten pleasure.

I suppose it's heaven, in a way.
And I am waving down at you.
Ha ha! I hope you hate it where you are.
I see you – a grubby speck beneath me,
and it's all your own damned fault.
You don't know what you're missing.
Watch me exploit the magic
of my somersaulting powers. Up here

we're worshippers of education by experience;
with only another life of heartbreak still to go
before we accept ourselves, each as one of you.
From my new world I'm waving.
See how far I've come?

Cut-out

This love has cut me
from my background –
snip like a pair of scissors
snip – too close to the heart,
look out for blood.
At last I'm extrovert.

And I remember
when a child, pasting
my heroines and heroes
in a scrapbook. Snip –
the privilege
of being chosen scrap.

THOMAS W. SHAPCOTT

Enemies

Stretch forth your right hand you will see
    the five betrayers move
    familiar as old love
to turn your words to perjury.

Take up your wrist and you will feel
    the armies of your blood
    rehearse the every deed
mocks at the language you can spell.

Clutch at your flesh to mark the nerve
    sell out the secrets of
    such symbols as you have,
those deepest gods that you believe.

But language is the mankind thing
    that body in its heat
    is lastly caged to beat
though it rend each man's covering.

Quetzalcoatl

for Rodney Hall

'I will return' said Quetzalcoatl the god
among bright birds, attendants singing and wondering.
'You, who shall remember me as silver and shells,
wind into the morning, the plumes of the serpent,
you must rehearse and await me.' Crying birds wheeling,
plunging around him, and all the limitless ocean.

'In the erosive sun, restless and wondering
long after all has been decided, dead shells

tossed on the sand, dead skin husked from the serpent,
flesh into pelt with the offal tossed to the wheeling
carolling sea-birds, you shall crouch by the ocean,
quarrelling, awaiting my promise. Keep vigil.' *'You are
God.'*

All the waves to forever broke on the shells
at their feet, and his craft was a diminishing serpent,
a speck, a shadow, and all the morning was wheeling
among them already; they gazed East at the ocean,
crested with brightness, sun, like a usurping god,
and they counted their loss, questioning, wondering.

Remembering was hardest. Bearing the husk of the serpent
before them, they danced in the evenings to their own
blood wheeling
high among drum-beats and drowned in the impatient
ocean
within them, distending and altering the texture of the god.
But something remained. In the uneasy ritual, the
wondering
chafed and persisted, a voice in the dead shells.

'Keep vigil.' And they rehearsed for his return among his
wheeling
and feathered bright attendants, dead birds on an ocean
of lights and minutes, intoning: 'It is the might of God
to reverse his pattern – pelt into flesh (wondering
and animate), molluscs restored to their shells,
the skin regrafted on to the shrunken serpent;

Yes, it can all be achieved!' Out of the ocean
they picked up tokens of Quetzalcoatl; the god
was corn swelling, life quickening and wondering –
oh, the seasons did not falter. Each tide threw up shells.
The winds were birds prophesying, plumes of the serpent . . .
or shadows of bone? dead cages pivoting and wheeling?

At last, at last a messenger: 'Hail Montezuma! The god
returns; amazing craft from the East.' Crowding,
       wondering,
they saw from the beach dark Spanish ships rut the ocean.

Party in Room 21

'Put on a record; the one that Terry liked –
I'm in that sort of mood.' 'What was it called?'
'*Au fond du temple saint.*' 'Who's Terry, anyway?'
One a.m. The window-ledge is filled

by empty bottles: even Tom is smoking,
it's at that stage. 'Coffee, anyone?'
Who's Terry, anyway? – name from a past
without shire or shape to most of us, gone

before we came here to the boarding-house,
tarnish of a rented privacy
only. 'Terry left for the States last June.
He lived here.' 'Will you remember me

when I've shot through? It's brandy with soda, darling.'
'I always think of Terry, with this song.'
'Then think of me with brandy.' 'O.K., I will.'
The music is picked for a phrase to skim along

before the talk skids elsewhere. Peter, Bob;
Helen; Nell. These present names we know
enough to wrap a week, a year, a place
around; enough to pin this moment to.

'Here's to the New Year, everyone.' The glass
of the empty window bottles glints and winks;
somewhere the record grinds (*Ô Pêcheurs des perles!*)
that no one bothers to turn off; it sinks
through the noise alive of voices, glasses, drinks.

Death of the Minotaur

He is trapped within his labyrinth, choked by a cord
of cheap thread that slits language out of his throat
and sets brash Theseus loose to run and greet
his Ariadne. The Minotaur is dead;
his flesh with all its passageways of blood
is only meat in a butcher's stall, the sting
and stink of his breath is exorcised. Bring
your baskets to the marketplace, divide
the carcass severally. Here is your piece,
a strict apportionment: take it to your pale daughter –
flesh is nutritious, if she eats she may
grow strong once more, and again rejoice
in our simple village rites. We take what we need.
The Minotaur makes an oblation from his blood.

RANDOLPH STOW

b. 1935

Dust

'Enough,' she said. But the dust still rained about her;
over her living-room (hideous, autumnal)
dropping its small defiance.

                       The clock turned green.
She spurned her broom and took a train. The neighbours
have heard nothing.

Jungles, deserts, stars – the six days of creation –
came floating in, gold on a chute of light.
In May, grudging farmers admired the carpet
and foretold a rich year.

Miraculous August! What shelves of yellow capeweed,
what pouffes of everlastings. We worship nature
in my country.
Never such heath as flowered on the virgin slopes
of the terrible armchairs. Never convolvulus
brighter than that which choked the china dogs.
Bushwalkers' Clubs boiled their billies with humility
in chimneys where orchids and treesnakes
luxuriantly intertwined.

A photographer came from *The West Australian,* and ten
teenage reportresses. Teachers of botany
overflowed to the garden.

Indeed, trains were run from Yalgoo and Oodnadatta.
But the neighbours slept behind sealed doors, with feather
dusters beside their beds.

Ruins of the City of Hay

The wind has scattered my city to the sheep.
Capeweed and lovely lupins choke the street
where the wind wanders in great gaunt chimneys of hay
and straws cry out like keyholes.

Our yellow Petra of the fields: alas!
I walk the ruins of forum and capitol,
through quiet squares, by the temples of tranquillity.
Wisps of the metropolis brush my hair.
I become invisible in tears.

This was no ratbags' Eden: these were true haystacks.
Golden, but functional, our mansions sprang from dreams
of architects in love (*O my meadow queen!*).
No need for fires to be lit on the yellow hearthstones;
our walls were warmer than flesh, more sure than igloos.
On winter nights we squatted naked as Esquimaux,
chanting our sagas of innocent chauvinism.

In the street no vehicle passed. No telephone,
doorbell or till was heard in the canyons of hay.
No stir, no sound, but the sickle and the loom,
and the comments of emus begging by kitchen doors
in the moonlike silence of morning.

Though the neighbour states (said Lao Tse) lie in sight of
        the city
and their cocks wake and their watchdogs warn the
        inhabitants
the men of the city of hay will never go there
all the days of their lives.

But the wind of the world descended on lovely Petra
and the spires of the towers and the statues and belfries fell.
The bones of my brothers broke in the breaking columns.

The bones of my sisters, clasping their broken children,
cracked on the hearthstones, under the rooftrees of hay.
I alone mourn in the temples, by broken altars
bowered in black nightshade and mauve salvation-jane.

And the cocks of the neighbour nations scratch in the straw.
And their dogs rejoice in the bones of all my brethren.

Sleep

Sleep: you are my homestead, and my garden;
my self's stockade; identity's last fortress. . . .

All day I have stood the siege, and my hands are shaking;
my paddocks are charred and fuming, my flocks are
    slaughtered;

my lands mirror the moon in desolation.
But the moon has come. And the tribes, like smoke, seep
    campward.

And turning, barring the wall-slits with jarrah shutters,
my rifles leaned to the door, I cede; conjuring

Sleep: who are silence; make me a hollow stone
– filled with white blowing ash, and wind, and darkness.

Starshine, or hostile beacon: all light is welded.
So far, so sweet, I know I shall some day love them,

the warchants of cicadas trill in my caverns,
and all is fused, dimmed, healed, in a general grieving.

And man I mourn; till the hurts are as wrongs in childhood
– and a child forgets; though he weep, asleep, forever. . . .

Sleep: you are the month that will raise my pastures.
You are my firebreak. My homestead has not fallen.

Ishmael

Oasis. Discovered homeland. My eyes drink at your eyes.
Noon by noon, under leaves, my dry lips seek you.

The red earth arches away to gibber and dune.
I shall not return to this uncharted spring.

Antarctic seas work statuary of ice,
and sand-toothed wind, in the hungry waiting country,

raises unseen its pale memorials
to lioness, sphinx and man. These blinding images

I call to mind to mould the mind, inviting
desert and sky to take me, wind to shape me,

strip me likewise of softness, strip me of love,
leaving a calm regard, a remembering care.

Whoever loves you, whoever is loved by you,
speaks from my heart. That said, enough of speaking,

a clean break now. My ghost will not come creeping.
One night for words, and then my tenure ends.

The hawks wheel in the dawnlight, the dawn breeze blows
from the heart of drought, from the hungry waiting country

– and what have I to leave, but this encumbering
tenderness, like gear for ever unclaimed.

JUDITH RODRIGUEZ

b. 1936

Nu-Plastik Fanfare Red

I declare myself:
I am painting my room red.
Because they haven't any
flat red suitable for interiors,
because their acres of colour-card
are snowy with daylight only,
because it will look like Danger! Explosives,
or would you prefer a basement cabaret?
a decent home where Italians moved in,
Chiswick House (yes, I've gilded the mirror)
or simply infernal —

I rejoice to be doing it
with quick-drying plastic,
for small area decoration.
I tear at the wall, brush speeding:
let's expand this limited stuff!
It dries impetuously in patches,
I at edges too late scrub; this is a fight.
I accepted the conditions,
and the unbroken wall is yet to come.
Clear stretches screech into clots,
streak into smokiness.
Botched job this, my instant
hell! and no re-sale value, Dad;
a cliché too. Well, too bad.

It's satisfying to note
this mix is right for pottery.
(Good glad shock of seeing
that red-figure vases *are*.

Not 4th-edition-earthy, but stab-colour,
new-wine, red-Attis-flower, the full howl.)
My inward amphora!

Even thus shyly to surface:
up we go red, flag-balloon,
broomstick-rocket!
Brandishing blood and fire, pumping
lungs external as leaves!
Ours is a red land, sour
with blood it has not shed,
money not lost, risks evaded,
blood it has forgotten, dried
in furnace airs that vainly
figure (since wool and mines are doing well)
the fire. Torpor
of a disallowed abortion.

Why not a red room?

NORMAN TALBOT

b. 1936

Ballad of Old Women
& of how they
are constrained to simulate youth in
order to avoid shocking the young

Three old ladies in an apple tree
swinging their dimity legs,
eating one apple with a sharp fawn tooth
& a laugh could be heard for leagues.

One old girl in a swanny swing
whisking her toes in the summer,
showing the wrinkles behind her knees
& making the branches simmer.

Three skinny madams in bikini tags,
their midriffs carved like posts
with names that answer to the creaky hands
in their threefold persistent past.

A nice old lady with a nice young man
is plucking his hairs off his chest
to decide if to die & be beautiful
or live so lewdly chaste.

I love old ladies with a memorable twist
dancing to the back of the years –
only stopping en route for a hardwon kiss
& experienced stout like yours.

I love old women with their own age on
& snakes in their hair saying no –
a snakedancer only has to wriggle a bit
but a charmer has to know.

DON MAYNARD

b. 1937

How to write 2 poems

at the one go
(or how to believe)

I have a natural love
of cummings & goings

Tibet
sends me
up
Krishna & beautiful
Buddha & holy Jesus
blasphemed

for once

they were
nonplussed
(   )

I believe
e.e. died
of ampersands

(God grows

B. A. BREEN

b. 1938

Fragments of O'Flaherty

I

O'FLAHERTY IN A SERIOUS MOOD

Three dark men walk in my
waking dreams, in my night, in
my uneasy still-dark
awakenings three dark men
walk.

    Not even with footsteps, si-
lent that pad-fall behind
my mind; no flicker of lips, no
twitch of nostrils; Rodin-eyed
they walk . . .

        SPEAK
YOU BASTARDS but
only their coming is any
response only
        their coming.

II

O'FLAHERTY'S CONFESSION

Bless me father doctor cell
I have sinned . . . thus
I have sinned
and
    thus . . . I
have slithered with cold-smooth
snakes have
      sinned thus.

III

O'FLAHERTY CONSIDERS A CRUCIFIX

What we need is
more blood and mottled
flesh-drained-of-its-blood lips
and none of these half-shut
drowsing eyes but eye-balls
bulging pain
              pain and blood – how
would your fingers twitch
with your palms twisted
around a nail? blood
and pain and all
the knotted guts of it
then
we might be after all
able to forget . . .

IV

O'FLAHERTY PASSING THROUGH

I had
a beer in their bars and used
their piss-houses and met
a talkative drunk in a hotel
yard, I slept
in a room where the cobwebs
talked   moved
on next day   they say
it's a bloody nice little
town that.

433

V

O'FLAHERTY WRITES HIS
WEEKLY LETTER

Dear People
            dear dead and
embryonic mad and middling
people this is my
weekly letter the weather is
and yesterday I
                the doctor
held my balls and made me
cough and so
did the nurse but didn't
make me cough
            oh I
am a reprobate these days
these gutside-out
dark days and mumbling
nights
        and I am well
            regards
                O'Flattery.

VI

O'FLAHERTY ON THE
ESTABLISHMENT

You climb
into his and I'll
climb into yours and if
I'm seen climbing into
yours while you're seen
climbing into his we'll
both be IN
            suck
blow suck blow . . .

VII

O'FLAHERTY IS ASKED TO BE
POLITICALLY ACTIVE

Thump drums for them? Not
on your bloody! Why should I
put my hand to the bum of some
loose-mouthed mediocrity and
push?
    To build a better world.
Listen to them – better
beer for the men and pills for
the ladies and gin-dipped
dummies maybe for babies more
money for
education, farmers, public shit-houses and
               politicians. Hell
and they expect me
to spit into their trumpets.

VIII

O'FLAHERTY WAXES LYRICAL
AT A PARTY

       Atchoo
       there's many things to do
       drinks to drink
       girls to woo
       atchoo
       and I
       have had a few
       and jeez
       the flowers make
       me sneeze.
       Do you?

IX

O'FLAHERTY ON EDUCATION

One two three four
one two three
four one two
three four one two
three
four one two three
four one two
three four
one . . .

X

O'FLAHERTY TO HIS MISTRESS

Now thickened
ankles. God! girl
how you danced, your
belly circling out
to raze my eyes; arms high-held
bunching and tightening breasts
that droop now
and the long
line of you from breast to hip
is a tide now, and the thighs
once taut and tight and telling my
every nerve now
squelch under my hand
and chuckle like jelly.

LES MURRAY

b. 1938

A New England Farm, August 1914

August is the windy month,
The month of mares' tails high in heaven,
August is the fiery month,
The windswept doorstep of the year.

But who is this rider on the road
With urgent spurs of burning silver?

August is the winter's death,
He dries the rotted June rain in the earth,
Stiffens fat roots, ignites within the peach tree
Flower and seed. August is time to think
Of facing ploughshares, getting our new boots,
And of the first calves shivering in the grass
Still wet with birth-slime.

But who is this rider at the gate?
Why do the people run to listen?

August is the new year's hinge:
Time out of mind we've stacked the raddled autumn
Cornstalks on the river bank for burning,
Watching the birds come dodging through the smoke
To feast on beetles. Time out of mind
We've retraced last year's furrows with the plough:
How can this August fail us?

Why do the young men saddle horses?
Why do the women grieve together?

The Princes' Land

For Valerie, on her birthday

Leaves from the ancient forest gleam
In the meadow brook, and dip, and pass.
Six maidens dance on the level green,
A seventh toys with an hourglass,

Letting fine hours sink away,
Turning to sift them back again.
An idle prince, with a cembalo,
Sings to the golden afternoon.

Two silver knights, met in a wood,
Tilt at each other, clash and bow.
Upon a field semé of birds
Tom Bread-and-Cheese sleeps by his plough.

But now a deadly stillness comes
Upon the brook, upon the green,
Upon the seven dancing maids,
The dented knights are dulled to stone.

The hours in the hourglass
Are stilled to fine fear, and the wood
To empty burning. Tom the hind
Walks in his sleep in pools of blood. . . .

The page we've reached is grey with pain.
Some will not hear, some run away,
Some go to write books of their own,
Some few, as the tale grows cruel, are gay.

But we who have no other book
Spell out the gloomy, blazing text,
Page by slow page, wild year by year,
Our hope refined to what comes next,

And yet attentive to each child
Who says he's looked ahead and seen
How the tale will go, or spied
A silver page two pages on,

For, as the themes knit and unfold,
Somewhere far on, where all is changed,
Beyond all twists of grief and fear,
We look to glimpse that land again:

The brook descends in music through
The meadows of that figured land,
Nine maidens from the ageless wood
Move in their circles, hand in hand.

Two noble figures, counterchanged,
Fence with swift passion, pause and bow.
All in a field impaled with sun
The Prince of Cheese snores by his plough.

Watching bright hours file away,
Turning to sift them back again,
The Prince of Bread, with a cembalo
Hums to the golden afternoon.

Blood

Pig-crowds in successive, screaming pens
We still to greedy drinking, trough by trough,
Tusk-heavy boars, fat mud-beslabbered sows:
Gahn, let him drink, you slut, you've had enough!

Laughing and grave by turns, in milky boots,
We stand and yarn, and whet our butcher's knife,
Sling cobs of corn – hey, careful of his nuts!
It's made you cruel, all that smart city life.

In paper spills, we roll coarse, sweet tobacco.
That's him down there, the one we'll have to catch,
That little Berkshire with the pointy ears.
I call him Georgie. Here, you got a match?

The shadow of a cloud moves down the ridge,
On summer hills, a patch of autumn light.
My cousin sheathes in dirt his priestly knife.
They say pigs see the wind. You think that's right?

I couldn't say. It sounds like a good motto.
There are some poets who – He's finished now.
Melon-sized and muscular, with shrieks
The pig is seized and bundled anyhow

His twisting strength permits, then sternly held.
My cousin tests his knife, sights for the heart
And sinks the blade with one long, even push.
A wild scream bursts as knife and victim part

And hits the showering heavens as our beast
Flees straight downfield, choking in his pumping gush
That feeds the earth, and drags him to his knees –
Bleed, Georgie, pump! And with a long-legged rush

My cousin is beside the thing he killed
And pommels it, and lifts it to the sun:
I should have knocked him out, poor little bloke.
It gets the blood out if you let them run.

We hold the dangling meat. Wet on its chest
The narrow cut, the tulip of slow blood.
We better go. We've got to scald him next.
Looking at me, my cousin shakes his head:

What's up, old son? You butchered things before . . .
It's made you squeamish, all that city life.
Sly gentleness regards me, and I smile:
You're wrong, you know. I'll go and fetch the knife.

I walk back up the trail of crowding flies,
Back to the knife which pours deep blood, and frees
Sun, fence and hill, each to its holy place.
Strong in my valleys, I may walk at ease.

A world I thought sky-lost by leaning ships
In the depth of our life – I'm in that world once more.
Looking down, we praise for its firm flesh
The creature killed according to the Law.

The Wilderness

For Peter Barden

Penury in Sydney had grown stale
And, at twenty-two, my childhood was in danger
So I preceded you, in all but spirit,
To the far-back country
Where the tar roads end.

In the silent lands
Time broadens into space.
Approaching Port Augusta, going on,
Iron-brown and limitless, the plains
Were before me all day. Burnt mountains fell behind
In the glittering sky.

At dawn, the sun would roll up from his lair
In the kiln-dry lake country, fire his heat straight through
The blind grey scrub, awaken me beside wheeltracks
And someone's car, and I would travel on.

At noon, far out in a mirage, I would brew
Tea with strangers, yarn about jobs in the North
And, chewing quietly, watch maybe an upstart
Dust-devil forming miles off, going high

To totter, darken
And, quite suddenly, vanish
Leaving a formless, thinning stain in the heavens.

Where the spirits of sea-cliffs
Hovered on the plain
I would remember routines we had invented
For putting spine into shapeless days: the time
We passed at a crouching trot down Wynyard Concourse
Tell each other in loud mock-Arunta and gestures
What game we were tracking down what haunted gorge . . .
Frivolous games
But they sustained me like water,

They, and the is-ful ah!-nesses of things.

An Absolutely Ordinary Rainbow

The word goes round Repins, the murmur goes round
    Lorenzinis,
At Tattersalls, men look up from sheets of numbers,
The Stock Exchange scribblers forget the chalk in their
    hands
And men with bread in their pockets leave the Greek Club:
There's a fellow crying in Martin Place. They can't stop
    him.

The traffic in George Street is banked up for half a mile
And drained of motion. The crowds are edgy with talk
And more crowds come hurrying. Many run in the back
    streets
Which minutes ago were busy main streets, pointing:
There's a fellow weeping down there. No one can stop him.

The man we surround, the man no one approaches
Simply weeps, and does not cover it, weeps
Not like a child, not like the wind, like a man
And does not declaim it, nor beat his breast, nor even
Sob very loudly – yet the dignity of his weeping

Holds us back from his space, the hollow he makes about
    him
In the midday light, in his pentagram of sorrow,
And uniforms back in the crowd who tried to seize him
Stare out at him, and feel, with amazement, their minds
Longing for tears as children for a rainbow.

Some will say, in the years to come, a halo
Or force stood around him. There is no such thing.
Some will say they were shocked and would have stopped
    him
But they will not have been there. The fiercest manhood,
The toughest reserve, the slickest wit amongst us

Trembles with silence, and burns with unexpected
Judgements of peace. Some in the concourse scream
Who thought themselves happy. Only the smallest children
And such as look out of Paradise come near him
And sit at his feet, with dogs and dusty pigeons.

Ridiculous, says a man near me, and stops
His mouth with his hand, as if it uttered vomit –
And I see a woman, shining, stretch her hand
And shake as she receives the gift of weeping;
As many as follow her also receive it

And many weep for sheer acceptance, and more
Refuse to weep for fear of all acceptance,
But the weeping man, like the earth, requires nothing,
The man who weeps ignores us, and cries out
Of his writhen face and ordinary body

Not words, but grief, not messages, but sorrow
Hard as the earth, sheer, present as the sea –
And when he stops, he simply walks between us
Mopping his face with the dignity of one
Man who has wept, and now has finished weeping.

Evading believers, he hurries off down Pitt Street.

PETER STEELE

b. 1939

Matins

Out there in darkest Parkville it's a kind
   of animal country. Morning displays –
I thought it was the gardener – someone trotting
   hale and compulsive, barely attached
to four maleficent greyhounds, sleek and dumb.
   He's Bogart or Camus, a bigboned ghost
easing himself and his charges round the block;
   they move as sweetly and as bloody-minded
as if their talent were for treachery,
   not coursing and a would-be kill.
We've traded words on form in wetter days,
   sodden together into comradeship,
but not this morning. I'm praying in his trail,
   a sort of christian and a sort of man,
watching him get between us the police
   the park the children's hospital
the bolted shelter for old derelicts
   and the zoo, that other eden, where
some cruciform and prestidigious monkeys
   hang in the sunlight, and the sombre bears
rove their concrete to sweat out the duration.

GEOFFREY LEHMANN

b. 1940

The Pigs

For Chris Koch

My grey-eyed father kept pigs on his farm
In Tuscany. Like troubled bowels all night
They muttered in my childhood dreams, and grumbled
Slovenly in moonlight, sprawled in night-slush,
While chill winds dried the mud upon their hides.
I lay in the faint glow of oil-lamps,
In a musk-scented stillness,
And from the icy paddocks heard the pigs.

My thoughts were haunted by pig-greed, how pigs
Surge to their food-troughs, trample on each other,
And grunt and clamber swilling themselves full.
Often we emptied food on top of them,
So that they swam in muck. And then one day
When the wind splattered us with dust, my father
Heard a pig squealing, crushed beneath the press,
And we began to stone the pigs, and drew
Blood with our stones, but they just shook their buttocks,
And grunted, and still tore at cabbage leaves.

Passing a dozing boar one summer morning
My father pointed at two dead-pan eyes
Which rolled up quizzing me (and yet its head
And snout snoozed motionless, and flies
Fed and hopped undisturbed among the bristles).
Only a pig, my father now explained,
Could glance out of the corner of its eye.
I watch two bead-eyes turn and show
Their whites like death-flesh.

One dusk this huge old boar escaped and chased
Me through an olive-grove upon a hillside.
Dumpy, it thundered after me,
With murder in its eyes, like someone damned,
A glow of Hades perfuming the air.
That night my father took me in his arms
And told me that of all the animals
Only pigs knew of death

And knew we merely fattened them for slaughter.
Puddles of hatred against man, they wallowed
In greed, despair and viciousness,
Careless of clinging slops and vegetable scraps,
And the sows even eating their own young.
The knowledge of death made pigs into pigs.

Later that year this old boar ate
A peasant woman's baby and was burned
Alive one night by public ceremony.
My father stood there by my side,
His toga billowing in the rush of heat,
But in the flames my child-eyes saw
Not a pig, but myself,
Writhing with stump-legs and with envious eyes
Watching the men who calmly watched my death.

A Voyage of Lions

Sea-water stained with lion's blood.
Our arrows caught a lion
Escaping in the foam.
The crowds edged cautiously back to the quay
And so our convoy with its lions set out
For Rome and arenas foul with blood.

At night we sleep in snatches.
In lulls a sudden roar will go

447

From lion to lion and ship to ship.
They smell each other in the night-wind.
Anchored in a bay we heard
A lion's voice from the hills,
And the darkness resounded with every lion
Roaring for freedom and Africa.

We are dogged by fear and guilt on our voyage,
Imagining the death in the arena
Of these amiable friends
Who happily take raw meat we throw them.
Gently and casually a male
Lays a paw upon his female and looks about
Snarling at any threat to her.

Having mastered the lions, we find
The lions have mastered us.
Our clothes are musty from lion hair and dung,
And some nights we dance and sing songs by torchlight,
Watched by lions, their whiskers sensing the air.
Asleep we dream of cages for ourselves,
From which cooped up we stare at lions
Freely roaming on deck and sniffing the sea.

Five Days Late

Late, five days late. At night in sleep they fumble
To feel the cool gold ring which is not there,
The space beside them which is sometimes man,
The single girls who laughed and ran from Daddy.
The wind-chimes stir. From their high rented rooms
The city is a wave of black stars breaking
In violet abysses, clouds of gasoline.
Pads of rouge, scent bottles, eyelash brushes
Are mummified in the dressing table mirror.

They travel nightmare elevators up
And down with flimsy shift fanned by ozone,
In an empty building, buttons pressed by no one.
Memories of kisses hang around their necks
Like stones, dolls fall from burning aeroplanes,
And ghosts of children crawl in moonlit playpens,
Clamber and strain for milk from dormant breasts,
Breasts which have never existed, dangling playthings
Craving the press of life, the tug of lips,
Anguished wombs twisting, curving to be filled
With Baby and his big blind head of bread,
The bawling nightmare spilling porridge on floors,
The handful of tears blowing a paper trumpet,
The bib daubed with chocolate kissing the stars goodbye.
In rented rooms the coffee cups are cold,
And single girls toss in their night of doubt.
When morning wakes with blood, they weep, are safe.

Pear Days in Queensland

For James Wansfell, on whose article this poem is based

Days of pear-madness, nights of pear-murder we spent
Digging and burning the prickly pear,
Poisoning, crushing with rollers drawn by bullocks,
Standing in pubs and swapping pear yarns,
Scraping the spines off with knives,
Sponging our thorn wounds with mustard,
Scratched brown and purple with Condy's and gentian
    violet,
While beyond the pressure lamp's wavering circle
The pear massed its nightmare armies by moonlight
And peered with balloon green faces over pub railings.

Our horses whinneyed with pain
Fetlocks swollen to pumpkins where big thorns wedged.
Sometimes pear-happy our cattle romped through the cacti.

We hacked, we poisoned, we crushed but the segments
Just split and sprouted again.
A tree grew from a burned green ear.
Munching amongst the yellow flowers a cow
Ate the soft red fruit and wandered five miles
And seeds passed with her stools became ten plants.
The pear flew in the stomachs of birds,
Breathed on the fur of bees, explored the nightwind.
A pad lived for three years hung in a room.

How could we fight what stuck to our boots and travelled
The red volcanic soil on our clothes and horses?
We sweated, were smeared with pear.
Pear cities covered millions and millions of acres,
Through a green Babylon we galloped flat out,
Pear leaves flying in all directions,
The roads just narrow tracks through walls of pear.
Mustering cattle we climbed up trees
To spot their heads amongst the plazas of cactus.

But we learned to live with pear-megalomania, these miles
Of green intestine digesting the world into pear.
We mashed the pads for feed,
Fermented them into alcohol
And extracted second grade dyes and oils.
We used the big yellow thorns for gramophone needles
And heard Enrico Caruso husky and faint
Sing from a thorn as we boiled in hot pear nights.

Then a moth came and Troy fell overnight.
The land was cleared, the arcades of pear collapsed.
The cactoblastis chewed its way through green cities
And we stood stunned in the pear-free open air,
Incredulous, a trifle uneasy
At the hemisphere of grassland tilting to the sea.

Now in winter we burn the sugarcane,
The hillside a honeycomb crumbling with fire

In blue indigo twilights blowing with orange smoke.
Our rivers and country daze us with largeness.
But at night we doze in mosquito nets
And smell ghost armies of cactus
In the heart of the rain forest, deeper than we can reach,
New resistant strains sending out clouds of pollen.

CRAIG POWELL

b. 1940

Nembutal Rock

One o'clock in the morning
she sat up in bed,
a fist full of yellow capsules
and screaming in her head.

Open the door and the window,
let the stars blow in!
Her lungs are full of thunder
and there's spittle on her chin.

Who cares if you didn't love her
and you meant to go away?
Forget the slanging quarrels
you spat out every day.

Drag her to the ambulance,
go howling through the night,
cry like a silly school-boy
and screw your knuckles tight.

But it's no use calling the doctor.
She's learning how to die –
face grown blue as the water,
foam on her mouth gone dry.

Four o'clock in the morning
they stretched her out in bed,
her fist uncurled and empty,
a cold sheet across her head.

ANDREW TAYLOR

b. 1940

The Sistine Spiders

Cracks
in masonry
and plaster
sceptically explore
this artistry.

Visitors
utterly exclaim
at Adam
lolling from sleep
and at the God Almighty
proof eternal
in awe.

At night
spiders
clamber from their cracks
wander the Creation
and wait
for prey.

Visitors
don't see any spiders.
Spiders
from their homes in cracks
at God's right hand
aren't much
impressed
by admiration.

ROGER McDONALD

b. 1941

1966-1866

We have become so personal that words are ungainly.
Intimacy contradicts itself;
We don't see each other clearly.

And yet there is a life an arm's length from each other;
Lean back to find it. Use my surname in letters to your
    mother.
Address the servants with a sharp
'Consult the master,'
And when speaking to the Dean
Preface my name with 'Mister'.
Apply yourself to this
And I will undertake an equal deference;
'The mistress is in the village'
Will issue roundly from my lips
When I am called from my study.
You may weave your way through Ladyships
On my crooked arm, when the Queen is at hand,
And our names are murmured in bent ears
Against the blare of the regimental band.
I'll have a daguerreotype prepared to signal our success.
We'll call it 'Doubled Singleness' . . .

But we are young and unmarried
And far south from such a century.

JOHN TRANTER

b. 1943

The Moment of Waking

She remarks how the style of a whole age
disappears into your gaze, at the moment
of waking. How sad you are
with your red shirt, your features
reminiscent of marble, your fabulous
boy-girl face like a sheet of mist
floating above a lake.

Someone hands me a ticket
In Berlin a hunchback
is printing something hideous;
my passport is bruised with dark blue
and lilac inks. Morning again,
another room batters me awake
you will be haunting the mirror like silver.

Now the nights punish me with dreams
of a harbour in Italy – you are there
hung in the sky on broken wings
as you always have been, dancing,
preparing to wound me with your
distant and terrible eyes.

ROBERT ADAMSON

b. 1944

Toward abstraction/possibly a gull's wing

The most disconcerting feature is an absolute flatness
especially the sand. I've been here in love
and having passed the perfectly calm ocean had only
noticed the terns – If there was some way
back, some winding track to follow I'd possibly find
the elusive agents for creativity.

As now for instance, I am completely indifferent
to the sad way that fellow moves over the sand . . . who?
ah, let's be pure in observation, let us drop opinions –
Look he stops, and throwing off his towel
runs into the surf, where stroking out he attracts the terns
and they curve above him.

Now look back to the beach, it is mid winter.
The sand's deserted and eddies of windcaught grit are left
to dance and fall unhindered . . . At the far end of the
    beach
is an object, a rifle – rusting. He comes out from
the surf stubbing his toes, heading towards the place
where the rifle lies melting.

The sand whispers beneath his feet as he by passes the gun.
Dazed he goes in no particular direction.
The surf rolls a dead tern onto the sand and he kicks it.
Its wing unfolds like a fan, sealice fall
from the sepia feathers and the feathers catch fire.

PETER SKRZYNECKI

b. 1945

The Farmer

The place of birth that his relatives gave
Was a little town somewhere west of the mountains;
But he hardly seemed to care whether or not
They were talking: just gripped the sides
Of the cot they'd strapped him into,
And his small blue eyes followed
The orange dot on the cardiograph monitor.
When they left, tip-toes and apologetic,
He asked for water and perhaps for the leads
To be taken off: it was all too uncomfortable
Like that.

Slumping back he'd watch the dot rise and fall
Crazily – disappear and reappear, sometimes non-stop.
All the while his fingers strained inwards
At himself and at the black thin leads.
About twelve hours later he was dead.

He'd talked about his farm and the winds
That came off the slopes in winter:
The frosts, grass parrots, and the orchards he'd planted:
About his late wife and her love of books:
About the early years spent in northern Queensland,
Till he returned and settled down after the war.

Even now his strong voice comes back
Like a soft rainstorm moving in the brain –
More incisive than the high frequency pitch
Of that machine when he died:
When eighty-four summers were written off as dead,
And the full stop was a fading scribbly line.

MICHAEL DRANSFIELD

b. 1948

epiderm

Canopy of nerve ends
marvellous tent
airship skying in crowds and blankets
pillowslip of serialised flesh
it wraps us rather neatly in our senses
but will not insulate against externals
does nothing to protect
merely notifies the brain
of conversation with a stimulus
I like to touch your skin
to feel your body against mine
two islets in an atoll of each other
spending all night in new discovery
of what the winds of passion have washed up
and what a jaded tide will find for us
to play with when this game begins to pall.

ground zero

wake up
look around
memorise what you see
it may be gone tomorrow
everything changes. Someday
there will be nothing but what is remembered
there may be no-one to remember it.
Keep moving
wherever you stand is ground zero
a moving target is harder to hit.

CHARLES BUCKMASTER

b. 1951

To This Place

How we are
     crashing through the bracken, a power out
of any earth, how my worlds revolve
        in great circular
    scrapings, of fire, of light
       and soil; my greying
conscience

hard facing the sky. And she
like a magnet, evoking that instant, refuses
               to flinch
in the sharp heat of our dying.

And this; in this; this
mine; a delicate balance, I acknowledge
      the turnings, turn to move
   to this place.

ACKNOWLEDGEMENTS

For permission to reprint the poems in this anthology, acknowledgement is made to the following:

ROBERT ADAMSON: 'Towards abstraction/possibly a gull's wing' from *Canticles on the Skin* (1970), Illumination Press, to the author.

DOROTHY AUCHTERLONIE: 'Apopemptic Hymn' from *The Dolphin* (1967), to Australian National University Press.

WILLIAM 'BAYLEBRIDGE' (Blocksidge): 'On Moral Laws' from *This Vital Flesh* (1961), to Angus & Robertson.

BRUCE BEAVER: 'Exit' and 'Holiday' from *Seawall and Shoreline* (1964); 'Letters to Live Poets, I' from *Letters to Live Poets* (1969), to South Head Press; 'Sittings by Appointment Only' to the author.

JOHN BLIGHT: 'Death of a Whale' and 'Mud' from *A Beachcomber's Diary* (1963); 'Helmet Shell' and 'Lamprey' from *My Beachcombing Days* (1968), to Angus & Robertson.

B. A. BREEN: 'Fragments of O'Flaherty' from *Behind My Eyes* (1968), to Melbourne University Press.

CHRIS BRENNAN: 'The Wanderer' and 'Epilogue' from *Verse* (1960), to Angus & Robertson.

JOHN LE GAY BRERETON: 'The Silver Gull' from *Sea and Sky* (1908), to Lothian Publishing Company.

VINCENT BUCKLEY: 'Late Tutorial' and 'Colloquy and Resolution' from *Masters in Israel* (1961), to Angus & Robertson; 'Places', 'Burning the Effects', 'Fellow Traveller' and 'Youth Leader' from *Arcady and Other Places* (1966), to Melbourne University Press.

CHARLES BUCKMASTER: 'To This Place' to the author.

DAVID CAMPBELL: 'Men in Green', 'Windy Gap', 'Night Sowing', 'Under Wattles', 'Droving' and 'Windy Nights' from *Selected Poems 1942-68* (1968), to Angus & Robertson.

NANCY CATO: 'Moon and Pear-Tree' from *The Dancing Bough* (1957), to Angus & Robertson.

C. B. CHRISTESEN: 'The Desecrated Valley' from *The Hand of Memory* (1970), to The Meanjin Press.

LAURENCE COLLINSON: 'Hand in Hand' from *Who Is Wheeling Grandma?* (1967), to Overland and the author.

JOHN COUPER: 'A Sydney Scot' and 'For You Angela' from *East of Living* (1967), Edwards & Shaw, to the author.

ALEXANDER CRAIG: 'Sea at Portsea' from *The Living Sky* (1964), to Angus & Robertson.

JOHN CROYSTON: 'Reconciliation' from *Australian Poetry 1962* (1962), Angus & Robertson, to the author.

BRUCE DAWE: 'How to Go On Not Looking' from *A Need of*

Similar Name (1965); 'The Not-So-Good Earth', 'Life Cycle' and 'A Victorian Hangman Tells His Love' from *An Eye for a Tooth* (1968); 'Home-Coming' from *Beyond the Subdivisions* (1969), to Cheshire Publishing.

ROSEMARY DOBSON: 'The Mirror' from *Child with a Cockatoo* (1963); 'Cock Crow' and 'Jack' from *Cock Crow* (1965), to Angus & Robertson.

MICHAEL DRANSFIELD: 'epiderm' and 'ground-zero' from *Streets of the Long Voyage* (1970), to University of Queensland Press.

GEOFFREY DUTTON: 'Abandoned Airstrip' and 'January' from *Flowers and Fury* (1962); 'Ky in Australia: A Postscript' and 'Our Crypto-Wowsers' from *Poems Soft and Loud* (1967), Cheshire Publishing, to the author.

W. S. FAIRBRIDGE: 'The Consecration of the House' from *Poems* (1953), to Angus & Robertson.

R. D. FITZGERALD: 'The Hidden Bole', 'This Night's Orbit', 'The Face of the Waters', 'Heemskerck Shoals', 'Song in Autumn', 'Bog and Candle', 'Macquarie Place' and 'The Wind at Your Door' from *Forty Years' Poems* (1965), to Angus & Robertson; 'Invocation of Josefa Asasela', to *Meanjin Quarterly* and the author.

MARY GILMORE: 'Eve-Song', 'Never Admit the Pain', 'The Men of Eureka', 'The Yarran-Tree', 'An Aboriginal Simile' and 'Old Botany Bay' from *Selected Verse* (1969), to Angus & Robertson.

RODNEY HALL: 'The Hunter' from *Eyewitness* (1967), to South Head Press; 'The Two Staircases of Consummation' from *The Autobiography of a Gorgon* (1968), to Cheshire Publishing; 'Heaven, in a Way' and 'Cut-Out' from *Heaven, in a Way* (1970), to University of Queensland Press.

MAX HARRIS: 'A Window at Night' and 'The Death of Bert Sassenowsky' from *A Window at Night* (1967), Australian Book Review, to the author.

WILLIAM HART-SMITH: 'The Inca Tupac Upanqui' from *Poems of Discovery* (1959); 'Postage Stamp' and 'Razor Fish' from *The Talking Clothes* (1966), to Angus & Robertson.

GWEN HARWOOD: 'The Wound', 'The Glass Jar' and 'Triste, Triste' from *Poems* (1963); 'Estuary' and 'Cocktails at Seven' from *Poems Volume Two* (1968), to Angus & Robertson.

WILMA HEDLEY: 'Isaac' from *Identity* (1968), Realist, to the author.

JILL HELLYER: 'The Way to the Headland' from *The Exile* (1969), Alpha Books, to the author.

DOROTHY HEWETT: 'Go Down Red Roses' from *Windmill Country* (1968), *Overland* in conjunction with Peter Leyden, to the author.

ACKNOWLEDGEMENTS

CHARLES HIGHAM: 'Still Lives' and 'Dusk at Waterfall' from *The Earthbound and Other Poems* (1959); 'Harbourscape' and 'The War Museum at Nagasaki' from *Noonday Country* (1966); 'The Creature' from *The Voyage to Brindisi and Other Poems* (1970), to Angus & Robertson.

HARRY HOOTON: 'Moonlight' and 'The World Is Too Much Withered' from *It is Great to be Alive* (1961), to Leon Fink.

A. D. HOPE: 'Australia', 'The Wandering Islands', 'The Death of the Bird', 'Imperial Adam', 'Pasiphae', 'Letter from the Line', 'Ode on the Death of Pius the Twelfth' and 'Crossing the Frontier' from *Collected Poems* (1966); 'Moschus Moschiferus' and 'On an Engraving by Casserius' from *New Poems 1965-1969* (1969), to Angus & Robertson.

PETER HOPEGOOD: 'Snake's-Eye View of a Serial Story' from *Snake's-Eye View of a Serial Story* (1964), Edwards and Shaw, to Mary Hopegood.

FLEXMORE HUDSON: 'Our World' from *Pools of the Cinnebar Range* (1959), Robertson & Mullens, to the author.

REX INGAMELLS: 'Earth-Colours', 'Black Mary' and 'History' from *Selected Poems* (1945), Georgian House, to the author's widow.

EVAN JONES: 'Noah's Song' from *Inside the Whale* (1960), Cheshire Publishing, to the author; 'Boxing On' from *Understandings* (1967), to Melbourne University Press.

T. H. JONES: 'My Grandfather Goes Blind' to *Meanjin Quarterly*.

NANCY KEESING: 'The Goat with the Golden Eyes' from *Poetry Australia 1964* (1964), to the author.

HENRY LAWSON: 'Middleton's Rouseabout' and 'The Song of Old Joe Swallow' from *Collected Verse*, vol. I (1967); 'One-Hundred-and-Three' from *Collected Verse*, vol. II (1968), to Angus & Robertson.

GEOFFREY LEHMANN: 'The Pigs' from *The Ilex Tree* (1965), to Australian National University Press; 'A Voyage of Lions' from *A Voyage of Lions* (1968), to Angus & Robertson; 'Five Days Late' from *Australian Poetry 1969* (1969); 'Pear Days in Queensland' from *Australian Poetry 1970* (1970), Angus & Robertson, to the author.

NOEL MACAINSH: 'A Small Dirge for the Trade' from *Australian Poetry 1962* (1962), Angus & Robertson, to the author.

JAMES MCAULEY: 'Tune for Swans', 'Celebration of Divine Love' and 'A Leaf of Sage' from *A Vision of Ceremony* (1956); 'St John's Park, New Town', 'Pietà' and 'Because' from *Surprises of the Sun* (1969); 'Terra Australis', 'Aubade', 'The Cloak' and 'The Incarnation of Sirius' from *Collected Poems 1936-70* (1971), to Angus & Robertson.

ACKNOWLEDGEMENTS

HUGH MCCRAE: 'Ambuscade', 'I Blow My Pipes', 'Enigma' and 'Fantasy' from *The Best Poems of Hugh McCrae* (1961), to Angus & Robertson.

RONALD MCCUAIG: *'Au Tombeau de Mon Père'* from *The Ballad of Bloodthirsty Bessie and Other Poems* (1961), to Angus & Robertson.

NAN MCDONALD: 'The Bus-Ride Home' from *Selected Poems* (1969), to Angus & Robertson.

ROGER MCDONALD: '1966-1866' from *Citizens of Mist* (1968), to University of Queensland Press.

J. A. R. MACKELLAR: 'Football Field: Evening' and 'Twelve O'Clock Boat' from *Collected Poems* (1932), to Angus & Robertson.

KENNETH MACKENZIE: 'The Moonlit Doorway', 'The Wagtail's Nest', 'Derelict' and 'An Old Inmate' from *Selected Poems* (1961), to Angus & Robertson.

DAVID MALOUF: 'At a School Athletics Day' from *Bicycle* (1970), to University of Queensland Press.

J. S. MANIFOLD: 'The Tomb of Lieut. John Learmonth' and 'The Showmen' to the author.

DAVID MARTIN: 'Gordon Childe' from *The Gift: Poems 1959-65* (1966), to Jacaranda Press.

FURNLEY MAURICE: 'Plunder', 'Apples in the Moon' and 'The Agricultural Show, Flemington, Victoria' from *Poems* (1944), to Lothian Publishing Company.

DON MAYNARD: 'How to write 2 poems' from *Australian Poetry Now* (1970), to Sun Books.

TOM INGLIS MOORE: 'Align Your Act' from *Bayonet and Grass* (1957), to Angus & Robertson.

IAN MUDIE: 'They'll Tell You About Me' and 'In Sunny Days of Winter' from *The Blue Crane* (1959), to Angus & Robertson; 'The North-Bound Rider' from *The North-Bound Rider* (1963), Rigby, to the author.

R. D. MURPHY: 'In the Train' from *Australian Poetry, 1964* (1964), Angus & Robertson, to the author.

LES MURRAY: 'A New England Farm, August 1914' from *The Ilex Tree* (1965), to Australian National University Press; 'The Princes' Land', 'Blood', 'The Wilderness' and 'An Absolutely Ordinary Rainbow' from *The Weatherboard Cathedral* (1969), to Angus & Robertson.

SHAW NEILSON: 'The Orange Tree', 'Song Be Delicate', 'May', 'Schoolgirls Hastening' and 'Native Companions Dancing', to Lothian Publishing Company; 'Beauty Imposes' from *Poems of Shaw Neilson* (1965), to Angus & Robertson.

BERNARD O'DOWD: 'Australia' from *Collected Poems* (1944), to Lothian Publishing Company.

ACKNOWLEDGEMENTS

VANCE PALMER: 'The Farmer Remembers the Somme' from *The Camp* (1920), Sydney J. Endacott, to Aileen Y. Palmer and Helen G. Palmer.

A. B. PATERSON: 'The Man from Snowy River' and 'Saltbush Bill' from *The Collected Verse of A. B. Paterson* (1921), to Angus & Robertson.

GRACE PERRY: 'Red Scarf' from *Red Scarf* (1963), Edwards & Shaw, to the author; 'Time of Turtles' from *Two Houses* (1969), to South Head Press.

JAMES PICOT: 'For It Was Early Summer' from *With a Hawk's Quill* (1953), to The Meanjin Press.

HAL PORTER: 'Hobart Town' from *Elijah's Ravens* (1968), to Angus & Robertson.

PETER PORTER: 'Your Attention Please' from *Penguin Modern Poets* vol. 2 (1962), to the author; 'Competition is Healthy' and 'Moaning in Midstream' from *A Porter Folio* (1969), Scorpion Press, to the author.

CRAIG POWELL: 'Nembutal Rock' from *I Learn By Going* (1968), to South Head Press.

ALAN RIDDELL: 'Goldfish at an Angle' and 'At the Hammersmith Palais' from *The Stopped Landscape* (1968), to Hutchinson & Co.

ELIZABETH RIDDELL: 'After Lunik Two' from *Forbears* (1961), to Angus & Robertson.

ROLAND ROBINSON: 'I Had No Human Speech', 'Altjeringa' and 'Passage of the Swans' from *Deep Well* (1962), Edwards & Shaw, to the author; 'The Seed Goes Home' from *Grendel* (1967), to The Jacaranda Press.

JUDITH RODRIQUEZ: 'Nu-Plastik Fanfare Red' from *Australian Poetry Now* (1971), to Sun Books.

ERIC ROLLS: 'Sheaf Tosser' and 'The Knife' from *Sheaf Tosser* (1967), to Angus & Robertson.

DAVID ROWBOTHAM: 'The Candle Is Going Out' and 'First Man Lost In Space' from *The Makers of the Ark* (1970), to Angus & Robertson.

J. R. ROWLAND: 'Canberra in April' and 'Dawn Stepping Down' from *The Feast of Ancestors* (1965), to Angus & Robertson.

THOMAS W. SHAPCOTT: 'Enemies' from *The Mankind Thing* (1964), Jacaranda Press; 'Quetzalcoatl' and 'Party in Room 21' from *A Taste of Salt Water* (1967), Angus & Robertson, to the author; 'Death of the Minotaur' from *Inwards to the Sun* (1969), to University of Queensland Press.

R. A. SIMPSON: 'Student' and 'Carboni in the Chimney' from *After the Assassination and Other Poems* (1968), to Jacaranda Press.

ACKNOWLEDGEMENTS

PETER SKRZYNECKI: 'The Farmer' from *There, Behind the Lids* (1970), Lyre-Bird Writers (Sydney), to the author.

KENNETH SLESSOR: 'Thieves' Kitchen', 'Fixed Ideas', 'Metempsychosis', 'Sensuality', 'South Country', 'Captain Dobbin', 'Elegy in a Botanic Garden', 'The Night-Ride', 'Five Bells' and 'Beach Burial' from *Poems* (1957), to Angus & Robertson.

VIVIAN SMITH: 'Dialogue' and 'Late April: Hobart' from *An Island South* (1967), to Angus & Robertson; 'Balmoral, Summer' from *Australian Poetry, 1969* (1969), Angus & Robertson, to the author.

PETER STEELE: 'Matins' to the author.

DOUGLAS STEWART: 'Rock Carving', 'The Dosser in Springtime', 'The Brown Snake', 'One Yard of Earth', 'B Flat', 'The Silkworms', 'Firewheel Tree', 'Fence' and 'Professor Piccard' from *Collected Poems 1936-1967* (1967), to Angus & Robertson.

HAROLD STEWART: 'Orpheus and the Trees' from *Orpheus and Other Poems* (1956), to Angus & Robertson.

RANDOLPH STOW: 'Dust', 'Ruins of the City of Hay', 'Sleep' and 'Ishmael' from *A Counterfeit Silence* (1969), to Angus & Robertson.

NORMAN TALBOT: 'Ballad of Old Women' from *Poems for a Female Universe* (1968), to South Head Press.

ANDREW TAYLOR: 'The Sistine Spiders' to *Meanjin Quarterly*.

COLIN THIELE: 'Up-Country Pubs' from *Selected Verse* (1970), to Rigby.

JOHN THOMPSON: 'A Latter-Day Polonius to His Sons' from *I Love and I Hate* (1964), Cheshire Publishing; 'Attis' from *Meanjin Quarterly* (1964), to Patricia Thompson.

JOHN TRANTER: 'The Moment of Waking' from *Parallax* (1970), to South Head Press.

ANN TREGENZA: 'The Priestess of the Temple' from *Poetry Australia No. 20* (1968), to South Head Press.

BRIAN VRÉPONT: 'The Net-Menders' from *Beyond the Claw* (1943), to Angus & Robertson.

KATH WALKER: 'We Are Going' from *We Are Going* (1964); 'Municipal Gum' from *The Dawn Is at Hand* (1966), to Jacaranda Press.

CHRIS WALLACE-CRABBE: 'Melbourne' and 'A Wintry Manifesto' from *In Light and Darkness* (1963); 'The Secular', 'Nature, Language, the Sea' and 'Rustum' from *The Rebel General* (1967), to Angus & Robertson.

FRANCIS WEBB: 'On First Hearing a Cuckoo', 'The Yellowhammer', 'Pneumo-Encephalograph', 'Harry' and 'Wild Honey' from *Collected Poems* (1969), to Angus & Robertson.

JUDITH WRIGHT: 'The Company of Lovers' from *The Moving Image* (1946), to The Meanjin Press; 'Bullocky', 'South of My

ACKNOWLEDGEMENTS

Days', 'Woman to Man', 'The Cycads', 'Our Love is So
Natural', 'Black-Shouldered Kite', 'The Harp and the King'.
'Clock and Heart', 'Typists in the Phoenix Building' and 'The
Beanstalk, Meditated Later' from *Collected Poems 1942-1970*
(1970), to Angus & Robertson.

Every effort has been made to trace copyright holders, but in a
few cases this has proved impossible. The publishers would be
interested to hear from any copyright holders not here acknow-
ledged.

INDEX OF POEM TITLES

INDEX OF FIRST LINES

Other Australian titles available in Penguin

The Penguin Book of
Modern Australian Verse

Edited by Professor Harry Heseltine

An ideal companion to *The Penguin Book of Australian Verse* is Professor Heseltine's latest collection, *The Penguin Book of Modern Australian Verse* published in 1981. In this anthology Professor Heseltine has collected the most vital Australian poetry in the period between 1955 and 1980. The fifty-seven poets range from the Aboriginal poet Jack Davis, Dorothy Hewitt, Vincent Buckley to the promising younger poets, Chris Wallace-Crabbe, Bruce Beaver, Rodney Hall, Les Murray, Bruce Dawe and David Malouf.

As well as providing a select bibliography on each poet, Professor Heseltine has contributed an introduction to the book in which he discusses his choice of material and a survey of modern Australian verse.

The Penguin Australian
Song Book

Edited by John Manifold

John Manifold, who has an international reputation as
an authority on folk music and as a poet in his own
right, has brought together a magnificent variety of
words and music in *The Penguin Australian Song Book*.
His material comes from traditional sources but is all
alive today.

Some eighty songs are divided into the following
sections: Seamen and Transports: Immigrants and
Diggers; The Bushrangers; Pastoral Australia; The
Nomads; The Poets.

The versions given are based on meticulous scholar-
ship tested by public performance, and notes to each
song are provided. These are the songs of a new nation,
ready for singing by one or many voices.

The Penguin Book of Australian Ballads

Edited by Russel Ward

Australia's songs and ballads grew as swiftly as her history. They did not record all of that history, but certain aspects of the young and vast country's traditions, legends, true and tall stories are expressed in the ballads with a simplicity and zest not to be found elsewhere. Dr Russel Ward, author of *The Australian Legend*, is an expert in the subject who has collected many old bush songs and ballads himself. From the vast amount of material available he has made a selection which shows all its liveliness and variety, from old anonymous convict and bushranging songs and ballads to the literary ballads of *The Bulletin* to modern verse in the ballad tradition. In his introduction he has tackled the thorny subject of the composition of many of the ballads, and justified his use of the word 'ballad' to cover all the different types of work he has included in this book. But authorship or questions of category have had little to do with the immense popularity of many of these ballads. 'Bold Jack Donahoe', 'The Wild Colonial Boy', 'Waltzing Matilda' and 'The Man from Snowy River' are as much a part of Australia as is the River Murray; but as well as these Dr Ward has included many others, which like lesser creeks and billabongs are no less refreshing.

The Literature of Australia

Edited by Geoffrey Dutton

Since it was first published in the mid 1960s, *The Literature of Australia* has proved to be a popular and widely-used guide to the most important literary work on Australian themes from 1788 until recent times. In addition to its important critical assessments of writers and their work, it provides a much-needed bibliographical guide to the literature and to criticism of it. Long introductory chapters surveying the social background and the fiction or verse of the whole period are followed by chapters on individual writers, groups of writers and the drama.

The twenty-three contributors are not only experts in their fields, but through their writing or teaching they have themselves been part of the exciting development and reassessment of Australian literature. Several of them are, in their own right, subjects of chapters in the book. The editor, Geoffrey Dutton is the author of more than a dozen books and has lectured on Australian Literature in England, the U.S.A. and throughout Australia.